The PHANTOM WAR

The PHANTOM WAR

The German struggle against Soviet partisans 1941-1944

Matthew Cooper

MACDONALD & JANE'S
LONDON

To James Lucas

First published in 1979 by
Macdonald and Jane's Publishers Limited
Paulton House, 8 Shepherdess Walk
London N1 7LW

ISBN 0 354 01220 7

Design: Judy Tuke
Maps: Alec Spark

Printed in Great Britain by
Biddles Ltd, Guildford, Surrey

Contents

Illustrations

Introduction

Evil devours itself. Perhaps no other single aspect of the Second World War so well exemplifies the truth of this saying as the German struggle against the Soviet partisans from 1941 to 1944. Unpleasant tale though it is, its telling provides some important truths concerning the nature of the Third Reich and of its Führer, Adolf Hitler; it reveals that National Socialism contained within itself the seeds of its own failure. Had it not been for the brutality of its racial dogma, the complexities and contradictions of its organisation, and the intransigence and narrowness of intellect of its leader, it is at least arguable that Germany could have pacified the occupied territories of Russia, harnessed for its own purposes the discontent with the Communist régime that was widespread among the Russian peoples, and thereby brought to an end the Soviet Union. The failure to achieve this was the primary cause, in its turn, of the defeat of the Third Reich.

But, interesting though such a thesis may be, it is purely hypothetical. What is certain, however, is that, by their savage repression of the Eastern peoples, the German invaders lost the support of the indigenous population, created hostility where none previously existed, and, despite the great weaknesses inherent in the partisan movement, were forced to surrender large areas of occupied territory to the Soviet guerrillas. Although the Germans could claim, with reason, that the partisans had not succeeded in their primary task – the dislocation of the vital supply lines to the armies at the front – they themselves were brought to the realisation that their ruthless measures, born of an intolerant racialism, could only fuel the fires of resistance, and foster, rather than subdue, partisan activity. But by the time this truth had penetrated the prejudices of Führer, High Command, and régime, it was too late; the war in the East had been lost.

The history of German rule in occupied Russia in general, and of its security measures in particular, also reveals much about Hitler's responsibility for the immeasurable atrocities that took place during the war. Certainly, although he gave orders of great cruelty concerning the policies to be pursued towards the Russian people, they included no mention of any desire to commit genocide. Perhaps, therefore, it could be argued that he had no intention of allowing his political officials and soldiers to engage in the destruction of twenty million Russians, of whom at least 750,000 were Jews – the enormity of which figures becomes clear when it is realised that the number of Soviet soldiers and partisans killed in battle amounted to around one third of the total. Perhaps, even, it might be said that the Führer had no knowledge that such wholesale slaughter, initiated solely by subordinates such as Heinrich Himmler, was taking place. Perhaps. But what can be established beyond doubt is that it was Hitler, and he alone, who created the conditions whereby such evil could be done. He shaped the mentality of the invaders. Without his diatribes against the Slavs and the Jews – the *Untermensch* – and without his orders, or those emanating at his instigation and with his approval from his military staffs, the High Commands of the Wehrmacht and the Army, the atrocities perpetrated by his SS men and his soldiers would not have taken place. As Erich von dem Bach-Zelewski, Chief of the SS Anti-Partisan Formations, was to tell the International Military Tribunal at Nuremberg after the war: 'if, for decades, a doctrine is preached that the Slav race is an inferior race, and the Jews not even human at all, then such an explosion is inevitable'. For that, Hitler must bear responsibility.

The struggle behind the German front lines in the East was immense; at its peak, it involved some 250,000 partisans against 500,000 men in the security forces. At times it could cause the invader much consternation. In 1943, for example, the Luftwaffe was forced to issue to its pilots a map on which, in red, were marked areas over which it was dangerous even to fly – areas that were in the German-held rear areas themselves. Claims for the efficacy of the Soviet guerrilla war have been many. General Ponomarenko, Chief of the partisan Central Staff, asserted that up until the middle of 1943, Soviet guerrillas in Belorussiya alone killed more than 300,000 Germans, caused more than 3,000 railway accidents, and destroyed 3,263 bridges, 1,191 tanks, 4,097 lorries, 378 heavy guns; and 895 supply depots. A well-known British military writer, Major-General J.F.C. Fuller, wrote: 'The partisans, whose numbers were always increasing, sowed fear in the hearts of the German soldiers, who were scattered along the endless railways. In the immense spaces which these crossed, the partisan detachments played the same role as did the submarine packs in the Atlantic' – packs which, it should be remembered, nearly brought about the economic demise of Great Britain. Others, however, have been less sure of the value of the guerrillas. Sir Basil Liddell Hart, for example, believed their activities to have been both ineffective and counter-productive, rarely being more than just a nuisance value and having direct consequences for the civilian population by provoking the enemy into taking severe reprisals. Such writers point to the fact that the partisans were but an auxiliary force of the Red Army; that their activities did not become serious until the second half of the occupation; that, even then, they were limited to the poorer, less populated, and often less strategic areas; and that, in any case, Soviet claims for their successes are wildly exaggerated. Indeed, if early Soviet accounts are to be believed, the Germans suffered more than one million casualties from guerrilla activity alone – about one-sixth of all their soldiers who fought in the East. At the Nuremberg War Trials, General Jodl, Chief of Operations in the Wehrmacht High Command, in whose interest it would have then been to exaggerate the menace of the partisans, doubted whether German casualties in the Soviet Union at their hands were as high as 50,000. Recent studies suggest they were even less, at between 15,000 and 20,000, not including those of the Eastern volunteers who also took part in security operations. In this sense, at least, the phantom war lived up to its name, appearing to possess immense form but, in reality, having little substance. This, however, was often overlooked by the Germans, who, in the extreme violence of their security measures, appeared not only to have misunderstood the proper conduct of anti-guerrilla warfare, but also to have overestimated the partisan danger. As the Head of the SS, Heinrich Himmler, admitted a few months before the Germans were driven from the Soviet Union: 'Perhaps we have overreacted to these bandits, and by this have caused ourselves needless problems.'

This book is the result of research undertaken while writing my previous book, *The German Army 1933–1945; Its Political and Military Failure*, but which could not be incorporated because of limitations of space. Many of those who helped me so greatly before have done so again. Foremost among them is, as always, my cousin, Miss Elaine Austin, who reads with such care and much valuable criticism everything I write. My thanks to her, and to James Lucas, whose collaboration over the past years has been a source of great strength to me. Michael Stevens and Sidney Jackson of Macdonald and Jane's also deserve special mention, for it was only with their help and support that my words have ever appeared in print. I should also like to express my gratitude to Graeme Wright who has edited with such care my manuscript, as well as to all those at Macdonald and Jane's who helped in the production of this book. Mrs Dora Clarke and Dr John Poole, of the House of Commons Library, have also been particularly helpful, as has Alex Vanags, also of Macdonald and Jane's. Others whom I should like to thank are: Dr Anthony Clayton, of the Royal Military Academy, Sandhurst; Dr Eric Taylor, of the House of Commons; Mr Terry Charman, of the Imperial War Museum; David Henson, Miss Philippa Morgan; Miss Karen Kundert; Miss Celia Hall; and Herr L. Klein; together with Miss Jane Howard and Miss Clare Pearson who typed the manuscript. To them all, my thanks.

Matthew Cooper
LONDON, JULY 1978

Chapter 1

The Rule of Terror

The Russian is no more than an animal; he has no right to exist other than in the service of Germany.
ADOLF HITLER *August 1941*

Ruthlessness was a basic principle in both guerrilla and counter-guerrilla warfare in the Soviet Union during the Second World War. Two weeks after the German invasion in June 1941, Joseph Stalin announced Soviet aims: 'In the occupied regions, conditions must be made unbearable for the enemy and his accomplices. They must be hounded and annihilated at every step. . . .'[1] In response, Adolf Hitler declared: 'This partisan warfare has some advantages for us; it enables us to destroy anyone who opposes us.'[2] By savage action did the guerrillas seek to fight the invader and neutralise the collaborator; by savage action, also, did the invaders hope to rule the Russian people and defeat the partisan. Its use played a key role in both the nature and the outcome of the struggle. Ruthless methods, instead of subduing, fuelled resistance and created it where none existed; without German barbarity to aid its cause, the Soviet partisan movement might well have been still-born. Certainly, the combination of German and Soviet aims brought to the guerrilla struggle a perverted morality, making brutality a virtue and mercy a vice, both hunter and hunted pursuing their objectives with a complete disregard for human suffering. Seldom in time of war had life been held so cheap.

Brutality was no stranger to German ways. During and after the Polish campaign, which took place almost two years before the invasion of the Soviet Union, the inescapable consequences of National Socialist racial dogma had become evident. Fast behind the attacking armies had moved the SS *Einsatzgruppen* (Action Groups), designed for what was euphemistically called 'house-cleaning'[3] – the elimination of the Polish intelligentsia, aristocracy, clergy, Jews, and other 'disruptive' elements. The Poles, in Hitler's view, were 'especially born for low labour',[4] and, according to their new Governor-General, Hans Frank, were to become 'the slaves of the Greater-German Reich'.[5]

Some Germans, among the few who were aware of what was going on, were horrified at the results of such an attitude, as much on practical as on moral grounds. One, Generaloberst Johannes Blaskowitz, a military commander in Poland, sent a memorandum, dated 6 February 1940, to the Army High Command, in which he stated: 'the worst damage that will accrue to the German nation from the present situation is the brutalisation and moral debasement which, in a very short time, will spread like a plague among valuable German manpower.' He foresaw the 'rule of the thug', when 'like-minded people and those with warped characters ... can give full expression to their animal and pathological instincts'. Moreover, Blaskowitz understood the practical results of the indifference to the sufferings of the conquered people shown by German officials and the SS, an indifference which could serve only to imbue hatred among the population, to provoke both passive and armed resistance in the occupied territories, and to provide powerful propaganda material for the enemy. He prophesied: 'The idea that one can intimidate the Polish people by terrorism and rub their noses in the dirt will certainly prove false. The people's capacity for enduring suffering is too great for that ...'[6] Time and experience were to prove Blaskowitz right; his opposition to National Socialist policy, however, went unheeded, except that thereby he, one of the German Army's most able generals, was denied a Field-Marshal's baton. The same mistakes committed in Poland were to be perpetrated again in the Soviet Union, but on a far larger scale. The 'rule of the thug' reigned supreme.

Hitler's aim of destroying the Soviet régime and undermining its creed – 'Jewish inspired Bolshevism' – was shared by most of the leaders of the Third Reich; so, indeed, was his intention of subduing the Eastern peoples and of establishing *Lebensraum* (living space) for the survival of *Grossdeutschland* (Greater Germany).[7] Almost without exception, those who guided the destinies of the nation had long coveted the great economic and agricultural resources that lay in the Baltic regions, Greater Russia, the Ukraine, and the Caucasus; moreover, they believed that, if the Bolshevik system were not crushed, the *Mongelsturm*, as the Führer called the Eastern peoples, would some day sweep into the West as their forefathers had done in the days of Attila the Hun and Genghis Khan. The time appeared ripe for action; as Hitler asserted, the door of Russia was rotten – it only needed to be kicked in. The new Russian state that had emerged since 1917 was far from being an integrated, homogeneous nation; indeed, its very title – the Union of Soviet Socialist Republics – indicated that it was an agglomeration of distinct peoples united only by political circumstances. The Soviet Union was to a great extent the victim of its imperial heritage, from which even the 'cleansing process' of the Revolution in 1917 had not succeeded in breaking it free. In the nineteenth century, it was written that the Russian Empire was 'a dust-bin held together by the rusty hoops of Tsardom'[8]; by 1941, little had changed in this respect, except that the autocratic Tsar had been replaced by a dictator, and the idea of the monarchy by Marxism-Leninism.

The Soviet 'Empire', like its imperial predecessor, was a mosaic of subjugated peoples, united by no common language or heritage and condemned by history to dislike and distrust each other.[9] The Russians were a Slavonic people who, in the sixth century AD, had made their appearance in the vast exposed plain that stretches from the Baltic Sea in the north to the Black Sea in the south, and from the Ural mountains in the east to the Carpathian mountains in the west. In the ninth century, this rich, but strife-ridden, land had been conquered by Swedish Vikings, and its inhabitants given the nordic name of 'Russ'. Thus, the Russians came to be separated for ever from the other Slav races. But not for long were they to remain a single people. From all points of the compass came invaders, in particular Tartars from the east and Poles and Lithuanians from the west. Partition and isolation for many centuries resulted, and from this there developed three quite distinct areas of 'European Russia': Greater Russia, centred around Moscow, Little Russia, the area now known as the Ukraine, and White Russia, or Belorussiya. Greater Russia was first dominated by the Tartars and then by Muscovy, while the other two formed part of the Polish-Lithuanian kingdom. The three areas came to develop their own distinct language, culture, and heritage, the subsequent history of Imperial Russia being, to a large extent, the result of the nationalist and minority tensions caused by the expansion of the Greater Russians and their attempts to subject, or to 'russify', the White Russians, Ukrainians, Estonians, Latvians, Lithuanians, Finns, and Poles, together with various Asiatic nationalities such as the Cossacks, Caucasians, Mongols, Siberians, and Armenians. Much blood was shed. As Lenin wrote: 'Nowhere in the world is there such oppression of the majority of the country's population as there is in Russia: the Greater Russians form only 43 per cent of the population, i.e. less than half; the rest have no rights as belonging to other nationalities. Out of 170,000,000 of the population of Russia, about 100,000,000 are oppressed and without rights.'[10]

The Revolution in 1917 brought no diminution of the old separatist tendencies. Although the Communist doctrine of universal brotherhood officially spurned nationalism, and although many of the Soviet leaders were not themselves Greater Russians – Stalin, for example, was a Georgian – the problems of racial antipathy and separatism remained, as is evidenced by the nationalist uprisings in the early days of the Revolution. These tendencies were increased by the authoritarianism of

Lenin, and made immeasurably worse by the atrocities committed by his successor. Repression was endemic from the beginning. Purge followed purge throughout the 1920s and 1930s; wave after wave of prisoners were either transported to camps or killed as, daily, new political crimes against the Soviet people were found to exist. Still more arrests were deemed necessary, still more trials, and yet more purges. Men, women, and children were found guilty of espionage, malingering, plotting rebellion, failing to fulfil production quotas, and even of believing in God. During the years of collectivisation, from 1929 to 1938, some ten million people were either killed, starved to death, or transported to isolated labour camps. Hatred of the régime fuelled the fires of nationalism; political disaffection, though not always vocal, was rife. In the Ukraine, White Russia, and the Baltic States alone, some forty million people yearned for liberation from Communism and the tyranny of Moscow. The time was ripe for the dissolution of the Soviet Union.

In the early part of the previous century, when Russia was under the rule of Tsar and aristocracy, and had just successfully overcome an invasion by Napoleon's *Grande Armée*, the Prussian soldier and military theorist, Karl von Clausewitz, had written: 'Such a country can only be subdued by its own weakness, and by the effects of internal dissension. In order to strike these vulnerable points in its political existence, the country must be agitated to its very centre.'[11] More than one hundred years later this truth was just as pertinent; as an old Russian woman told a German soldier in 1941: 'the Russian people will not be saved by the man with the bigger gun, but by the man with the greater soul.'[12] But this, the German invader did not possess. Hitler's creed, the directives of his subordinates, and the actions of his security services, political officials and troops denied any hope to the various Russian nationalities. The Führer, together with such close associates as Martin Bormann, Reichsleiter and head of the Party chancery, Heinrich Himmler, Reichsführer SS and chief of the security services and police, and Hermann Göring, Reichsmarschall and, among other posts, head of the Luftwaffe, had no wish to foster national consciousness in the Eastern peoples. They regarded them all as 'Slavs'; no distinction was to be made. Hitler's goal was 'to deprive them of any form of state organisation and, consequently, keep them on as low a cultural level as possible';[13] his 'guiding principle' was that these peoples, like the Poles, had but one justification for their existence: to be of economic use to the Germans. Colonisation and exploitation were to be the lot of the conquered territories; it mattered not at all what happened to the various nationalities who inhabited them, provided they posed no threat to German domination.

Others, however, such as Alfred Rosenberg, Party 'philosopher' and Reichsminister for the Occupied Eastern Territories, recognising that the

Soviet Union was composed of various dissatisfied nationalities, wished to exploit this reality for German ends. Rosenberg argued that it was the Greater-Russians who had to be subjugated and contained, for it was only they who represented the real danger; Muscovy should become the dumping-ground for all the undesirable elements of the East. As for the various separatist movements, especially those in the Ukraine and the Caucasus, he wished to recruit them as allies against the Greater-Russians, although at the same time he was adamant that, while each would be allowed some form of self-government, they would be fully dependent on the Reich and subject to a large measure of economic exploitation. He also considered that the Baltic area should, in time, become part of the Greater-German Reich. For all the contradictions in his policies, and his evident desire to subjugate the Slavs, Rosenberg nevertheless had the intelligence to perceive that 'The worst that could happen . . . would be if the people, in the face of our measures of economic exploitation, would come to the conclusion that the present [German] régime causes them greater want than did Bolshevism.'[14]

A few, a small minority, went further than the Reichsminister. These were the 'pro-Russians', men who could be found in the Foreign Ministry and in some branches of the Armed Forces. They favoured a direct appeal to the Russian peoples to join in the fight against Bolshevism, and advocated the institution of national states, independent but under the protection of Germany, to act as a buffer against the Asiatic Russians. But such a concept, put forward by men with little influence, had no impact whatsoever on the counsels of the Reich. Rosenberg, too, his ideas betrayed even by his own subordinates, was impotent. The Führer's policy reigned supreme.

If it was axiomatic that the separate Russian nationalities should cease to exist, then it was a matter of indifference to Hitler whether the people who composed them should live, suffer, or die; their existence would be guaranteed only if their German masters so decreed. The Führer's attitude was symbolised by his reduction of the Russian man to the status of an *Untermensch*, a sub-human; in National Socialist ideology, the Easterners were predestined to an inescapable, perpetual inferiority to the *Herrenvolk*, the Nordic master-race embodied in the blue-eyed, fair-haired, German. 'The Slavs', Hitler declared, 'are a mass of born slaves',[15] and, worst of all, were dominated by Jewry. Conflict was inescapable, he argued, and of this he made no secret: 'The Nordic race has a right to rule the world, and we must take this racial right as the guiding-star of our foreign policy. It is for this reason that, for us, any co-operation with Russia is out of the question, for there on a Slav-Tartar body is set a Jewish head.'[16]

What made the *Untermensch* particularly unacceptable, and, indeed, dangerous to the National Socialists was their addiction to Communism. As Joseph Goebbels, Reichsminister for Propaganda and Public Enlightenment, wrote in his diary, the National Socialists believed that the Russians were 'not a people, but a conglomeration of animals.... Bolshevism has merely accentuated this racial propensity of the Russian people.'[17] The general antipathy felt by Germans for Communism had been turned by the National Socialists from a political argument into a moral crusade designed to save a civilised Europe from the Bolshevik-Slav horde. 'Some day', Hitler believed, 'they are bound to turn against us.'[18] Their destruction was the only solution. Such a policy was regarded simply as a development of the traditional struggle between the Germans and the Russians that had existed since the days of Charlemagne and beyond; Bolshevism was but 'a contemporary form of the drive that animated Attila and Genghis Khan'.[19] Thus, the Third Reich had as its mission the age-old task of liberating Europe from the Eastern menace garbed in its present, but transitory, form of Jew-inspired Bolshevism.

Hitler's attitude to war in the East was well summed up in a speech to the leaders of the Wehrmacht, given on 30 March 1941. Generaloberst Franz Halder, Chief of the Army General Staff, recorded his Führer's comments thus:

> 'Struggle between two *Weltanschaungen* ['world-outlooks']. Devastating assessment of Bolshevism: it is the equivalent of social delinquency. Communism is a tremendous danger for the future. We must get away from the standpoint of soldierly comradeship. The Communist is from first to last no comrade. It is a war of extermination. If we do not regard it as such, we may defeat the enemy, but in thirty years' time we will again be confronted by the Communist enemy.... The struggle will be very different from that in the West. In the East toughness now means mildness in the future. The leaders must make sacrifices and overcome their scruples.'[20]

Hitler's policy was to be carried out by all participants in the German expansion in the East, for, in contrast with previous campaigns, the exercise of repression was not limited solely to Himmler's men and to politicians; the Army was also closely involved. As Hitler made clear to his senior generals on 30 March, the fight in Russia had to ensure the destruction of the Soviet leadership and intelligentsia, the only elements of society capable of subversive action against the occupying force; such a fight could not be won by court-martials. 'The leaders of the troops must know what is involved. They must take the lead in the struggle. The troops must defend themselves with the methods with which they are attacked. Commissars and secret service personnel are criminals and must be treated as such.'[21]

Guidelines were laid down for the conduct of soldiers in the forthcoming invasion, code-named Operation 'Barbarossa'. On 13 May, OKW (the High Command of the Armed Forces) issued its 'Order concerning the exercise of Military Jurisdiction and Procedure in the area "Barbarossa", and Special Military Measures',[22] which advocated the harshest measures against all signs of resistance. It enabled soldiers to shoot all civilians, either in action or in flight, who participated, or attempted to participate, in hostile acts, or who in any way resisted or threatened the German Armed Forces. If they were captured, an officer could order their death on the spot. Reprisals, or 'collective measures of force', as they were called, were to be taken against areas from which insidious and malicious attacks of any type had taken place. If, out of bitterness against the Jewish-Bolshevik system, troops committed acts punishable under military law, prosecution was not compulsory; indeed, officers were instructed that 'When judging such offences, it must be borne in mind, whatever the circumstances, that the collapse of Germany in 1918, the subsequent sufferings of the German people and the fight against National Socialism which cost the blood of innumerable supporters of the Movement, were caused primarily by Bolshevik influence and that no German has forgotten this fact.'[23]

In a subsequent addition to this order, dated 6 June 1941, and known as the 'Commissar Order',[24] it was instructed that Soviet political officials and leaders were to be liquidated either when they were captured or, at the latest, when they arrived at the prisoner-of-war transit camps. Another order, dated 16 June and issued by OKW, dealt with the treatment of prisoners-of-war;[25] it also stated that ruthless action was to be taken against any sign, however slight, of restiveness or resistance, either active or passive. In the view of two leading military conspirators against Hitler, Generals Beck and Oster, both of whom were to die for their opposition, such orders systematically transformed 'military law concerning the conquered population into uncontrolled despotism'.[26]

Behind the front-line troops came the SS, who were destined to play the major role in the policy of extermination. The *Einsatzgruppen*, the first SS formations to enter Russia, were given 'special tasks in preparation for the political administration . . . tasks which result from the final encounter between two opposing political systems'.[27] In common with the rest of the SS, the men who composed these units were imbued with propaganda concerning the *Untermensch*, one example of which declared that 'these millions have been moulded with all the means of mass psychology, rendered stupid, provided with blinkers, proletarianised, their bestial drives fanaticised, themselves made into machines . . . for killing and blind destruction.'[28] Reinhard Heydrich, SS Obergruppenführer and Chief of the Reich Security Main Office, instructed the leaders of his *Einsatzgruppen* that, provided there was no economic, political, or military use for them, Communist Party members, Jews, and other 'subversive elements', such as saboteurs, propagandists, snipers, assassins, and agitators, were to be executed without hesitation. He also ordered that any purges initiated by any of the populace hostile to Communists or Jews were to be secretly encouraged.[29] In short, the *Einsatzgruppen* were to proceed against the 'Eastern criminals' as they thought fit.

In such a manner did the Germans intend to make war upon the Russians.

As early as 3 July, an elated Franz Halder entered in his diary: 'the campaign has been won in the course of two weeks.'[30] On the same day, Stalin spoke to the Russian people over the radio; in a lengthy address he emphasised that the Soviet Union was fighting for its existence. To halt the enemy, no loss of life or human suffering was to be considered too great; guerrilla warfare, the most potent expression of a people's resistance to an invader, was to be organised. The Soviet dictator declared: 'In areas occupied by the enemy, guerrilla units, mounted and on foot, must be formed; diversionist groups must be organised to combat enemy troops, to ferment guerrilla warfare everywhere, blow up bridges and roads, damage telephone and telegraph lines, set fire to forests, depots and trains. In occupied territories, conditions must be made unbearable for the enemy and all his collaborators; they must be pursued and annihilated wherever they are, and all their measures must be brought to nought.'[31]

Thus began the Soviet partisan struggle, a phantom war waged in the shadows. It was one in which the guerrilla was exhorted to use 'courage touching insolence' in all his dealings with the enemy. Together with some of the first tactical instructions sent to the units came an article written in 1906 by Lenin, entitled simply 'Partisan Warfare', and his statement: 'We [the Party] have never rejected terror on principle, nor can we do so. Terror is a form of military operation that may be usefully applied, or may even be essential at certain moments.'[32] If the partisan was not to be restricted by moral considerations, neither was he to be limited solely to a military role; behind the enemy lines he was to be the embodiment of the Communist belief that a conflict with imperialist states should be turned into a civil war of the proletariat against the bourgeoisie.[33] The guerrilla was not simply a man fighting for his country; he was a political-being struggling for a powerful and pervasive cause, against his own race as well as against the enemy. Militarily, he was to assist the progress of the Red Army by creating unbearable conditions in the enemy's rear; politically, he was to be the champion of the class-struggle in the furtherance of the Communist millenium.

Before the German invasion in 1941, as now, Communism in Russia was a goal still to be attained, rather than an order already firmly established, and the Soviet régime was active in imposing a new series of institutions on society and a new psychology on the individual. After more than twenty years of Soviet rule, the Russian leaders believed, with justification, that many of the pre-Revolution attitudes of the old order remained, especially among the peasants, whose dislike of the new ideology and its practice was widespread, if not vocal. Indeed, to rid the nation of what they considered to be this evil still in their midst, the Communists were glad to avail themselves of the opportunity that the war provided. Lenin had once declared: 'war tears down false façades, lays bare the weaknesses of governments, and uncovers internal putrefaction.'[34] A new society was being formed in the Soviet Union, and, as the years of Lenin's and Stalin's purges had so ably demonstrated, blood was bound to be shed in the process. In this, the partisans had their part to play. They were fighting not to preserve, but to destroy the old form of society, and, in its place, help create a new one. This was especially true of those areas that had only recently been brought under Soviet rule – the Baltic States and the western Ukraine – where antipathy to the régime was strong, but it also pertained within the borders of old Russia. Thus, with a vested interest in social disruption, there was no need for the Soviet partisans to avoid extreme civilian loss, nor to allow moral considerations to interfere with any action deemed necessary to rid the country of the invader. The class-war had acquired a new aspect.

Furthermore, the Soviet system in peacetime had been based not simply on police action, but on the maintenance of an atmosphere of terror, a feeling by the ordinary citizen that, whatever he said or did, he could not escape the omnicompetent and omnipresent organs of state authority. In war, it was essential that the population in the enemy-occupied territories should continue to believe that they were still under the watch of the Soviet security services; nobody should be allowed to accustom himself to the idea that Soviet power was at an end. This aim the partisans fulfilled; they were the representatives of the Soviet régime, evidence that neither it nor its ideology was defeated but, on the contrary, that it was active against the enemy and his collaborators. Anti-Soviet activity was never to become safe; those who took part in it would always feel themselves in danger; and the task of re-establishing Soviet authority in previously occupied territory would be made considerably easier by the fact that, even during the darkest times, its long arm of retribution had never completely vanished.

Ruthlessness, therefore, in the pursuit of both political and military aims, was demanded as much from the Soviet defender as it was from the German invader. No regard, either for personal safety or for any humanitarian principle, would be allowed to impede the partisan; this is exemplified by the recollection of one guerrilla commander of his motives for the execution of one, minor, operation: 'I knew, of course, that the Hitlerites might send a punitive expedition to the village, accuse its citizens of contacts with the partisans and cruelly avenge themselves on the peaceful population. But I also knew that the population, which was driven to repair the enemy's road, whether voluntarily or involuntarily, delayed the hour of victory by some time. But who can determine what a minute of military activity costs?'[35] The destruction of innocent civilians counted for little in the guerrilla war. The attitude was evident in the oath sworn by every member of the movement:

> 'I, a citizen of the Soviet Union, a true son of the heroic Russian people, swear that I will not lay down my weapons until the Fascist serpent in our land has been destroyed.
>
> 'I commit myself without reservation to carry out the orders of my commanders and superiors, and to observe the strictest military discipline. I swear to work a terrible, merciless, and unrelenting revenge upon the enemy for the burning of our cities and villages, for the murder of our children, and for the torture and atrocities committed against our people. Blood for blood! Death for death!
>
> 'I swear to assist the Red Army, and by all possible means to destroy the Hitlerite dogs without regard for myself, or my life.
>
> 'I swear that I would die in terrible battle rather than surrender myself, my family, and the entire Russian people to the Fascist deceivers.
>
> 'If, out of fear, weakness, or personal depravity, I should fail to uphold this oath and should betray the interests of my people, may I die a dishonourable death at the hands of my own comrades.'[36]

With such thoughts in mind, the partisan leaders sent their men to fight both the Germans and their own countrymen.

Chapter 2

The Failure of the Partisan Movement – 1941

Soviet rule has been eradicated in the occupied territories; the building of a new empire has begun.
ALFRED ROSENBERG November 1941

Before the invasion, General der Artillerie Alfred Jodl, Chief of Operations in the High Command of the Wehrmacht, had confidently predicted: 'The Russian colossus will be proved to be a pig's bladder; prick it, and it will burst.'[1] Certainly, in the summer and autumn of 1941, it appeared as if this prophecy would come true. On 22 June, Hitler had launched some three million German and allied troops into the Soviet Union; within five months they had penetrated more than 600 miles eastwards and had reached the gates of Moscow, having killed or captured nearly seven million Russian soldiers in the process. At least forty per cent of the Soviet Union's total population lay within the occupied area, as did roughly half its economic potential. The Soviet war machine had shown itself to be quite incapable of meeting the invader on equal terms, this being nowhere more apparent than in the partisan movement, where lack of preparation and organisation was endemic – and this despite the fact that guerrillas had previously played a distinguished part in modern Russian history.

In 1812, guerrillas had participated in the crushing of Napoleon's *Grande Armée* while on Russian soil;[2] Leo Tolstoy recorded in *War and Peace* that 'the cudgel of the people's war was raised in all its menacing and majestic power . . . it rose and fell and belaboured the French till the whole invading army had been driven out.'[3] Relying greatly on this experience, the Prussian military theorist, General Carl von Clausewitz, analysed the characteristics of a 'people's war' and likened it to 'a slow, gradual fire' which 'destroys the basis of the enemy force'.[4] Understandably, the revolutionary socialists spent much time considering what lessons could be learnt from such an experience.[5] Karl Marx claimed that only by such unorthodox methods could a weaker force defeat a stronger one, but Lenin, although recognising that a combination of terrorism, robbery, and ambush had its role to play in the revolutionary struggle, warned that 'the party of the proletariat must never regard guerrilla warfare as the only, or even the principal, method of struggle'.[6] This set the tone for succeeding Soviet writings on the subject. Analysts of the Russian Civil War of 1918–20, while they lauded the Red partisans for their militancy and dedication to Communism, always relegated their efforts to merely assisting the regular conscript army – the main element of war. Leon Trotsky, creator of the Red Army, rarely mentioned guerrillas in his writings, for he, in common with many others, believed in the fundamental importance of a mass army in any conflict with capitalist countries; irregular units were to be used only outside Soviet borders, to help to spread the revolution, while the defeat of the enemy would be the work of the regular forces. Stalin continued this policy, giving it further impetus. Although, as a former guerrilla-revolutionary in the Caucasus mountains, he possessed direct experience of such warfare, which led him to advocate mobilising subject-races against their colonialist rulers, Stalin nevertheless saw war in terms of the offensive, refusing to believe that there would be anything other than a brief and partial occupation of Soviet soil by an enemy. Why, therefore, was there any need for an internal partisan organisation? Indeed, he and his subordinates argued that this would be positively dangerous: not only would it be an admission of the possibility of losing territory in the event of war, but it would also encourage the individualist and independent tendencies that were a hallmark of irregular fighting-men but were an anathema to the régime. To place arms in the hands of people over whom the Soviet leaders had not the strictest control would, it was believed, be dangerous, especially in those regions, such as the Ukraine, most exposed to attack. Moreover, by 1941 the Soviet leaders were psychologically unprepared for underground resistance against an occupying power. Stalin's purges had ensured the premature demise of the Old Guard – the men of the revolution, the conspirators and fighters of the Party – and in their place had come the bureaucrats, the state organisers who were accustomed to undisputed power rather than to revolution.

Before the war, guerrilla warfare was a subject for general study by the central authorities in Moscow rather than for any active planning. Indeed, no plans, however generalised, were even circulated to those in the lower administrative levels, and, after his purge of the military command in 1937, Stalin put an end to all such preparations. As a result, the first official instructions for the development of a partisan organisation did not appear until five days after the German invasion had begun, and even then were issued only by the regional administration of the Ukraine, being signed by Nikita Krushchev, then head of the Ukrainian Communist Party. It was eleven days before there was any formal signal for the creation of a partisan movement for the Soviet Union as a whole. This was when, on 3 July, Stalin made a major radio address to the Russian people. His declaration, echoing a resolution of the Central Committee taken on 28 June, caught many by surprise; the Soviet administrative machinery, neither the fastest nor the most efficient in the world, moved ponderously into action. Regional partisan staffs were instituted by local Party initiative, but in a purely haphazard fashion: in Karelia in August, followed by Leningrad in September, Moscow in October, and the Ukraine and the Crimea in November. Meanwhile, the Soviet leadership was arguing as to where supreme control should lie – with the Party, or more specifically with the NKVD (the secret state police), or with the Red Army. It took ten months, during which time the partisan movement was nearly destroyed, before a compromise was agreed on and the Soviet guerrillas given a central command to co-ordinate their operations and supply their needs. Until then, their fortunes were dependent on voluntary co-operation between the *ad hoc* partisan organisations of the Communist Party, the NKVD, and the Red Army.

Not surprisingly, in the face of this lack of planning and strong central direction, together with the devastating German advances in the field and the widespread antipathy of the population towards Soviet rule, the first attempts at guerrilla activity were a failure. The general plan, on which the movement was based, called for the uniform distribution, regardless of terrain, targets, or population, of small, highly mobile *Otryadi* (units) within the former Party and NKVD administrative divisions. The theory was that the units, based, as far as possible, in forests, controlled by headquarters located usually in towns or cities, and reliant upon clandestine contacts with local inhabitants, were to undertake hit-and-run attacks on small enemy troop units, communications, and supply depots, and to terrorise collaborators. The reality, however, was to be very different.

The *Otryadi* themselves were far from uniform, being formed either by local Party organisations, Red Army units, or the NKVD. The latter had already instituted 'Destruction Battalions', units only little suited for guerrilla activity. They comprised between 100 and 200 men, too young or too old for military service, under the leadership of secret state policemen, their duties originally being to guard important installations and prevent sabotage. However, on Stalin's call, unreliable elements within the battalions were dismissed, Party and NKVD personnel were appointed officers, and then, in common with all other partisan units, the units withdrew to the most inaccessible areas available, built camps and began training, all the while waiting for the enemy advance to sweep over them. But the speed of the German attack all too often made this process impossible, and, in addition, prevented close co-operation with the Red Army, a co-operation which would, in any case, have been extremely difficult because of the acute shortage of radios. Most of the partisan units in western Russia were organised after their regions had been occupied, usually with inadequate equipment, and always without proper co-ordination with their neighbours. Food was sometimes so short that the guerrillas had to raid villages to feed themselves. Often, Red Army units that had been bypassed in the advance and had adopted the role of irregulars proved most effective of all Soviet units behind German lines.

Not all was a shambles, however. Deep in the Russian interior special schools were instituted to train partisan commanders and specialists in underground activity, teaching such arts as the derailment of locomotives and the destruction of bridges, as well as a hundred and one ways of killing a German sentry. The men who entered these establishments were thoroughly dedicated, forsaking not only their families but also their real names. On completion of their training, they were either assigned to regions in the path of the invader, or infiltrated or parachuted into occupied territory. They first began their operations in July 1941, but these were as a drop in the ocean and could do little to offset the lack of equipment, the poor training, and the inadequate leadership under which the hastily-formed *Otryadi* laboured. These, because of their inexperience, suffered unusually high casualities in their brushes with the enemy; moreover, owing to the territorially-based organisation of the movement, many found themselves in areas where targets were either lacking or were of little importance. This forced units to move to more suitable areas, thereby causing them to spend much valuable time moving across large distances, in addition to searching for food and weapons and constructing hidden shelters, instead of fighting the invader.

Shortly after entering Soviet territory, the German forces began to feel the first effects of partisan activity. The head of Soviet propaganda, Losovski, announced on 21 July 1941 that 'hundreds of partisans keep attacking the German communications. Everywhere there are tens of thousands of men sufficiently armed for fighting the invaders.'[7] Like his counterpart in Berlin, Losovski was prone to exaggeration, but there was, nevertheless, some truth in his assertion. The commander of Army Group North, Field-Marshal Wilhelm von Leeb, reported to the Army High Command in July that large numbers of Red Army troops, many in peasant clothes, were roaming the swamps and forests, and that he was prevented from destroying them by the vastness of the country and his lack of troops. In late July, a report[8] from 256th Infantry Division operating in north-east Belorussiya (White Russia) spoke of 'partisan regions' having been established, and mentioned that roads were mined daily. Sniping and assassination of sentries became more frequent. On 25 July, the first report on Soviet guerrillas was issued by the High Command of the Army (OKH), which stated that partisans were beginning to constitute danger to supply lines. Derailment of trains and ambushes on motor convoys were by then not unknown. Two months later, on 25 October, the Army Commander-in-Chief, Field-Marshal Walther von Brauchitsch, issued the first directive for the combating of partisans, as much in anticipation of activity to come as in reaction to what had gone before.[9] On 14 November, Generaloberst Erich von Manstein, commander of 11th Army in the Crimea, was told by his counter-intelligence officers that there was a well-organised, centrally-directed partisan organisation operating in the southern part of the region, and, as a result, he formed special anti-partisan staffs and units to deal with the menace;[10] guerrilla activity continued, however, and, during the night of 5 January 1942, some 900 partisans combined with the Red Army to mount a fairly large-scale operation against the 11th Army on the shore of the Black Sea.

For most German units, the experience of such activity on the part of Soviet partisans was the exception rather than the rule. On 1 December 1941, for example, a report from Area Commander 1/593 at Vyazma, some fifty miles east of Smolensk in the central sector, stated: 'There is still no indication of the formation of partisan groups or of partisan activity. . . .'[11] The territorial system instituted by the Soviets in the first hectic weeks of the war had proved ill-considered; as the Germans established their control, many *Otryadi* simply disappeared, their men either being captured or deserting. To this disastrous lack of preparation, common to all areas, were added two further factors – popular hostility and unsuitable terrain – both of which were to prove decisive in the history of the partisan movement throughout the war.

In the former Baltic republics of Estonia, Latvia and Lithuania, the inhabitants were particularly unsympathetic to the guerrillas. Having been incorporated into the Soviet Union against their will as late as June 1940, the people had never ceased to express their dissatisfaction with their new masters, often quite forcibly. Immediately on the Soviet occupation, nationalist bands had been formed to carry out acts of sabotage and terrorism against Russian authority, and in retaliation some 100,000 Balts had been arrested by the NKVD by mid-1941. The German invasion was the occasion for revenge; the nationalists rebelled against the Russians and welcomed the invaders as liberators. Not surprisingly, there was little local support for the formation of a partisan movement, and large numbers of Soviet agents assigned to the task were consequently withdrawn. East of the three republics, however, the Germans encountered more substantial opposition. The terrain of the Russian Soviet Socialist Republic west, south, and east of Leningrad, with its forests and swamps, was better suited to guerrillas, who were also un-hampered by any nationalist elements opposed to Soviet rule. As a result, by the end of October some 3,000 partisans had established themselves in the region. Even then, however, the sparse population and the poor local economy made both recruits and, more important, food difficult to come by; losses were particularly high and many units were wiped out. Although anti-Soviet nationalism was lacking, the peasants were nonetheless antipathetic towards the Communist cause – sharing an opposition that was widespread throughout Russia – and this made them unsympathetic, if not hostile, to the partisan units, largely composed, as they were, of representatives of the hated system. Consequently, the Germans had no difficulty in finding supporters and informers to aid their anti-guerrilla operations.

In the central sector, the partisans, although shaken by the rapid German advance, had more success, primarily because of the help afforded them by the thousands of Red Army stragglers who remained uncaptured and sought refuge in the impenetrable forests and swamps with which the region abounded. But, as in other areas, popular hostility limited the effectiveness of the movement. Many were the instances of betrayal by the local inhabitants. The commander of a detachment sent from Moscow to Belorussiya, G. Linkov, recounted how, when his fifty-five men were dispersed over a large area because of a bad parachute drop, it took him several months to find them, simply because of the indifference and hostility of the population; peasants even gave a detailed description of him to the German soldiers who were busy hunting down his detachment. Another partisan told how, despite the absence of enemy troops, the uncertainty of receiving a friendly reception from villages forced him to trail his dying comrade twelve miles before reaching a place of safety. Such experiences were widespread throughout the Soviet Union, and the need to become self-sufficient that was thereby forced on the guerrillas often proved unbearable, especially with the onset of winter.

In the central region, as in other areas, desertion was a particular problem, and a further manifestation of popular antipathy. In the Smolensk province, although more than 6,000 Party and Youth League members were left behind to work against the Germans, there were only 2,000, some of them newly recruited, still operating in the area by the autumn. In the Orel province, the situation was similar; seventy-five Destroyer Battalions, totalling 10,000 men, had been formed, but when the invader arrived only 2,300 stayed to fight, many of whom faded away in the following weeks. Only in the Moscow region did the partisans come up to expectation; there, some 2,000 men and women operated with considerable bravery and tenacity when the capital was under threat of occupation during the later stages of the German advance. One, an eighteen-year-old girl named Zoya Kosmodemyonskaya, was captured, tortured, and hanged by the Germans; for her undoubted bravery she received the title of 'Hero of the Soviet Union', the highest award in the gift of Stalin, and, thanks to the Party propaganda machine, became a national heroine and symbol of resistance for millions of Russians. Her name now graces a tank regiment of the East German Army.

In the Ukraine,[12] where the swiftness of the German advance prevented the Soviets from establishing many *Otryadi*, the area west of the river Dnepr was almost totally free of irregular activity. Further east, too, it proved impossible to harass the invaders, despite all endeavours, which included the sending of 33,000 Party members into occupied territory. In the open steppes of central and southern Ukraine, there was neither natural cover nor a sympathetic population; indeed, the people there held the Soviet régime in particular contempt. The few units formed in this region seem to have been totally destroyed by early 1942, although some underground groups, mainly located in cities, remained to carry on the Communist struggle. The forests and swamps to the north, too, were largely cleared of guerrillas by the end of 1941, although a few remained around Polesye. Not until the summer of 1943 were partisans to become more than a passing nuisance in any part of the Ukraine. In the Crimea, also, the guerrillas were in a very difficult position, largely because of the hostility of the Tartars, who eagerly gave help to the Germans. By the end of the year, most of the guerrillas had been driven into the Yaila mountains, where they were to suffer severe food shortages and deprivations of all kinds. Their effectiveness, accordingly, was low. From the beginning, however, the Crimean partisans distinguished themselves by establishing a carefully organised system of command which was to survive until the end of the war, and by adapting the territorial organisation to suit the dire circumstances in which they found themselves.

By the end of 1941, then, of the seventy million people in the occupied regions of the Soviet Union, probably no more than 30,000 were in the partisan movement, scattered, uncoordinated and unevenly, over 850,000 square miles; most were poorly equipped and many undernourished. The territorial organisation was in ruins; the leaders of the *Otryadi* were largely state officials, inexperienced and unaccustomed to the hardships and methods of guerrilla warfare; the system of communications was in a parlous state, in some areas non-existent; and the necessary central command, supply, and replacement organisations had yet to be formed.

In such disarray, the partisans were forced to exist through one of the severest winters in modern Russian history. In some areas temperatures fell to around –40° Fahrenheit, marshes froze over, and the land became covered with snow, in places up to a depth of 28 inches. Heating and food often gave out; foot-prints in the snow revealed hiding-places; the lack of foliage on the trees exposed the camps to aerial spotting. Some guerrillas died, others were captured, a few surrendered. The Russian winter, no friend to the invader, was no ally of the Soviet partisan. As spring began, fewer than 30,000 bedraggled survivors emerged to continue the fight in the German rear. The prospects for success looked poor.

Chapter 3

The Revival of the Partisan Movement – 1942

The occupied territories are seething with discontent.
The time has come for decisive action.
HEINRICH HIMMLER August 1942

The early spring of 1942 was a decisive period for the Soviet partisans. Defeat seemed probable. The Germans had survived the Red Army's counter-offensive and were making ready for a new advance, while the guerrilla movement, which had been badly mauled, still lacked both central control and coherent organisation. Only in the few regions where they could avail themselves of both natural protection and a friendly attitude from the inhabitants, could the guerrillas hope to survive German counter-measures. In February, a German security report noted that, with modest resources assigned to the task, the guerrilla danger could soon be overcome[1]; few on either side would have quarrelled with this statement. By the end of the year, however, matters were to look very different, the High Command of the Army reporting that 'unless measures are taken immediately, the partisan menace will endanger the entire front'.[2] For this state of affairs, the Germans had themselves to blame.

Over large areas of the Soviet Union, the German invaders had initially been greeted by the population as heroes, as liberators rather than as conquerors. A corporal in a tank regiment in the southern sector of the front wrote: 'nowhere have I seen even the slightest sign of hatred from the civilians. We are greeted only by smiling faces.'[3] Large numbers of Ukrainians, Cossacks, Tartars, Georgians, Turkomens, and Armenians deserted to the German Army; whole villages turned out to greet the men in field-grey, with posies of flowers and food. Generaloberst Heinz Guderian, Commander of Panzer Group 2 which led the attack in the centre, remembered that 'women came out from their villages on to the very battlefield bringing wooden platters of bread and butter and eggs, and in my case at least, refused to let me move on before I had eaten'.[4] Even the Führer's guard unit, the *Leibstandarte* SS 'Adolf Hitler', was met in the south by 'laughing and cheering people', and the dictator himself was regarded, at least by the Ukrainians, as the 'Saviour of Europe'.[5] Ukrainian nationalists in eastern Galicia rose against their Soviet masters even before the German advance had reached them, although they were only to suffer savage reprisals.

General Anders, commander of the Free Polish Army, wrote that the battles in 1941 'disclosed the widespread disinclination of the Soviet soldier to fight in the defence of the "fatherland of the proletariat", and his hatred of the régime, which was shared by the great majority of the population of the USSR. Many soldiers, seeing the war as an opportunity for a change of order in Russia, wished for German victory and therefore surrendered in great masses. . . .'[6] Although the general exaggerated, there was more than a little truth in his statement. In a highly secret order dated 16 July, Stalin noted that 'on all fronts' there were numerous elements 'given to panic and even orientated towards the enemy', who, 'at the first pressure, throw away their weapons . . . and drag others along with them'. Furthermore, he added, 'the number of firm and steady commanders and commissars is not very great'.[7]

Nationalism, important though it was in areas such as the Baltic States, the western Ukraine, and the Yaila mountains in the Crimea, had meant little to the mass of peasants who made up two-thirds of the population of the USSR (in Belorussiya, four-fifths of the inhabitants were peasants). Instead, their motivation arose from a simple hatred of Communism and the Soviet régime. In the Ukraine, with its rich black soil, the effects of the forced establishment of *kolkhozes* (collective farms) in the 1930s, and the elimination of the *kulaks* (peasants who had a large influence over rural economic life) had been disastrous; mass famine had ravaged the population, peasants had been uprooted, imprisonment and death were common, and dislike of collectivisation, of high production quotas, and of the absence of any profit motive were universal. Further to the north, in Belorussiya, where the ground was poorer, the impact of the *kolkhozes* had been less, but resentment was equally great. Thus, whether from reasons of nationalism or dissatisfaction, the overwhelming majority of the population in the occupied areas were, at the very least, indifferent to the invaders, and, for the most part, welcomed them as a catalyst that would bring about change for the better. Indeed, it was because of this lack of loyalty to the Soviet cause that Stalin introduced the idea of the Great Patriotic War, in which the vital issue at stake was not the Union or Communism, but sacred Mother Russia.

Had the Germans recognised the advantage to them that lay in the political realities behind the façade of the Soviet Union and accordingly treated the peoples of the occupied areas as allies in the fight against Bolshevism, the collapse of the Soviet system might well have been brought about. But they did not. The ruthlessness that had been so evident in the official pronouncements, directives, orders, and propaganda before Operation Barbarossa found virulent expression during the conduct of the campaign. The Easterner, whether he was Ukrainian, Belorussiyan, or Muscovite, was treated as an *Untermensch*, subject to exploitation, deprivation, humiliation and death. Army units varied in their attitude towards the Russians, whether soldiers and civilians; sympathy co-existed uneasily with brutality. A clinical harshness was, however, most common. The Commissar Order was applied in the field by most commanders, often against their own inclinations, and even by those who opposed everything that Hitler stood for. Generaloberst Erich Hoepner, for example, commander of Panzer Group 4 in the north, who ended his days hanging by piano wire from a meat-hook for his part in the Bomb Plot of June 1944, reported on 10 July 1941 that his men had 'liquidated' no fewer than 101 commissars. Many generals issued their own orders to their troops, telling them to show no mercy to the Slavs. In October, for example, Field-Marshal Walter von Reichenau, commander of 6th Army in the Ukraine, told his soldiers that 'Feeding inhabitants and prisoners-of-war who do not work for the German Armed Forces from army messes is as much an act of misplaced humaneness as giving away bread or cigarettes. . . .'[8] Such exhortations had their effect on the troops. One, a sergeant who had bayoneted a youth who was shouting curses at the marching troops, when put before a court-martial, was acquitted unconditionally; another, an infantryman aged nineteen who had set fire to a cottage with five bound woodcutters inside, was similarly absolved from his crime. Such instances were far from uncommon. Red Army personnel who surrendered were often shot rather than taken prisoner; civilians who acted in a suspicious manner were likely to be killed without question; reprisals against innocents were, in many areas, commonplace. Only in cases of rape and of thieving was German military law to be applied with its usual severity.

The treatment of Soviet prisoners-of-war was particularly terrible. By mid-December, the German Army held more than 3,800,000 military captives. On 25 July, the Army High Command had instructed that 'In line with the prestige and dignity of the German Army, every German soldier must maintain distance and such an attitude with regard to Russian prisoners-of-war as takes account of the bitterness and inhuman brutality of the Russians in battle. . . . In particular, fleeing prisoners-of-war are to be shot without preliminary warning to stop.'[9] Fraternisation was forbidden, and punished severely; any form of resistance was to be dealt with by force. At first, some prisoners were released almost immediately upon capture – men from the Baltic States and the Ukraine – but this practice was soon ended. The majority who remained were treated barbarically; many spent weeks, even in the severe winter, without shelter and with little food. Epidemics were rife, starvation an everyday occurrence, and cannibalism not unknown. Even the commandants of the SS concentration camps complained of the low condition in which Soviet prisoners arrived into their care. Many men, especially of Jewish and Asiatic origin, were handed over to the SS for extermination; so indiscriminate did this selection become that on occasion it sufficed merely for a man to have black hair and brown eyes for him to be earmarked for certain death. During the four years of war with the Soviet Union, no fewer than three million of the five million Russian prisoners-of-war were estimated to have died in German captivity.

While many, though by no means all, Army units indiscriminately killed and maltreated soldier and civilian alike, as they believed the occasion demanded, the SS carried out its task of extermination in a far more systematic manner. Mass murders of Jews and Communists were undertaken in towns and villages, and the reports from the SS *Einsatzgruppen* are full of stark figures which serve to represent unimaginable human suffering. On 19 October 1941, for example, a commando of *Einsatzgruppe* A entered Borisov, in the central sector, and killed the whole Jewish population, numbering 7,620; *Einsatzgruppe* D reported towards the end of the autumn that, in the previous few days, 3,176 Jews, 85 partisans, 12 looters, and 122 Communist functionaries had been eliminated, bringing the total for the campaign to 79,276. By the winter, the four *Einsatzgruppen* had reported the death of almost half a million persons, three-quarters of them Jews. Behind the *Einsatzgruppen* came yet more SS forces, this time under the command of Higher SS and Police Leaders who were responsible for police security in the occupied regions. Further executions took place, again mostly of Jews but including a large number of Communists and other 'subversive' elements, to the tune of at least 100,000 by the end of the year. Even the SS murderers were exhausted, mentally as well as physically, by their tasks.

After the Army and the SS had wreaked what they would in the occupied areas of the Soviet Union, the *Goldfasanen* (Gilded Pheasants) arrived to complete the task of subjugation. These were the officials of the *Ostministerium*, the Ministry for the Occupied Eastern Territories, men of generally low intelligence, of whom the other numerous agencies of the National Socialist Party and State had been only too anxious to rid themselves. Hitler had spoken of them as 'new type of men . . . real masters . . . viceroys';[10] those who saw them in action had a different view, one remarking that they were 'Bürger without horizon or sophistication; the philistines who like to play Lord'.[11] Their qualities and attitudes differed, from the ineffectual planning of Rosenberg and the self-interest of Heinrich Lohse, Reich Commissar of Ostland, to the ruthlessness of Erich Koch, Reich Commissar of the Ukraine, but their repression of the Russians remained constant. In the north, Lohse introduced excessive centralisation of administration and laid down scores of orders, directives, and regulations to control the population and the economy, including such intricate details of everyday life as the prices of geese with or without heads. Although he himself was not inspired by any hatred of the peoples over whom he ruled, his subordinates often were, foremost being Wilhelm Kube, General-Commissar for Belorussiya, whose dislike of Greater-Russians and Jews was matched by the harshness of his measures. To the south, Koch's biological hatred for the Slavs ushered in an era of oppression that was an anathema to all who wished to foster good relations with the Ukrainians. His belief was that 'the Ukraine is for us only an object of exploitation ... the people must, as a second-grade people, be utilised to a certain extent for the solution of military problems, even if they have to be caught with a lasso.'[12] Despite regional variations, economic exploitation and destruction of the intelligentsia, Jews, and any potential opposition were standard throughout the occupied territories; only the degree of intensity with which this policy was carried out, varied.

The rise of a strong Soviet partisan movement largely as a direct consequence of German occupation policy is well illustrated by two examples.[13] In the summer of 1941, the eastward advance of a front-line infantry corps was temporarily halted in the Bobruysk area of the central front. For the purposes of administration and the acquisition of supplies from the locals, the corps area was subdivided and placed under the control of its component divisions. One particular division covered territory of forty square miles between the Bobruysk-Roslavl highway and the Berezina river. Under enlightened supervision, which included the abolition of collectivisation and the introduction of financial incentive, the local economy, which had been paralysed by the war, flourished better than it had done for years. A large measure of autonomy was allowed the Russians. As a result, the division was able to make a considerable contribution towards the overall supply system without robbing the locality, and engendered a feeling of confidence among the inhabitants. A certain amount of fraternisation was allowed, and any arbitrary act by the troops against persons or property was punished most severely. Disaffection and resistance were unknown; co-operation was widespread. In August, the front-line soldiers moved on, to be replaced by the rear-area military administrators. The population was immediately treated in a markedly different manner. Curfews were rigidly enforced, and every rule of common-sense was replaced by strict adherence to the letter of the law. Co-operation was largely withdrawn. This, Soviet agents were quick to exploit; within a short time the partisans had gained a foothold in the area, and it was not long before they had gained the upper hand over the Germans. Disruption of communications, and a fall in the economic value of the region, were the result. That autumn, a similar advantage was taken by the partisans in the area around Mglin, west of Bryansk. A successful administration was established by a division that had been temporarily halted and, although the front line was no more than 25 miles away, peaceful conditions prevailed. But again, after the division had left and the occupation forces had moved in, conditions changed rapidly. Persecution of Jews and conscription of labour transformed the area, within six months, into a hotbed of partisan activity.

The connection between popular dissatisfaction with German rule and the rise of the guerrilla movement was recognised by a number of Germans at the time. Even the SS was occasionally aware of it; as early as the middle of July 1941, an SD (the SS Security Service) report from Belorussiya noted that 'The positive attitude towards the Germans is being jeopardized by the indiscriminate requisitions by the troops, which become generally known, further by individual instances of rape, and by the way the Army treats the civilian population, which feels handled as an enemy people'.[14] The Army, in its turn, blamed the SS and the political officials, although it was prepared to admit its own mistakes. A report from the 255th Infantry Division, dated 13 November 1941, spoke of 'the great danger which the large number of [German] stragglers in all parts of the area [Yelnya-Dorogobuzh] constitutes both for the maintenance of discipline and for the pacification of the country. These soldiers, who have been left behind by other units to guard munitions or . . . vehicles which have become stuck, continuously requisition and loot in the villages in a manner which embitters the population and practically drives it into the arms of the partisans.'[15] Physical abuse was held to have been particularly important in stimulating hatred of the German masters. The next year, on 13 May 1942, Rosenberg felt himself constrained to write to his headstrong deputy, Koch, in the following manner: 'There exists a direct danger that, if the population should come to believe that the rule of National Socialism would have worse effects than Bolshevik policy, the necessary consequence would be the occurrence of acts of sabotage and the formation of partisan bands.'[16] This belief, Rosenberg echoed a year later in a letter to Dr Lammers, Chief of the Reich Chancery, when he stated: 'The partisan bands . . . have become a magnet for all the disappointed elements among the indigenous population.'[17]. On 22 May 1942, even

Goebbels wrote in his diary: 'Basically, I believe we must change our policies essentially as regards the peoples in the East. We could reduce the danger from partisans considerably if we succeeded in winning some of these peoples' confidence.'[18]. But no change was forthcoming; the endangered population often chose to flee to inaccessible areas and join the guerrillas. As Rosenberg wrote to Fritz Sauckel, Plenipotentiary-General for Labour Allocation, on 21 December 1942: 'the increase of the guerrilla bands in the occupied Eastern regions is largely due to the fact that the methods used for procuring labourers . . . are felt to be forced measures of mass deportations, so that the endangered persons prefer to escape their fate by withdrawing into the woods or going to the guerrilla bands.'[19]

In October 1942, Otto Bräutigam, Head of the Main Political Department of the Ministry for Occupied Territories, wrote a long criticism of the invader's policy; he described how the proper treatment of the peoples of the Soviet Union 'would have kindled the greatest enthusiasm and would have put at our disposal a mass consisting of millions', as well as have reduced the powers of resistance of the Red Army, and he demonstrated how this potential was wasted by the refusal to acknowledge even the modest wishes of the population. Bräutigam regarded the treatment of prisoners-of-war as 'a factor of primary importance'. He wrote:

> 'it is no longer a secret from friend or foe that hundreds of thousands of them have literally died of starvation and cold in our camps. It is alleged that there were not enough supplies of food on hand for them. But it is strange that food supplies are lacking only for prisoners-of-war from the Soviet Union, while complaints about the treatment of other prisoners – Poles, Serbs, French and English – have not been voiced. It is obvious that nothing is more calculated to strengthen the resistance of the Red Army than the knowledge that in German captivity they are faced with a slow and painful death.'

Bräutigam recognised other German mistakes: the shipping of thousands of forced-labourers to the Reich, in miserable conditions [begun in mid 1942]; the failure to institute proper agrarian reform, to announce the restoration of religious freedom and individual ownership, to provide guarantees about the future of the conquered peoples, and to institute an indigenous alternative government to the Soviet régime; and, generally, the treatment of the peoples of the occupied territories as 'second-class Whites, to whom providence is alleged to have given the task of slaving for Germany and for Europe'. The results were obvious. Bräutigam wrote:

> 'As the population has become aware of our true attitude towards it, so to the same degree has the resistance of the Red Army and the strength of the partisan movement increased.... Our political policy has forced both Bolsheviks and Russian nationals into a common front against us. The Russian today is fighting with exceptional bravery and self-sacrifice for nothing more or less than the recognition of his human dignity.... The forty million Ukrainians who greeted us joyfully as liberators are today indifferent to us and are already beginning to swing into the enemy camp. If we do not succeed in checking this situation at the last moment, we risk the overnight emergence in the Ukraine of a partisan movement which would not only eliminate the Ukraine as a source of food supply, but would also tie up the reinforcements of the Germany Army, threaten its existence and thereby involve the danger of a German defeat....'[20]

The partisans, themselves, were aware of the importance in this change of mood among the people. One brigade, operating south of the river Dno in the area of Army Group North, reported:

> 'The most characteristic feature in the relations between the population and the occupying forces [is] that now, after two months of occupation, all, and that includes the most reactionary category of the workers, turn an unfriendly and united face to the Fascists, based on the facts of life.
>
> 'Everything has gone to show that to stand aside from the struggle between the Soviet people and German Fascism is impossible....
>
> 'The command of the brigade considered very rightly that without close contact with the population, without a fight to re-establish the collective farms, to establish soviets and the laws of the Soviet state, it was impossible to create for the partisan movement a powerful economic and political basis, and it was impossible to win the sympathy and support of the population.'[21]

Added to this, the effect of German atrocities on the partisans' will to resist was considerable. In his memoirs, the guerrilla leader, Sidor Kovpak, remembered one incident: 'The girls [in the partisan band] now knew there was no fouler evildoer in the world than the Hitlerites, but what they saw in blood-drenched Novaya Sloboda, literally stupefied them. In the past we had tried to take care of the girls, not to take them on very dangerous operations, but after they had been in Novaya Sloboda, it was impossible to do so.... It was thus that peaceful Soviet men and women became terrible avengers of the people.'[22]

To German brutality was added German failure, even in 1941. At the end of the year they had proved unable to take Moscow despite all efforts; during the Soviet counter-offensive that followed, they were forced to yield much hard-won ground and to lose a significant proportion of their men and equipment. The much-vaunted Wehrmacht was seen to be fallible; the prospect of Hitler's victory, so certain in the heat of summer, seemed more unlikely in the intense cold of the Russian winter. If the prospect of Communist success did not exactly elate most of the population, especially the peasants, the possibility of German defeat did make the idea of co-operating with the invader and incurring the wrath of the Soviet régime distinctly unacceptable. From this, the partisans were bound to benefit. Furthermore, the same increase in partisan activity that German brutality and defeat had encouraged was in itself a further sign of German failure; as the commander of the rear area of Army Group Centre wrote in April 1942: 'The confidence of the population in the strength of the German Army is declining as it gets the impression that we are not subduing the partisans. It is therefore more inclined to support or even to join the partisans.'[23] Another German report remarked that the attitude of the average citizen was: 'If I stay with the Germans, I shall be shot when the Bolsheviks come; if the Bolsheviks don't come, I shall be shot sooner or later by the Germans. Thus, if I stay with the Germans, it means certain death; if I join the partisans, I shall probably save myself.'[24]

Time and experience were not to alleviate the oppression until it was too late: the Russian peoples had been irrevocably alienated from German rule. The partisans, although still disliked as representatives of the Soviet system, became the lesser of two evils. Guderian put it quite simply in his memoirs: 'The so-called Reich Commissars soon managed to alienate all sympathy from the Germans, and thus to prepare the ground for all the horrors of partisan warfare.'[25] As the remembrance of Soviet mismanagement and terror dimmed with time, and the experience of German behaviour became ever more unbearable, the people found themselves less alienated from the representatives of Communism than from those of National Socialism. At the same time, as the prospect of a German victory faded and the certainty of a Soviet return grew stronger, the advantages of alliance with the invader diminished and those of collaboration with the partisans increased. Although this development was far from uniform throughout the occupied territories, with nationalist bands being formed in both the Ukraine and the Baltic States with the intention of fighting both German and Russian, it is certain that, without this rejection of the invaders by the indigenous population behind the northern and, more particularly, the central fronts, the guerrillas would have stood little chance of survival. Their debt to the Germans was immense.

In 1942, the partisan movement was also particularly aided by the existence of large numbers of men from the Red Army and, to a far lesser extent, the NKVD who had eluded capture by the Germans in 1941. Although in the north and in the Baltic States the Germans had succeeded in taking prisoner the great majority of Soviet soldiers left behind by the retreating armies, numerous survivors were still hiding in the forests and swamps of Belorussiya, Bryansk, and the Russian Soviet Socialist Republic. Towards the end of 1941, these stragglers, amounting to three or four hundred thousand, many of whom remained in disciplined groups, were beginning to have an effect on German security, although this was usually because of their forays for food and arms rather than any planned guerrilla activity. Many of these groups surrendered, for, to those ignorant of the reality of the prisoner-of-war camps, the ravages of starvation and lack of protection from the elements made imprisonment seem preferable. However, those who resisted captivity, spurred as they were by the horror-stories which were circulating about German treatment, and realising that surrender would mean harsh imprisonment or death, had little alternative but to become partisans. Soviet agents sought them out to enroll them for the cause, and guerrilla bands welcomed them, providing for the fugitives much-needed food and shelter together with at least the appearance of security. From these groups, experienced officers were found to give the *Otryadi* the necessary military experience that their political leadership had so clearly lacked.

At the same time, a number of Soviet prisoners-of-war made determined attempts to break out of captivity and reach the partisans; one German report[26] tells of a rising planned by the inmates of a hospital near Voroshilov in conjunction with men in a camp and a factory, to take place in early January 1942. The prisoners acting as batmen to the German officers were to steal their masters' weapons and lead the uprising; if successful, there was to be a meeting, previously scheduled, with partisans near Minsk. But the Germans learnt of the plan through an informer and were able to foil it. Other attempts, however, were more successful, and a number of escaped prisoners-of-war found their way to the bands hidden in the swamps and forests of European Russia. There, they joined the large numbers of Red Army soldiers who were to become a key element in the partisan movement. A report from the Chief of the German Secret Field Police, dated 31 July 1942, suggested that this would not have happened had the occupying authorities pursued more enlightened policies. It noted that a number of stragglers and escapees had settled down in villages but, because of a lack of credentials and the reorganisation of the agricultural system, they had been unable to obtain work, and, hearing rumours of forced labour in Germany and of the fate of prisoners-of-war, they had 'left their places of employment in droves and went into the forests where they found partisan bands'.[27] By the summer of 1942, such men formed some sixty per cent of the guerrilla units, their military training and experience, their general lack of local family ties, and their legal and moral obligation to the Soviet state making them qualitatively by far the most important single element within the movement.

The alienation by the Germans of large numbers of the population and Red Army personnel, important though it turned out to be, was not of itself sufficient. What was required to turn popular discontent into something more than just an undisciplined reaction to enemy rule, without any guarantee of adherence to the Communist cause, was a new partisan organisation with a strongly centralised command to take full advantage of the fruits of German brutality. This, which had been singularly lacking in 1941, the Soviet régime provided in 1942.

By the beginning of 1942, the territorial control exercised by Party organisations had disintegrated, and the Red Army, which was better equipped for the task, took over direction of the guerrillas. Such a transfer was facilitated by the fact that most partisan activity at that time took place near the front line, the area of most concern to the military. Supplies were flown in from various front headquarters; army officers cut off behind the enemy lines assumed command of *Otryadi*, and even teams of parachutists led by men specially recruited by the Party were turned over to military control. Moreover, the gain in prestige by the Red Army during the relatively successful winter counter-offensive, encouraged partisan units to attach themselves to the military, a development that was furthered by direct contact with long-range scouting teams sent behind the German lines. Divisional, corps, as well as army and front commands, began to issue orders directly to the partisans, and so did much to co-ordinate their activities with those of the regular units. Although circumstances varied greatly throughout the occupied regions, as a general rule the military councils of the various front commands, on which sat Party representatives, played the major part in formulating the important decisions concerning guerrilla war. However, all this was a makeshift arrangement; there was no organisation within the Red Army capable of dealing with all the complex problems involved in a large-scale partisan movement. It was obvious that a new form of command was required, and on 30 May, after almost a year of guerrilla activity, this was provided.

The Central Staff for Partisan Warfare was an unusual organisation. Formally, it was attached to the Supreme Headquarters of the Red Army, and the Minister of Defence, Marshal Klimentii Voroshilov, was appointed commander-in-chief of the movement; in reality, however, its links with the Party were as great as, if not greater than, those with the military. Panteleymon Ponomarenko, First Secretary of the Belorussiyan Communist Party and a close associate of Stalin, was given the rank of Lieutenant-General and made Chief of Staff and effective leader of the partisans. Although he had had no military experience since 1919, it was he who appointed and dismissed guerrilla leaders, signed orders from the Central Staff, and generally directed operations. Moreover, other representatives of the Party also held positions on the Staff, which was itself attached to the Central Committee of the All-Union Communist Party, a link that was not often emphasised in propaganda and official pronouncements. The Communist Party, disturbed at the rapid gain in prestige and power of the military, had, by separating the partisan movement from the Red Army and creating a distinct command structure, diminished this in one important area. Although no open break was made with the previous system of control, the Party managed to increase its influence at the expense of that of the Red Army. It now had firm control of its representatives in the occupied regions – the partisans – but at the same time was able to draw on the expertise and resources of the Army. It was a compromise that worked well.

By instituting the Central Staff for Partisan Warfare, the Soviet régime had placed its faith in a strongly centralised, rather than a decentralised, system of command. Instead of appreciating the advantages of decentralisation to a guerrilla organisation – independence, flexibility, and simplicity – the Soviets feared its disadvantages – rebellion, stagnation, and disintegration. To prevent individual commanders from becoming a law unto themselves and an opposition to the régime (as had sometimes been experienced in the Civil War), and to ensure that the movement played its part in the war effort in co-ordination and not in conflict with the regular forces, a strong central control was necessary. Moreover, in the conditions that pertained behind the German lines – an area known to the guerrillas as the 'Little Land' – where the partisans could not always be sure of support from the local people, it was vital that sustenance could be obtained from the 'Great Land', as the unoccupied regions were called. This, the Central Staff provided.

The institution of the Central Staff, although the most important, was only one of the ways by which the Soviet régime established a strong control over the partisan movement. Every effort was made to introduce radio contact between the units in the field and Moscow; commissars, staff officers, and inspectors were sent to keep an eye on the guerrillas and their commanders; the NKVD maintained sections with every staff and band; partisan leaders were often called to the capital to receive orders; and only politically 'reliable' persons were chosen to command units – and even then they were subject to close supervision, and were frequently moved. Indeed, the very fact that a central command became the main, or the sole, means by which units could exist in the field, ensured a large measure of compliance by local leaders with Soviet authority.

Under the Central Staff, operational command was divided between the front staffs and the territorial staffs. The front staffs were formed at most Red Army front headquarters (the exceptions were in the Ukraine, where the small number of partisan units made a regular control unnecessary, and, until early 1943, in the area around Orel), and contained representatives of the major Soviet organisations, thereby institutionalising the joint Party and Army responsibility for the guerrilla movement. They were provided with a large technical organisation and had as their task the operational control, supply, reinforcement, and personnel direction of the partisan bands in areas near the front line. Below the front staffs, operational groups were instituted at army headquarters when necessary, their role being to co-ordinate guerrilla activities with those of the field armies. The territorial staffs of the partisan movement evolved from the early territorial commands instituted by the Party in the union republics occupied by the enemy towards the end of 1941. As with the front staffs, they were to control the recruitment, operations, supply, and personnel of partisan units, but only in those regions away from the front lines. Based in the 'Great Land', usually in Moscow, they were instituted for almost all the union republics, including Lithuania, Latvia, and, in February 1944, Moldavia. It appears that the Karelo-Finnish Soviet Socialist Republic was the only region not to possess such a staff, control there being exercised exclusively by the Karelian Front Staff. The Belorussiyan Staff was the most active, and except in the Crimea, the least active was the Staff of the South, which had control of only a few bands. The Leningrad Staff was unique, in that, in addition to its other duties, it also provided an intermediate level of command between the three front staffs of the region (North-West, Volkhov, and Leningrad), and the Central Staff; this was a legacy from the period in 1941 when control had been shared between the Party and the front staff (North-West) which then covered the whole area.

Between the main forms of control – central, front and territorial – there was no recognised chain of command down to the units in the field. Ambiguity, flexibility, and diversity were the keynotes, and this often made life extremely confusing and difficult for the guerrilla leaders. No one channel was used; the units in the field received orders directly from at least two of the higher levels of command, and even from the Red Army itself, as well as from other intermediate commands based in the occupied areas that were set up to control the day-to-day conduct of the units. At the same time, advice, which it was risky to disregard, came from various Party organisations (such as the *Komsomol*, the 'junior' Party, whose officials played a major role in controlling young partisans), and constant surveillance was undertaken by the NKVD. Only if a partisan commander had a strong personality, and if his success in the field made him valuable to the régime, could he disregard such 'advice'. Success brought its own immunity; failure when combined with disobedience was invariably fatal. Often, the representatives of Soviet authority in the units – the commissar, the NKVD section chief – would settle all differences between themselves, each compromising his own position and presenting a unified front to the central authorities. However, despite all this, the Central Staff remained supreme and could direct the partisan movement as it alone thought fit.

The creation of a centralised command was the signal that, henceforth, the Soviets would devote large resources to the partisan movement. More and better equipment and supplies were either flown to the units in the field or infiltrated through the various gaps in the enemy front line that had opened up as a result of the winter counter-offensive. Specialists were sent into the German rear in groups, often comprising a commander, commissar, radio operator, and explosives expert, with instructions to form new bands; doctors and nurses were made available to the field units; and, generally, the leadership of units was invigorated, trained men from the Army or the NKVD taking over from political officials. Between April and October alone, the Belorussiyan Staff sent 2,600 trained men into occupied territory. Training centres were then set up behind German lines; by the middle of 1942, for example, there were no fewer than fifteen situated around the city of Voronezh.

The guerrilla bands themselves also underwent many changes, the average size increasing considerably. They varied between 350 and 2,000 men – large enough to be able to operate independently and continuously against the enemy, and to make the best use of scarce commanders and commissars of suitable quality. By the summer, few bands possessed less than 350 men, those that had usually being engaged on special tasks; even fewer had more than 2,000. Increases in size were offset by the high losses incurred when fighting the Germans, and, if this were not so, by the commands placing a limit on recruitment for fear that more men would prove less mobile, unwieldy in operation, difficult to supply, and injurious to the principle that personal control by the commander was necessary for maintaining morale and discipline. Moreover, the Soviet régime was concerned that it should not be exposed to the possibility of opposition from an all-powerful leader with a large following of men loyal only to him.

The new organisation in the field was based on the independent brigade (known as a regiment in the Leningrad area), made up of several

Otryadi, usually up to five in number, which, in their turn, were divided into platoons and sections. A brigade could be dispersed over ten or twenty square miles, and a group of brigades sometimes occupied an area of several hundred square miles. For regional, operational, and historical reasons, units differed greatly in size, organisation, and equipment, and little attempt was made to impose unnecessary standardisation. Often a leader would favour his old *Otryad* at the expense of the others within his brigade, with the result that it would be significantly larger and better equipped than the others. Under the commander, the division of responsibility was distinctly military in style, with a commissar, a chief of staff, a chief of intelligence, a chief of counter-intelligence, and a chief of supply; each *Otryad* was led by both a commander and a commissar.

Nonetheless, despite all developments in organisation, training and equipment, the new partisan movement was still strictly limited by factors outside its control. Disregarding completely the old idea of units based on the territorial administrative divisions, which had proved so fatal the previous year, the guerrillas were forced to confine themselves to favourable terrain. Geographical features of the Soviet Union were always to be decisive in limiting their area of activity. The guerrilla, wherever he be, is heavily reliant on natural conditions, not only for protection from his hunter but also for food and shelter. For him, the ideal natural environment is one that is relatively impenetrable to regular military forces, capable of providing shelter and within striking distance of important enemy lines of communication, supply centres, and the like. The wide open, treeless, arid and sometimes sandy expanses of the Russian steppes, which covered more than half the territory occupied by the Germans, were clearly ill-suited to their activities. Early experience showed that, despite the predictions of some experts before the war, the relatively small, isolated forests and swamps found on the steppes proved totally inadequate to maintain partisan detachments. Unable to evade attack, they were quickly destroyed by the enemy. Thus, almost the entire Ukraine, together with substantial parts of the northern regions, bleak and economically desolate, were quickly found to be totally unsuitable for partisan operations.

Mountains have traditionally been kind to guerrilla movements, as was proved yet again by the Yugoslav experience during the Second World War. But in the area of the Soviet Union occupied by the Germans, mountains were few and far between; only in the north-west of the Caucasus range, in the small Yaila range of the Crimea, and that portion of the Carpathians which touches the extreme west of the Ukraine, were the protection of rock, ridge, ravine, and goat path to be found; and even there, because of the hostility of the local population, they provided

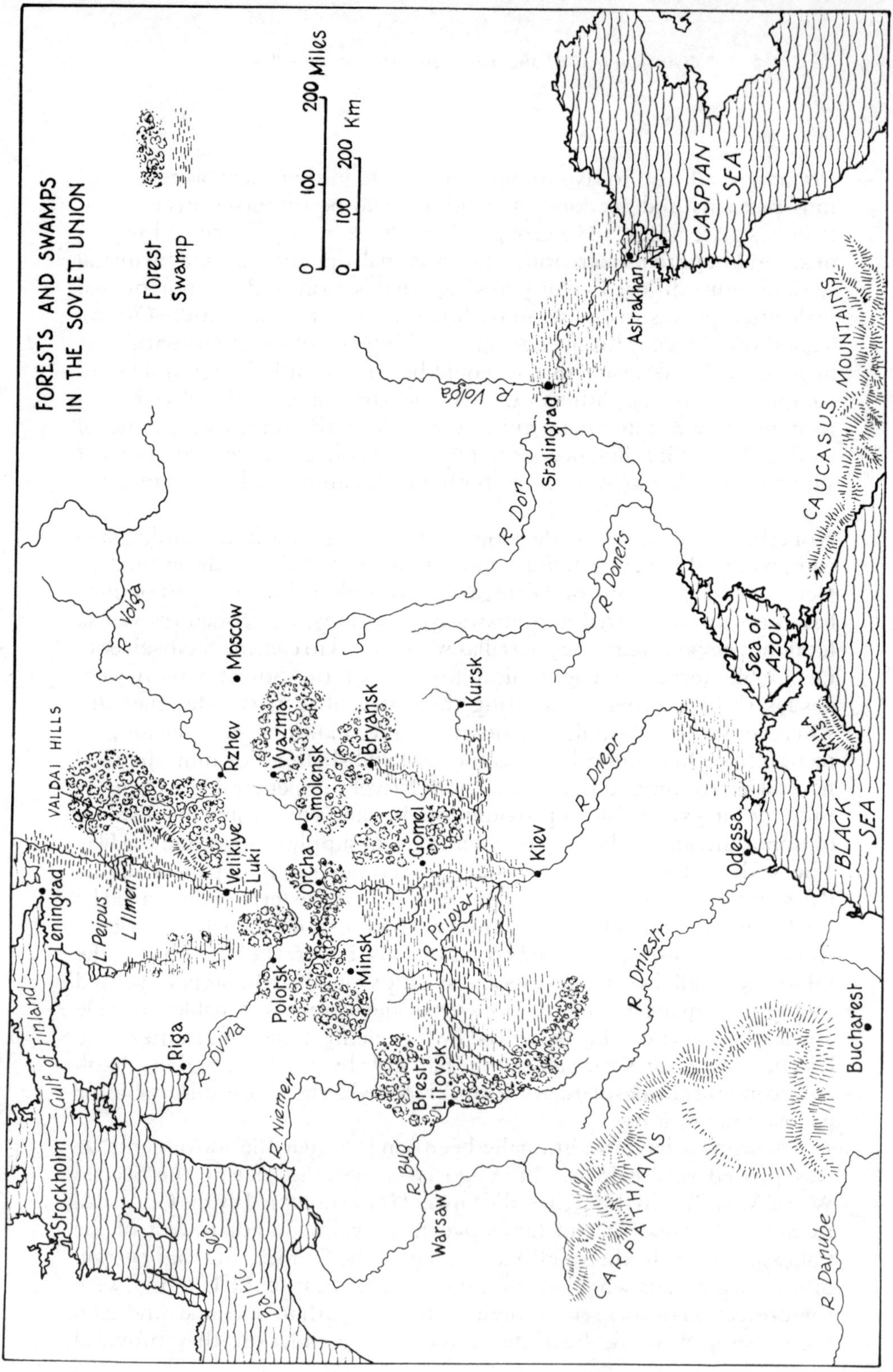
FORESTS AND SWAMPS
IN THE SOVIET UNION
Forest
Swamp
0
100
200 Miles
0
100
200 Km
VALDAI HILLS
Stockholm
Gulf of Finland
Leningrad
L. Peipus
L Ilmen
Velikiye
Luki
Rzhev
Moscow
R Volga
Riga
R Dvina
Polotsk
Orcha
Smolensk
Vyazma
Bryansk
Minsk
Gomel
Kursk
R Don
R Donets
Stalingrad
R Volga
Astrakhan
CASPIAN
SEA
CAUCASUS
MOUNTAINS
Sea of
Azov
YAILA
BLACK
SEA
Odessa
R Dnepr
Kiev
R Pripyat
Brest
Litovsk
R Niemen
Baltic
Sea
R Bug
Warsaw
R Dniestr
CARPATHIANS
Bucharest
R Danube

inadequate sanctuary for the guerrilla. In the Caucasus, the Moslem groups who inhabited the mountain regions had rebelled against the Soviet régime even before the invaders arrived, and they continued to provide active support to the Germans against all vestiges of the former authority. In the Yaila, many of the inhabitants were Tartars, violently opposed to the Communist system, and in the Carpathians, separated by huge distances from the Soviet front line, the population was so bitterly anti-Russian as to destroy any hope of effective partisan activity.

The Soviet guerrillas were, as a result, restricted to regions of thick forest and swamp and therefore to only about one-third of German-occupied territory. The large, deep forests and marshes, characteristic of so much of European Russia, begin east of Brest Litovsk. Foremost among them are those of the Pripyat region. The Pripyat is the only large river in western Russia that flows from west to east, clearly dividing the north and south. It is a region of contrast, with sandy plains, high forests, cultivated pastures, populated areas, canals, and paved causeways on one hand and, on the other, extensive swamp, bare reed flats, luxuriant weed-covered bogs, countless ponds and lakes full of sedge islands, bordered by meadow-like ground treacherous to walk on except in winter, when it is frozen hard. Birch and alder forests abound, where, according to the season, there may be a dry and firm ground surface, or a bottomless morass. A constantly changing maze of flood water and streams makes any movement off the few paved roads a hazardous undertaking; a sudden summer storm can wreck all plans. Even for the partisans, large parts of the region were unsuitable owing to shortage of food and lack of nearby targets; they therefore usually had to limit their operations to the settled fringes of the Pripyat. More suitable, however, were the smaller, better drained forests contiguous to the marsh, prominent among which were the wide belts of woodland around Minsk, Orsha, Vyazma, Bryansk, and Gomel; and further north, above the vital Smolensk-Moscow Ridge, the forests surrounding Polotsk and Velikiye-Luki, and the marshy lowlands along the courses of the rivers Lovat and Volkhov, nearby which are the forests of the Valdai Hills, the only hilly woodland in Western Russia.

The forest areas of European Russia defy general description. Their one common feature is that, in 1941, they were, unlike their counterparts in western and central Europe, essentially in their primeval state, with undisturbed natural growth. Inhabitants were scarce, and were usually found in clearings and along the river banks. Roads were few, most of them being built only to connect villages or as logging roads, having no more than local significance; during wet periods, they became rivers of mud, completely useless. In the rest of the regions, there was great variety, as in the Pripyat Marsh, already described, which covers some 62,000 square miles. The large forests around Bryansk and Vyazma are almost impenetrable during summer because of their swampy soil and dearth of roads, whereas those of Minsk and Borisov are completely dry. Only in winter is there any uniformity, when bogs and marshes freeze, trees lose their foliage, and roads and tracks remain hard. Winter was the most difficult season for the Soviet partisan. The loss of foliage revealed their camps; foot-prints left in the virgin snow indicated their presence; and the harshness of the weather caused them to seek shelter and eschew activity. Then the guerrillas became most vulnerable to attack, for they had lost that security which comes of being able to move at will without fear of observation and so avoid any counter-measures of the enemy. In an attempt to minimise their disadvantage, units would group together in the woods and establish camps capable of holding off all except large-scale assaults. If the Russian terrain limited the area of partisan activity, then the Russian winter dictated its nature and its timing. The Soviet guerrillas proved unable to overcome the restraints imposed upon them by nature.

Chapter 4

German Security Policy – 1941

Any sort of resistance will be broken . . .
by instilling in the population a fear which is
the only thing capable of depriving them
of any will to resist.
OKW DIRECTIVE 16 September 1941

Just as the Russians had made no provision for the conduct of guerrilla warfare, the Germans entered the Soviet Union in 1941 ill-prepared to meet any determined underground resistance. The prerequisites for such a policy were lacking: they possessed neither a single anti-partisan organisation to cover the entire occupied territory, nor any clear, uniform understanding of the conduct of anti-partisan warfare. Had their occupation policy been different, this need not have mattered, for it seems clear that an enlightened attitude towards the conquered peoples would have ensured the failure of the Soviet guerrilla movement. But, because of the general oppression practised on the Russians, it was disastrous. With neither proper organisation nor common methods and aims, German security was bound to fail. Just as the occupation policy was a mirror of the harsh realities behind the pseudo-philosophy of National Socialism, so were the security measures an image of the two fundamental weaknesses of the 'Thousand Year Reich': organisational complexity and racial dogma, both resulting from Hitler's ineptitude as a national leader. Never were these to be overcome, either within Germany or in the conduct of the war, and they are well exemplified by the struggle against the partisans and its outcome.

In late 1940 and early 1941, when the course of the war still appeared favourable to German arms, the planning of security arrangements in the East was undertaken. This was done not, as might have reasonably been expected, by one agency – the Army – but by three. In the First World War, the military were given responsibility for the areas they occupied during hostilities; in the Second, however, the German Army was not allowed anything approaching overall control of recently-taken and still-unsubdued territories. In occupied Poland, Norway, Denmark, Holland, Belgium, and France, only those areas that might be the scene of large-scale operations against Great Britain came under the direct control of the military; for the rest, the great majority, primary authority was given to the political officials and the security services. These were the men whom Hitler had made responsible for establishing the new German Order in Europe; the generals, for whom his distrust and contempt were daily growing, he limited solely to purely military security and administration. They, for their part, were not altogether displeased with this. Their soldierly instinct and training – together with their experiences of such matters during the First World War, their conflicts with the SS and civilian officials in Poland and elsewhere, and their growing understanding of the reality behind National Socialist dogma – had given them a deep dislike and distrust of the role of administrators and policemen. Furthermore, any form of organisation that would limit the calls on their already stretched resources was to be warmly welcomed.

The Führer's desire to restrict the powers of his soldiers was evident early in the planning for the occupation of the East. Hitler optimistically assumed that, even before operations had ended, civilian government would be capable of administering a large part of Russia. At a conference with Keitel on 3 March 1941, he stated that the tasks to be undertaken by the occupying authorities would be of such complexity and magnitude that they were quite unsuited to the military. Ten days later, OKW issued a directive embodying its master's wishes; it stated: 'The zone of operations of the Army is to be limited . . . as much as possible. . . . As soon as the zone . . . has reached sufficient depth, it is to be bordered off in its rear. The newly occupied area to the rear of the zone of operations will receive its own political administration.'[1] This was reaffirmed in a Führer Decree dated 17 July[2]: the controlling authorities in the East wherever possible were to be the *Ostministerium* and the SS; the military would be limited solely to their own administration and security. Moreover, the High Command of the Army (OKH), for whom Hitler had a particular mistrust, had its responsibility further restricted to the operational zone only; except here, control of all units was to be exercised by the High Command of the Wehrmacht (OKW), a relatively new organisation, set up in 1938, which owed its allegiance to the Führer and was, consequently, often antipathetic to the interests of the Army. Thus, there was to be no single overall security organisation in the East; instead, responsibility for administration and peace in the occupied territories was to be shared between the *Ostministerium*, OKH, OKW, and the SS.

Only in the operational area – the combat zone and the rear areas of the armies and army groups – was the German Army to have full control

Ukrainians greeting the Germans as liberators.

Red Army soldiers surrendering, July 1941.

Reichsführer SS Heinrich Himmler on a visit to the Ukraine, autumn 1941, seen here inspecting the *Untermensch*.

SS officers apprehending Jews on the road, 1941.

A welcoming hand-shake for the invader, Russia, 1941.

Partisans captured by a German Army patrol.

Soldiers in a Russian wood during a round-up of guerrillas and Red Army stragglers, 1941.

Opposite: German police searching partisan suspects, 1941.

A Red Army soldier/guerrilla being taken away for interrogation.

Opposite: A partisan and his captor in a wheat-field, 1941.

Partisans being brought in after a dawn raid, 1941.

Field Police erecting a notice warning drivers of partisan danger, and ordering that single vehicles wait for another before proceeding, with weapons at the ready.

SS men during an anti-partisan operation, 1942.

GERMAN ADMINISTRATION
IN OCCUPIED RUSSIA
BALTIC
SEA
Leningrad
Tallin
ESTONIA
NORTH
OSTLAND
Pskov
Riga
LATVIA
LITHUANIA
AREAS
OF
MILITARY
GOVERNMENT
Polotsk
Vilnius
Smolensk
CENTRE
Minsk
GERMANY
BELORUSSYA
Bryansk
Warsaw
Gomel
Kursk
GOVERNMENT
GENERAL
(POLAND)
SOUTH
Rovno
Zhitomir
Kiev
Kharkov
Lvov
UKRAINE
GALICIA
TRANSNISTRIA
HUNGARY
Dnepropetrovsk
Zaporozhe
ROMANIA
Reich Commisariats and
Military Government
National boundaries
Odessa
CRIMEA
0
200 Miles
0
200 Km
BLACK
SEA

of administration. Here, the Russians were administered by a system of commandants (*Kommandanturen*), both regional (*Feld-*) and urban (*Orts-*), which were generally based on the old Soviet administrative divisions. The rest of occupied Russia was under the administrative control of the *Reichsministerium für die besetzten Ostgebiete* – the Ministry for the Occupied Eastern Territories (*Ostministerium*) – under Reichsminister Alfred Rosenberg, whose permanent deputy was Gauleiter Alfred Meyer. This area was divided into two Reich Commissariats (*Reichskommissariaten*), Ostland and Ukraine (two others were planned, Caucasus and Muscovy, but never formed). Each was under the control of a Reich Commissar (*Reichskommissar*), nominally subordinate to Rosenberg: Heinrich Lohse in Ostland, and Erich Koch in the Ukraine. The Reich Commissariats were divided into General Commissariats (*Generalkommissariaten*), subdivided into Area Commissariats (*Gebietskommissariaten*) or large city areas. Russian officials appointed by the Germans administered the regions by means of an organisation based on groups of villages similar to the previous Soviet form. The military still maintained a presence in the Reich Commissariats, and in each there was stationed an Armed Services Commander (*Wehrmachtbefehlshaber*),[3] responsible to OKW, who possessed some authority for the maintenance of public order, prisoners-of-war, and the billeting and transport of troops.

Just as with administration, responsibility for security in the East was divided, but this time between the military and the SS.[4] In the operational areas, security was, in common with administration, the province of the Army; the SS and police units situated there, although they received orders from SS commanders, were, nevertheless, under the control of the military commanders in the field for matters concerning movement, billeting, and supply. Here, the Army had full authority to override all instructions, even from the Reichsführer SS, in order to prevent any interference with its operations. However, to the rear, in the administrative regions of the *Ostministerium*, it was the SS who possessed full responsibility for police security matters;[5] the Reichsführer SS was even allowed to give instructions to the Reich Commissars. This often overlapped military security, which remained the concern of the High Command of the Wehrmacht (and from which, it will be remembered, OKH was excluded), but if a major operation involving large numbers of troops was mounted against partisans, a senior general would usually be designated as commander. Transfers of units between the operational areas and the Reich Commissariats were made by OKW with the concurrence of either the Chief of the Army General Staff or the Reichsführer SS.

The command of the Army and SS security units, too, was complicated. In the operational areas, the military formations were under the control of the army group and army commanders, who themselves were under the direction of the Commander-in-Chief of the Army. The Army Quartermaster-General, Eduard Wagner, could give orders only to the supply formations under his control and, through the military government sections of the Army Group Headquarters, to the *Kommandanturen* in the rear area of each army group (*Rückwärtiges Heeresgebiet*). In the army rear area (*Rückwärtiges Armeegebiet*, commonly known as *Korücks*), however, the *Kommandanturen* came entirely under the control of the army headquarters in the field, and Wagner's authority held no sway. The Quartermaster-General himself received orders and advice from both his immediate superior, the Chief of the Army General Staff, and OKW. In the Reich Commissariats, military units – whether Army or Luftwaffe – were under the direction of the Wehrmacht commanders, who were responsible directly to OKW. The SS units were uniformly under the direction of the Reichsführer SS, the representatives of his authority in the East being the three Higher SS and Police Leaders (*Höhere SS und Polizei Führer – HSSPF*) allocated to three sectors, North, Centre, and South, which included both the army group rear areas, where the military commanders had ultimate authority over SS activities, and the Reich Commissariats (North and Centre in Ostland and South in Ukraine) where the civilian administrators were powerless to interfere in security matters. In the middle of 1942 a further HSSPF was appointed for the North Caucasus.[6] The HSSPF was responsible for all security matters that were the concern of the SS units, the police and the security services in his area, although these formations could also receive instructions direct from their superiors in Berlin, notably from Reinhard Heydrich, Chief of the Security Police and the SD (*Chef der Sicherheitspolizei und des SD – CSSD*). The system of command between the offices of the HSSPF and the CSSD was never fully defined, and tension existed between them; Himmler seemed quite content to let the HSSPF circumvent the CSSD and issue orders directly to the security units in the pursuance of 'special tasks', one of which was the destruction of the partisans.

To summarise: while the administration of the occupied areas was divided between the Army and the *Ostministerium*, the command of security forces in 1941 and 1942 was as follows: in the army operational areas, although SS units were present, the military had full control, responsibility being divided between the Quartermaster-General and the army commanders in the field; in the Reich Commissariats, police security was the exclusive province of the SS, and military security the responsibility of the High Command of the Wehrmacht, and when the two overlapped it was the latter which took charge of operations. No single organisation had overall control; only one man, Hitler, held that power.

Co-operation between the SS and the military was usually good. Relations between the Army formations and the SS *Einsatzgruppen* were at first particularly happy; a report from *Einsatzgruppe* A, covering the period from 22 June to 15 October 1941, noted:

> 'It must be stressed from the beginning that co-operation with the Armed Forces was generally good; in some cases, for instance with Panzer Group 4, under Generaloberst Hoepner, it was very close and almost cordial. Misunderstandings which cropped up with some authorities in the first days were cleared up mainly through personal discussions. . . . Close collaboration with the Armed Forces and the exchange of experiences which were collected in the fight against partisans, brought about a thorough knowledge of the origin, organisation, strength, equipment and system used by the Red partisans as time went on.'[7]

The Chief of the General Staff was told by army commanders in December 1941 that 'These people [the men of the *Einsatzgruppen*] are worth their weight in gold to us. They guarantee the security of our rear communications and so save us calling upon troops for this purpose.'[8] However, while relations between the men in the field were based on co-operation, those between the headquarters in Germany were not quite so harmonious. To a request from OKH in March 1942 for the SS to transfer units from the Reich Commissariats to the army group rear areas to help with the fight against the partisans, the Reichsführer SS refused, ending his letter with the gratuitous comment: 'the same people can be used only once at a given time.'[9] Problems over demarcation between army group rear areas and the SS and OKW in the Reich Commissariats were not unknown, and, although units from one region in hot pursuit of their game could cross into the other when necessary, such a division sometimes caused difficulties when operations were being planned which were to take place on the borders between the two. The greatest drawback lay in the inability to direct all security troops in the East according to one general plan for the whole of the occupied territories. Piecemeal operations directed by three autonomous authorities – the SS, the OKW, and the Army – were not the best solution to counter guerrillas over whom the Central Staff in Moscow had such strong control.

The division between the military and the SS was made more serious by the fact that, in matters of security, they held different aims. The soldiers, although motivated to a certain extent by National Socialist philosophy concerning the *Untermensch*, were nevertheless exclusively concerned with military security, the elimination of all opposition that would pose a threat to the continued existence of the armies in the front line. This goal was shared by both OKW and OKH, and also by the Wehrmacht commanders and the army group and army commanders. The SS, on the other hand, had no such aim; instead, theirs was the policing of the occupied territories to ensure the compliance of the local population with the representatives of Reich government, and, more ominous, the fulfilment of National Socialist racial policies. While these different aims were often pursued by similar methods, and could also result in similar conclusions, they were also at times diametrically opposed. To carry out a policy that aimed at reducing the indigenous population to the status of slaves, and involved the killing of all Jews, intelligentsia, and any form of human being who could be considered a danger to the Reich, could and did preclude military success by so antagonising the conquered peoples that their disaffection fuelled the fires of revolt, thus making possible the task of establishing the Soviet partisan movement. In this process, the Army was far from blameless, in the early days often enforcing military security with a barbarity that betokened acceptance of Hitler's racial creed; but, as events were to show, there can be no doubt that, had it not been for the political activities of the SS and police, the waging of the anti-guerrilla war would have been far more successful.

The vast expanse of Russian territory determined the German plans for military security from the beginning. From the border to Moscow was 600 miles; from the Soviet capital to the proposed end of operations was a further 200. The entire area to be occupied up to the line Archangel–Astrakhan was roughly one million square miles. Quite clearly, the vital supply and reinforcement routes to the armies at the front, running along the few, isolated roads and railway lines, would have to be considerably longer than in previous campaigns, and consequently more liable to disruption. No longer would the main danger to supplies be, as in previous campaigns, only in the area where the army was operating; instead, it would lie in the huge expanses to the rear, where the concentrations of troops close to the battle-lines would have no means of controlling the local population or the network of communications. Only near the front would it be possible to maintain a high degree of security, unless a large force were detailed especially for that purpose. But the Germans simply did not possess the manpower to secure the entire occupied territories; they realised that only those areas vital to the supply of the armies could be adequately protected from any guerrilla menace. At the beginning, therefore, they adopted a plan of security that was essentially 'passive', designed simply to protect existing lines of communications, major towns, and vital economic areas; 'active' measures, to destroy partisan units hiding in forests and swamp, would come later. It was expected that, by Christmas, the war would be over, with the defeat of the Soviet Union, and that then many front-line divisions would become available to pacify, once and for all, the rear areas that had been left untouched. Reality, however, was not to come up to expectation.

For the purposes of rear-area security, nine special formations, known as Security Divisions, were organised. These were, however, of poor quality. Most of their personnel were taken from older age-groups, and consisted mainly of veterans from the First World War or of men who had received insufficient training in replacement units. They were led by older reserve officers or retired officers recalled to duty, were armed and equipped with either obsolete or captured material, and possessed few weapons, such as light machine-guns and machine pistols, that were suitable for fighting guerrillas in forest and swamp. The divisions were small, consisting of one infantry regiment used for combat, and one *Landesschützen* (Territorial riflemen) regiment of three or four battalions intended for security tasks, together with supporting companies, a light artillery battalion, and a variety of pioneer and supply troops. Seven of the security divisions were accompanied by a motorised police-battalion. Each army group was allocated three such formations; in addition, Army Group North was provided with a police regiment and a security regiment mounted on bicycles, and Army Group Centre with a security regiment. Army Group South was able to augment its security forces with the allied units under its command, chiefly Hungarians. At the same time, the army groups made full use of all the various military or paramilitary units under their authority; transport troops, construction companies, field-gendarmerie, police, and Reich Labour Service units were all liable to find themselves combating partisans or guarding supply dumps and other vital installations.

Together with the Army security forces came the SS. Foremost among their formations were the four *Einsatzgruppen* – A, B, C, and D – fully motorised, armed with light automatic guns and varying in size between 500 and 1,000 men drawn from the SD, the Security Police, the Waffen SS, and the Order Police. *Einsatzgruppe* A was sent to the Baltic States; *Einsatzgruppe* B went in the direction of Moscow; *Einsatzgruppe* C and *Einsatzgruppe* D were assigned to the Ukraine, the latter being intended to move into the Caucasus. Behind these units came three regiments of *Ordnungspolizei* (Order Police, an armed variety of the London 'Bobby'), one under the control of each of the three Higher SS and Police Leaders who, for short periods, were also assigned certain Waffen SS units, such as cavalry regiments. Unlike those of the Army, these formations were not intended to guard supply lines and military depots; instead, they were to establish law and order in the Reich Commissariats and undertake the tasks of racial purification and colonial exploitation ordered by Hitler and devolved to the SS.

These security forces, to whose hands were entrusted the three tasks of pacification of the occupied territories, execution of racial policy, and preservation of the life-lines running to the armies at the front, were hopelessly inadequate for the task. They consisted of no more than 110,000 men at any one time to control an area which, by the end of 1941, covered more than 850,000 square miles. For example, by 1 October 1941, just three of these divisions and an SS brigade were employed in a region of no less than 125,000 square miles that composed the rear area of Army Group Centre. The 707th Infantry Division was required to guard 31,000 square miles, an area larger than Austria, in the forested terrain of Baranovichi and Minsk. The rear areas of the armies, too, experienced the same problem of a woefully inadequate ratio of men to space. In the rear of 9th Army in the centre, for example, an area of 43,000 square miles in which there were more than 1,500 villages and collective farms, there were fewer than 1,700 men available for security duties, of whom only 300 were assigned to active measures against the partisans. Against any determined guerrilla movement, their task would be impossible. Indeed, even with the low level of partisan activity encountered in 1941, the security forces seldom had great success when they took the initiative against the few strongly organised guerrilla bands that had established themselves in the thick forests and treacherous swamps of central Russia; it was too easy for the partisans simply to split up and disappear to areas where the few German troops could not hope to find them.

The Germans soon realised that they had more success in the passive security measures they introduced,[10] such as placing guards at important bridges, sending vehicles through endangered areas only in convoys, instituting a block system of successive guard posts along main roads, and safeguarding trains from mines and ambush. Attempts were made to bring the population near towns and lines of communication under close scrutiny. Collaborationist mayors, village elders, or district chiefs were ordered to compile lists of all those living within their areas; each person was registered, and all houses were required to display a list of their occupants, together with their ages. Strangers were ordered to report to the authorities immediately on arrival; failure to do so resulted in imprisonment or worse. Anyone caught harbouring an unregistered person would be shot. Special permits were required to travel outside a village, and these were usually valid for only one day. Travel in army operational areas was prohibited altogether. Persons caught after curfew, or near sensitive military areas, or without a permit, were shot. Experience soon taught the Germans to be suspicious of everyone. On 14 March 1942, a memorandum from 11th Army noted: 'In view of the credulity of German soldiers, the Soviet partisans frequently use cripples, primarily as agents. Some cases are also known in which healthy persons camouflaged themselves by putting on bandages or inflicting loathsome wounds upon themselves.'[11] As a result, harsh restrictions were introduced. In October 1941, for example, 4th Army decreed: 'Throughout the entire army rear area freedom of movement has been cancelled. During the day all persons of military age (17 to 65), who are wandering back and forth between communities, are to be picked up and sent to prison camp. At night, any civilian on the highways and in open country will be fired on. . . .'[12] With the gaps in the German front caused by high losses and the Soviet winter counter-offensive, the problem of control of civilians became even more difficult; 2nd Panzer Army reported on 2 January 1942: 'It has become known that the Russians are making extensive use of information obtained from the local inhabitants. Repeatedly, it has been observed that the enemy is accurately informed about the soft spots in our front and frequently picks the boundaries between our corps and divisions as points of attack. The movement of the inhabitants between the fronts must, therefore, be prevented by all possible means.'[13]

Some success greeted German efforts. On 31 July 1942 the Provost-Marshal General reported:

> 'The appointment of reliable mayors and indigenous policemen in communities recently cleared of partisans has proved to be an effective device for preventing the formation of new bands in such communities and in the adjacent woods. The mayors and police, in conjunction with German troops in the vicinity and with secret field police and military police detachments, watch closely over the pacified area, paying particular attention to the registering and screening of all persons newly arrived in the area. To combat the dangers arising from the migration of the population, the secret field police is constantly conducting large-scale checks. These revealed that among the migrating crowds, which are composed of evacuees, returnees, and food hoarders, numerous partisans and enemy agents can be found. Satisfactory results have been achieved by checking pedestrians on the streets.'[14]

In October, 3rd Panzer Army noted: 'The prohibition of civilian movements proved to be a very effective means of curbing hostile bands and enemy agents.'[15] However, these rigid, even harsh measures, which came to be associated with economic exploitation and the ravages of security troops, were not accompanied by any campaign to win for Germany the hearts and minds of the indigenous population. There lay the fatal flaw.

Until the Russian campaign, the German Army had been unequivocal in its attitude to guerrilla warfare. In the 'Ten Commandments for German Soldiers on Active Service', carried by every soldier in his pay-book, it was stated; 'Adversaries who surrender must not be killed, not even guerrillas or spies. These will be given their just punishment by the courts of justice.'[16] Moreover, Germany was a signatory of the two important agreements that governed modern warfare among 'civilised' nations: the Hague Convention concerning the Rules and Usages of Land Warfare, and the Geneva Convention concerning the Amelioration of the Fate of Wounded and Sick in the Active Army. Under the Hague Convention, signed on 18 October 1907, guerrilla warfare was not considered an offence, provided the guerrillas abided by the rules set out in Article 1:

> 'The laws, rights, and duties of war apply not only to armies, but also to militia and volunteer corps fulfilling the following conditions:
> 1. To be commanded by a person responsible for his subordinates.
> 2. To have a fixed distinctive emblem recognisable at a distance.
> 3. To carry arms openly.
> 4. To conduct their operations in accordance with the laws and custom of war.'[17]

But, should the guerrilla fighters not fulfil these conditions, they were to be regarded as *francs-tireurs* and deprived of protection under the Convention. The Soviet partisans followed consistently only the first. For the rest, they had no common uniform, often wearing civilian clothes; the Soviet star was usually worn as an insignia, but could not be seen at a distance; arms were carried openly only when it was to their advantage to do so; and they constantly broke the rules of war when dealing with captured German soldiers and their collaborators. The Soviet partisans, then, were quite legally considered *francs-tireurs*, or 'bandits' as the Germans called them, and as such were liable to the death penalty on capture. In theory, and perhaps in law, execution should have taken place only after trial, this being stipulated in the 'Ten Commandments', although not in the Hague Convention, but the German soldiers in the field chose to disregard the requirement as it was rendered ineffective by the orders and directives that emanated from OKW. The Germans also dealt with partisan suspects and supporters in the same way; General Eugen Müller, OKH Plenipotentiary for Special Assignments, briefed the Judge Advocate and army intelligence officers on 11 June 1941 thus: 'Every civilian who impedes or incites others to impede the German Wehrmacht is to be considered a guerrilla (e.g. instigators, persons who distribute leaflets, disregarders of German orders, arson raisers, destroyers of road signs, supplies etc.).'[18] This was followed on 13 September by a directive from the Commander-in-Chief of the Army, von Brauchitsch, who laid down the following guidelines to apply to Red Army personnel:

> 'Russian combat troops who are under the responsible leadership of officers and who are behind our front in situations in which they can carry out battle-missions . . . have the right to be treated as prisoners-of-war. On the other hand, Russian soldiers and units who, when the fighting has passed over them, come out of hiding, regroup, take up arms and go into action on their own initiative against our rear lines of communication, are to be regarded as *francs-tireurs*. It is a matter for unit commanders and/or commanders in individual cases to reach a decision according to the tactical situation.'[19]

In such a way the net was drawn wide for execution and reprisal.

From the beginning of the invasion, German security measures in Russia were intended to be harsh, thus following a German tradition of dealing with irregular fighters, whether in France in 1870, in Belgium and France from 1914 to 1918, and even against the Communists in Germany during the years 1919 to 1923. Even before the attack in 1941 was launched, the soldiers were told, in an order from OKW dated 13 May 1941, that the pacification of the vast areas of the East was possible only 'if the troops take ruthless action themselves against any threat from the enemy population'.[20] In the pursuit of this, 'Guerrillas will be relentlessly liquidated by the troops whilst fighting or escaping.' In direct contradiction of Article 50 of the Hague Convention, the order provided for the taking of collective sanctions against localities from which opposition stemmed. Reprisals were to extend to the innocent as well as the guilty. The OKW instructions were followed on 25 July by an order from OKH, which stipulated: 'The leading principle in all actions and for all measures . . . is the unconditional security of the German soldier. . . . The Russian has always been used to hard and unsparing action by the authorities. The necessary rapid pacification of the country can only be attained if every threat on the part of the hostile civilian population is ruthlessly taken care of. All pity and softness are weakness, and constitute a danger.'[21] Three months after the German attack, new instructions from OKW, dated 16 September and entitled 'Communist Insurrection in Occupied Territories', were issued to soldiers. They stated:

> 'The measures taken up to now to deal with this general insurrection movement have proved inadequate. The Führer has now

> given orders that we take action everywhere with the most drastic means in order to crush the movement in the shortest possible time.... In this connection it should be remembered that a human life in unsettled countries frequently counts for nothing, and a deterrent effect can be attained only by unusual severity. The death penalty for fifty to one hundred Communists should generally be regarded in these cases as suitable atonement for one German soldier's life. The way in which the sentence is carried out should still further increase the deterrent effect.'[22]

Consequently, the Germans, both military and SS men, came to commit horrible atrocities against the civilian population, often irrespective of age or sex. Village-burning, mass executions, torture, and indiscriminate shooting became common features of anti-partisan operations. Such measures, practised in the name of security from the moment German troops set foot on Soviet soil, could do nothing but alienate the people; they, as much as, if not more than, the other aspects of German rule, were the cause of the partisan movement avoiding the near-certainty of defeat and, instead, emerging, despite all its defects, as a potent force in large areas of the occupied territories.

The Army leaders themselves were not entirely unaware of the need to gain the confidence of the indigenous population in the conduct of anti-partisan warfare. On 25 October 1941, OKH issued instructions, circulated down to battalion level, entitled 'Guidelines for Combating Partisans',[23] in which special attention was paid to the attitude of the troops towards the civilians. The conduct of the soldiers, it stated, was to be strict but just, with the aim of instilling a feeling of safety and well-being under the protection of the German Armed Forces. Moreover, the population was to be encouraged to take part in providing their own security by the formation of indigenous militia units, raised with SS approval. Propaganda was to aim at turning the peasants against the Soviet guerrillas, and measures such as the release of prisoners-of-war to help with the harvest, and the granting of land to peasants, were rightly held to have great weight in gaining the co-operation of the Russians. Such advice from OKH reflected, in part, the concern felt by some field commanders about the severity of German measures. On 4 June, Field-Marshal Fedor von Bock, commander of Army Group Centre, had noted in his diary: 'An OKW order ... framed in such a way as to give every soldier the right to shoot, from in front or behind, any Russian whom he suspects of being a guerrilla ... is not acceptable and is not compatible with military discipline.'[24] On 29 July, the commander of the rear area of

Army Group South, concerned at guerrilla activity within his area, issued an order carefully worded so as not to conflict openly with Führer and OKW instructions:

> 'In his directive to the troops on this matter [the treatment of the civilian population, dated 13 May 1941], the Führer has authorised, during the course of operations and in the interest of the maintenance of the safety of the Armed Forces, that all evilly disposed civilians may be proceeded against with the strongest possible means. On the other hand, individual acts of violence against the civil population in the pacified area are purely vindictive. Therefore, the prosecution of justice in these areas is to be strictly maintained in every particular should soldiers act against the life and property of defenceless inhabitants. Those in authority who are not able to prevent this are unsuited to the position they hold.'[25]

However, such efforts, based on humanitarian as well as on practical considerations, were quite ineffective in stemming the tide of brutality and insensitivity towards the population of the East which the directives of Hitler, OKW, and even OKH had unleashed. Against these, OKH's 'Guidelines for Combating Partisans' had little effect. They were, as their title stated, only guidelines which simply enumerated a number of rather obvious security operations, and could not be regarded as a blueprint for the conduct of anti-guerrilla warfare. The difficulties against which the proponents of an enlightened, 'realist' approach had to battle are well illustrated by General Jodl's reaction to a report, produced in August by the OKW Propaganda Department, which urged that 'force, brutality, looting and deception should be avoided in order to win over the population'; in answer to this, the Chief of the Armed Forces' Operations Department wrote in the margin: 'These are dangerous signs of despicable humanitarianism.'[26]

Thus, in the absence of any detailed directives regarding the treatment of the civilian population in general and the Soviet partisans in particular, the commanders in the field were left to take practical measures themselves, and, with their limited experience, to evolve the best means of dealing with guerrilla action that Hitler's racial creed would allow.

During the campaign in 1941, General von Manstein, commander of 11th Army in the Crimea, was the first German soldier in the field to take practical measures against the partisans. In his view, 'it was necessary to direct the partisan combat from a central point in order to co-ordinate and make fullest use of information gathered. . . .'[27] In doing so, von

Manstein transferred responsibility from the Counter-Intelligence Officer of 11th Army to a special 'Staff for Combating Partisans', under a Major Stephanus. The order laying down the new organisation, dated 29 November 1941, stated: 'The annihilation of the many partisan groups that had been located, the prevention of the formation of further armed bands, and thus the protection of rear communications, are important prerequisites for the final mopping-up and occupation of the Crimea.'[28] In von Manstein's eyes, at least, the annihilation of the Soviet guerrillas, in which all formations of 11th Army were to take part, was of prime importance. The anti-partisan staff was to be accorded 'far-reaching assistance', and in emergencies Major Stephanus was entitled to issue orders to anyone on behalf of the army commander. The staff was to be responsible for obtaining information about the partisans, devising measures against them, and co-ordinating the necessary commitments of army units as well as of the SS security forces. Centralisation and co-ordination of effort could not have been taken further, and certainly the relationship between Army and SS guerrilla hunters was harmonious. By 15 December, 11th Army's 'Staff for Combating Partisans' had gained sufficient experience to issue a 'Memorandum on the Use of Troops against Partisans'. This provided, in more detail than did the OKH directive, the principles for conducting operations against guerrillas. Harsh action was regarded as fundamental. It was clearly stated: 'The population must be more frightened of our reprisals than of the partisans'. Concerning the treatment of partisans, it was laid down: 'Partisans captured in action will be interrogated and then shot (former members of the Red Army) or hanged (civilians). . . . Partisans who are caught will be hanged without exception. A label will be attached to them with the following legend: "This is a partisan who did *not* give himself up!" '[29]

11th Army's anti-partisan organisation, which met with much success, was soon regarded as a model for other such formations, although there was no official attempt to introduce it to the rest of the armies on the Eastern Front. On 10 January 1942 it was disbanded, its officers being incorporated into the staff of the newly appointed Leader of the Anti-Partisan Operations in the Crimea, a Dr Hermann of the Field Police. The following September, the SS took over responsibility for security in the region.

Another model for the German Army in 1941 in its conduct of rear area security was what has come to be known as the 'Reichenau Order', issued on 10 October. This was drawn up by Field-Marshal von Reichenau, who was at that time the commander of 6th Army operating in the Ukraine, and was intended solely for his own soldiers. However, Hitler so much approved of the sentiments expressed therein that he ordered the Army Commander-in-Chief to circulate them throughout the various army commands in the East. The subject of the order was 'The Conduct of Troops in the Eastern Territories', and its intent was to counter 'the vague ideas' held by the troops concerning their 'conduct . . . towards the Bolshevik system'. It was particularly specific in its attitude to partisans:

> 'The combating of the enemy behind the front line is still not being taken seriously enough. Treacherous, cruel partisans and unnatural women are still being made prisoners-of-war, and guerrilla fighters dressed partly in uniforms or plain clothes, and vagabonds, are still being treated as proper soldiers and sent to prisoner-of-war camps. . . . Such an attitude by the troops can only be explained as complete thoughtlessness . . . If isolated partisans are found using firearms in the rear of the army, drastic measures are to be taken. These measures will be extended to that part of the male population who were in a position to hinder or report the attacks. . . . The fear of German counter-measures must be stronger than the threats of the wandering Bolshevik remnants.'[30]

A month later, von Reichenau announced to the population under his jurisdiction: 'The Armed Forces will take away all foodstuffs and destroy the houses in those places where partisans find shelter and sustenance. In addition, ten male hostages from the population in the immediate vicinity of an incident will be shot.'[31]

The ruthlessness of security measures undertaken by the German Army in the first year of the campaign is confirmed by numerous examples. For instance, General der Infanterie von Salmuth, commander of XXX Corps in the Ukraine, ordered:

> 'The incidents which happened during the last days, during which several German and Romanian soldiers lost their lives in the course of partisan attacks, require severest counter-measures.
>
> 'The following persons are immediately to be taken as hostages in all places where troops are stationed:
> (a) persons whose relatives are partisans;
> (b) persons who are suspected of being in contact with partisans;
> (c) Party members, Komsomolzen, Party applicants;
> (d) persons who were formerly Party members;
> (e) persons who prior to the moving in of the German and Romanian troops had any official functions . . .
> (f) persons who are found outside the closed villages without a special permit.

'These hostages are to be accommodated in [eight] concentration camps. Their food must be supplied by the inhabitants of the village.

'From these hostages ten are to be shot for each German and Romanian soldier who is killed by partisans, and one of the hostages is to be shot for every German or Romanian soldier wounded by partisans; if possible they are to be shot near the place where the German or Romanian soldier was killed, and they are to be left hanging at that place for three days.'[32]

Generalleutnant von Roques, commander of the rear area of Army Group South, who was concerned to see 'justice' done towards the civilian population, ordered that, in case of sabotage to railway track, hostages (previously free men who had worked on clearing the surrounding countryside as an anti-guerrilla precaution) were to be strung up from poles along the lines as a reminder of the consequences of such action. General der Infanterie Koch, commander of XLIV Corps ordered: 'In case of sabotage of telephone lines, railway lines, etc., sentries will be posted selected from the civilian population. In the case of repetition, the sentry on whose beat the sabotage was committed will be shot. Suitable as sentries are only those people who have a family who can be apprehended in case the sentry escapes.'[33]

The 454th Security Division reported in November that in Kiev 'A total of 800 inhabitants were shot as a reprisal measure for acts of sabotage'. The town major of the city, in one of his public notices, declared: 'In Kiev a communication installation was maliciously damaged. Since the perpetrators could not be traced, 400 Kiev citizens were shot.' In Simferopol in the Crimea, headquarters of 11th Army, the Germans announced on 16 November:

'A mine reporting agency has been established in the German town major's office at Simferopol.

'Every inhabitant who knows about, or suspects the existence of mines, time fuses, explosives buried in houses or lying about, has to report this at once to the mine reporting agency in the town major's office. Information which proves correct, will be rewarded by money. On the other hand, everyone who in spite of having knowledge of the existence of mines, explosives, etc., omits to report to the mine reporting agency, will receive capital punishment.

'For every building in the town of Simferopol which is scheduled by the Soviets to be blown up, and which has not previously been reported to the mine reporting agency, *one hundred* inhabitants, each of the town of Simferopol, *will be shot*

> as a reprisal measure on the part of the German occupation troops.'

A few days later, the town major reported:

> 'On the 29th November, 1941, fifty male inhabitants of the town of Simferopol were shot as a reprisal measure:
>
> '(1) for the German soldier who was killed on 22nd November 1941 when entering an area that had not been reported as suspected of being mined.
>
> '(2) for the German sergeant who was fired at during the night of 27th–28th November, 1941.'[34]

The SS, too, conducted themselves in similar vein, but as much as a part of their general policy towards the Russian peoples and the Jews than as part of their security role. *Einsatzgruppe* B, for example, issued an order in November 1941 which stated: 'any of those people held that might be considered to be guerrillas should be executed at once and hung from the nearest tree or pole as a warning to local inhabitants';[35] the SS Hauptamt issued a directive in December that stated: 'As with all undesirable elements in the East, suspected partisans and their helpers are to be eliminated without hesitation, and reprisals taken whenever they have inflicted damage upon German property or personnel. None but the harshest measures are required. The initiative of the commanders on the spot will be unhindered.'[36] In an appendix to an operational order, dated 17 July and signed by Heydrich, it was noted that 'The special nature of the Eastern campaign calls for special measures, to be carried out on personal responsibility and beyond the range of any bureaucratic influences'.[37] In a survey of the activities of the *Einsatzgruppen* for the period 1 to 31 October 1941, the Chief of the Security Police and the SD provided details of all enemy killed in the operations undertaken by his men against partisans, Communist officials, and Jews. In the Baltic area 'The male Jews over sixteen were executed, with the exception of doctors and the elders. . . . After completion of this action, there will remain only 500 Jewesses and children in the Eastern territory.' In Belorussiya, under the heading 'Partisan activity and counter-action', Heydrich noted: 'In Vultschina eight juveniles were arrested as partisans and shot. They were inmates of a children's home. They had collected weapons which they hid in the woods. Upon search the following were found: three heavy machine-guns, fifteen rifles, several thousand rounds of ammunition, several hand grenades, and several packages of poison gas Ebrit.' Under the section entitled 'Arrests and executions of Communists, Officials and Criminals', he noted: 'A further large part of the activity of the Security Police was devoted to the combating of Communists and criminals. A special Commando in the period covered by this report executed sixty-three officials, NKVD agents and agitators.... The liquidations for the period covered by this report have reached a total of 37,180 persons'.[38] SS police measures, too, were harsh. In January 1942, SS Obersturmbannführer Strauch had the following notice posted throughout Latvia:

> 'The Commander of the German State Security Police in Latvia hereby announces the following:
>
> '... 2. The inhabitants of the village of Audriny, in the Rezhetz District, concealed members of the Red Army for over one-quarter of a year, armed them, and assisted them in every way in their anti-government activities.
>
> As punishment I ordered the following:
> That the village of Audriny be wiped from the face of the earth.'[39]

Such was the reality of German security policy in the East.

While Hitler, the SS, and the Army authorities were quite clear as to the general attitude that the security troops were to take against guerrillas and suspects, they gave no specific instructions as to how commanders were to act against individual partisans, bands, suspects, and innocent civilians. It was not made clear whether, on capture, partisans were to be taken prisoner or shot, how many civilians were to be executed in reprisal, or even who was to be considered a guerrilla or a suspect. In evidence to the International Military Tribunal at Nuremberg in 1946, the HSSPF for Central Russia and SS Chief of Anti-Partisan Units, Erich von dem Bach-Zelewski, admitted that 'since orders proved insufficient, a wild state of anarchy resulted in all anti-partisan operations.... Since there were no definite orders, and since the lower command was forced to act independently, many undertakings were executed according to the character of the officer in command and to the quality of the troops. These, naturally, varied considerably.... I am of the opinion that operations on numerous occasions not only failed in their purpose but they very often overshot their mark.'[40] When asked whether this meant that there was unnecessary killing of large numbers of civilians, he replied quite simply: 'Yes.'

In von dem Bach-Zelewski's opinion, the biggest contributory factor to the excesses on the part of the anti-guerrilla units was the lack of disciplinary power possessed by the higher commanders. In the OKW decree of 13 May 1941, part of which has already been quoted, there were inserted two provisions: that officers on the spot were allowed considerable initiative in deciding courses of action, and that soldiers who had committed offences against civilians could not be punished. They read:

> 'Where |extreme| measures [against civilians attacking German forces| . . . have been omitted or were not at first possible, suspected elements will forthwith be brought before an officer. This officer will decide whether they are to be shot. On the orders of an officer with the powers of at least a battalion commander, collective despotic measures will be taken without delay against localities from which cunning or malicious attacks are made on the Armed Forces, if circumstances do not permit of a quick identification of individual offenders. . . . With regard to offences committed against enemy civilians by members of the Wehrmacht and its employees, prosecution is not obligatory even where the deed is at the same time a military crime or offence.'[41]

Only if the maintenance of discipline or security were at risk would courts-martial result. As Generaloberst Reinhardt, commander of 3rd Panzer Army, ordered: 'the bands must be exterminated in combat. Any methods are permissible, and imply in any case exemption from punishment for the personnel ordered into action against bands.'[42] Such orders made against the background of the general tenor of official directives concerning the conduct of the war in the East ensured that the anti-partisan measures conducted by the Army, let alone the SS, took on more the aspect of an extension of National Socialist racial policies than of operations conducted according to military rules and practice.

In an affidavit submitted at the Nuremberg trial, General der Panzertruppen Hans Röttiger, Chief of Staff to 4th Army and later to Army Group Centre, who had close association with anti-guerrilla operations, wrote: 'I have now come to realise that the order from the highest authorities for the harshest conduct of partisan war can only have been intended to make possible a ruthless liquidation of Jews and other undesirable elements, by using for this purpose the military struggle of the Army against the partisans.'[43] This was echoed by no less a person than Generalleutnant Adolf Heusinger, Chief of the Operations Section of the General Staff from 1940 to 1944, when he stated: 'It had always been my personal opinion that the treatment of the civilian population and the methods of anti-partisan warfare in operational areas presented the highest political and military leaders with a welcomed opportunity of carrying out their plans, namely, the systematic extermination of Slavism and Jewry.'[44] In his testimony, von dem Bach-Zelewski spoke of Himmler's declaration in early 1941 of the need to reduce the Slav population by thirty million people, and that anti-partisan operations, at least on the part of the SS, were carried out with that aim in mind. He was convinced that 'this purpose was a decisive factor in the selection of certain commanders and of some quite definite formations'.[45] In a subsequent written testimony, he went further:

> 'when whole peoples rise, as was the case in the east and southeast, leaders at the top who are conscious of their responsibilities cannot abandon the execution of reprisals to the caprice of individual commanders. This lack of direction in responsible quarters is a cowardly devolution of responsibility on to lower echelons. But if it is obvious to everyone that lack of direction leads to a chaos of reprisals and nevertheless no clear orders are given, then the only possible conclusion is that this chaos is intended by the leaders at the top. There is no question but that reprisals both by Wehrmacht and by SS and Police units overshot the mark by a long way. This fact was repeatedly established at conferences with generals held by Schenkendorf [Commander, Army Group Centre Rear Area]. Moreover the fight against partisans was gradually used as an excuse to carry out other measures, such as the extermination of Jews and gypsies, the systematic reduction of the Slavic peoples by some 30,000,000 souls (in order to ensure the supremacy of the German people), and the terrorisation of civilians by shooting and looting. The Commanders-in-Chief with whom I came in contact and with whom I collaborated (for instance, Field-Marshals von Weichs, von Küchler, von Bock and von Kluge, Col.-General Reinhardt and General Kitzinger) were as well aware as I of the purposes and methods of anti-partisan warfare.'[46]

In his testimony at Nuremberg, von dem Bach-Zelewski commented: 'I am of the opinion that if, for decades, a doctrine is preached to the effect that the Slav race is an inferior race, and Jews not even human at all, then such an explosion is inevitable.'[47] At the conclusion of one anti-partisan operation, code-named 'Marsh Fever', in early 1942, the SS commander reported 389 partisans killed, 1,274 suspects shot, and 8,350 Jews liquidated. Heusinger was adamant in declaring that he 'always regarded such cruel methods as military insanity, because they only helped to make combat against the enemy unnecessarily more difficult'.[48]

Chapter 5

The Partisan Movement 1942–44

We have to be thankful to the Germans
that their policy enabled us to fan the flames
of the partisan movement. . . .
ALEXANDER SHCHERBAKOV Member of the Soviet Politburo

The growth in partisan activity in early 1942 took the Germans by surprise. On 1 March, OKH was forced to issue instructions to its units in the field to take immediate steps to protect their lines of communication to the front of the central sector; scarce divisions were even brought from combat duty to join in the hunt for guerrillas. In March, Goebbels wrote in his diary: 'An SD report informed me about the situation in occupied Russia. It is, after all, more unstable than was generally assumed. The partisan danger is increasing week by week.'[1] During that month, in the strategically important Bryansk region alone, guerrillas scored major successes in stopping trains on the Bryansk-L'vov railway line, in preventing the Bryansk-Roslavl line from operating, and in threatening the main roads from Bryansk to Roslavl, Karachev, and Zhizdra to such a degree that traffic could proceed only in convoy. During the year, the number of attacks on railways increased three-fold, from sixty-three in May to 199 in September. By December, the Central Staff directed the activities of some 130,000 partisans, of whom the majority operated in the forests and swamps of European Russia: in Belorussiya there were some 57,000 guerrillas; in the Smolensk region, 20,000; in the Bryansk area, 24,000, with the other 30,000 men dispersed throughout the Baltic States, the Ukraine, the Crimea, and the Caucasus which was occupied by the Germans from August 1942 to February 1943.

By the middle of 1942, the partisans had come to dominate large areas in the German rear. The Chief of the Army Field Police, in a report dated 31 July, believed the following regions to be 'particularly endangered':

'North: Marshy region south-east of Dno;
Eastern part of the Kudova district;

Region south of Opotschka;
Regions surrounding the Krasnoy-Sebesh and Opotschka-Novorschev roads;
Regions south and west of Puschkinskije Gery;
Wooded region east of Gdov, in particular east of the river Pijussa, as well as south and north of Gdov;
Wooded region east of Pleskau;
Wooded region south of the log road between Maramorka and Okonewo.

Centre: Region west of Vyama;
Region north of Gluscha, in particular south of Nowije-Tarrassowitschi;
Region north-west of Staryje Dorogy;
Region south of Glusk;
Region east of Potschep;
Region north of Bobruysk;
Region north of the railway line Klinzy-Unetscha;
Sector Klinzy;
Region north and south-west of Smolensk;
Region surrounding Tscherven and Berein;
Region north-east of Polotsk, including the railway line Polotsk-Nevel, and regions north-west and south-south-east of Polotsk;
Region surrounding Logi, north-west of Orsha; they control the whole region between the Minsk-Moscow log road and the Orscha-Vitebsk road up to Sonno;
Region east of Vitebsk;
Region south of Orsha;
All roads in the Gorki-Dropin sectors;
Region surrounding Schura atschi, south of Mogilev;
Region surrounding Lepel;
Region south-east of Luban.

South: Here the danger is not so great as in the areas North and Centre, but in the following regions partisan bands have also been located:
Region south of Kharkov;
Region near Polova;
Region surrounding Novgorod-Soverskij; this is completely under partisan control;
Southern part of the Crimea.'[2]

Not for nothing did Hitler state in a Directive dated 18 August: 'The bands in the East have become an unbearable menace during the last few months, and are seriously threatening the supply lines to the front.'[3]

But German alarm obscures the fact that, however impressive the efforts to restore the partisan bands appeared, the Soviet guerrilla movement still suffered from considerable weaknesses – weaknesses of which the invader proved incapable of taking advantage. Vast areas of the occupied territories had little or no guerrilla activity. In the central and southern sectors of the Ukraine, in the Baltic States, and in the Crimea, where the year saw the virtual destruction of the guerrilla force, the Germans went about their business virtually unhindered; their summer offensive into the Caucasus and to Stalingrad was affected not at all by partisan activities. In the northern Caucasus, too, the Wehrmacht was little troubled by the activities of some 7,000 guerrillas, whose operations were restricted mainly to the Kuban river delta and the forest-covered mountains around Krasnodar, and who received no support from the local population. Despite the cruelties perpetrated by the invaders, the Ukrainians and the Balts were still not prepared to accept the representatives of Soviet authority in their midst; underground communist cells might survive in the cities, but the vast steppelands remained inhospitable to the guerrilla bands. This was particularly unfortunate for the Soviets, for, in 1942, it was in the Ukraine that the decisive military events were taking place: in June, the Germans launched their summer offensive designed to reach the Volga river and the Caucasian oil fields; in November, the Soviets encircled the 6th Army at Stalingrad, and began their counter-offensive that was to end in the following February after the German evacuation of the Caucasus, the Don Bend, and part of the Donets Basin. In these events, the partisans took little or no part.

The Soviet régime also had cause for concern over the evident reluctance of many of the units within established partisan areas to embark on risky operations. It soon became apparent that the guerrillas in the field regarded the year, if not the war, as a time for consolidation rather than for action: comfort, liaisons with women, and the preservation of their own lives were to them more important than destroying the enemy within their midst. The units that were largely recruited from local inhabitants exhibited a particular reluctance to attack the invader, fearing that reprisals would be taken against their relatives who had remained in the villages. Clearly such a state of affairs could not continue. On 1 August 1942, the Central Staff ordered an immediate increase in guerrilla activity to aid the Red Army; this was shortly followed by articles in the Soviet newspaper, *Pravda*, calling for more attacks on German units and lines of communication. Later that month, twenty senior partisan leaders were

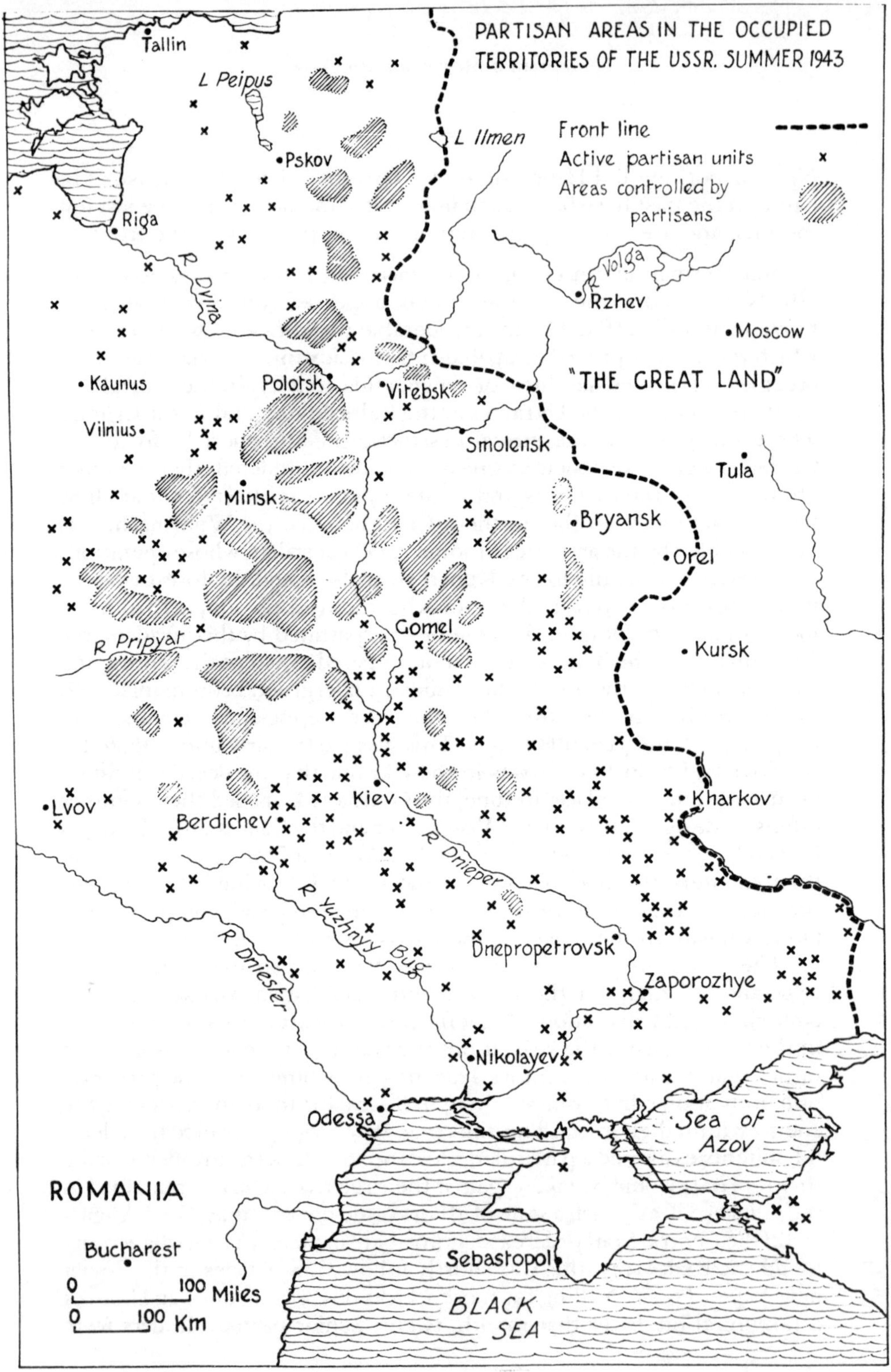
PARTISAN AREAS IN THE OCCUPIED TERRITORIES OF THE USSR. SUMMER 1943
Front line
Active partisan units
Areas controlled by partisans
Tallin
L Peipus
L Ilmen
Pskov
Riga
R Dvina
R Volga
Rzhev
Moscow
Kaunus
Polotsk
Vitebsk
"THE GREAT LAND"
Vilnius
Smolensk
Tula
Minsk
Bryansk
Orel
Gomel
Kursk
R Pripyat
Lvov
Kiev
Kharkov
Berdichev
R Dnieper
R Yuzhnyy Bug
R Dniester
Dnepropetrovsk
Zaporozhye
Nikolayev
Odessa
Sea of Azov
ROMANIA
Bucharest
0 100 Miles
0 100 Km
Sebastopol
BLACK SEA

called for a high-level conference in Moscow where, on the 31st, they were told by Stalin and other Soviet leaders that the movement had still not become as large and aggressive as it must, and could, be. Orders were given that partisan reserves were to be created and raids made into the Ukraine to destroy the main German lines of communication. At the same time, the Staff introduced a series of measures intended to promote a higher level of activity; these included the summary execution of lazy or cowardly commanders, and the movement of bands away from their place of origin. Almost at once, the guerrillas in the forests of Bryansk and Belorussiya stepped up their activity; in August, the German railway authorities in the central sector reported a dramatic increase in sabotage to railways, from 186 in June to 315.

However, it was not until the surging advances of the Red Army in 1944 that the partisans' desire for security was finally eliminated, and was replaced by an urge to prove their worth to the victorious Soviet régime. Indicative of the passive outlook during almost the whole period of guerrilla activity was the tendency towards the concentration of bands within one area. Instead of ranging freely, brigades tended to gather together to form centres of partisan territory. This was especially prevalent in Belorussiya, where more than a dozen centres developed, the largest, around Rossono, north of Polotsk, totalling 15,000 men. Others were situated along the Ushachi river between Polotsk and Lepel, in the swamps along the Berezina river between Lepel and Borisov, and near the towns of Minsk, Senno, and Vitebsk. By 1943, some three-quarters of the partisan movement were concentrated in such areas. Certainly, owing to the limited amount of terrain suitable for guerrilla activity, some form of grouping was inevitable, but it seems that the partisans overdid this tendency. Although their existence prevented great areas from falling under German control, the large centres were usually situated in those regions which had been by-passed by the invader during the initial occupation, and which were, in any case, of no particular use to him. As fixed bases, they required a large number of men to defend them, and their very size and lack of mobility made them easy targets for the Germans. It was only because the enemy could rarely find enough troops for the necessary large-scale operations that these centres provided security for the partisans. Soviet accounts of the condition of the major guerrilla area around Rossono, one which had never had more than a token German presence, are worth noting. The guerrillas were clearly suffering from inertia. One partisan wrote:

> 'I live passably and remember the times gone by which will certainly not return in the former fashion. You well know how our partisan life is – not as it was earlier. When we came here from the Soviet hinterland, the Germans were everywhere and it

> was not very pleasant. There were many police and other riff-raff who fought side by side with the Germans. The population was also against us. This last year [1943] has brought about perceptible changes. Our partisan area has become large. Now you see no Germans in the rayon centre. This work had to be carried out under difficult conditions; now, however, it has become easier; the population of the whole area stands behind us.'

Another wrote:

> 'My life passes quite tolerably at present. Food, footwear, and vodka are at hand in sufficient quantity.'[4]

During 1943, there was a considerable increase in the strength and activity of the partisan movement, despite the reduction in the area of occupied territory. Attacks on the German lines of communication were intensified. Sabotage attempts on railways rose from 500 in February to 1,460 in July. In March, for example, guerrillas blew up a railway bridge 330 yards long over the Desna river, on the route between Gomel and Bryansk, thereby complicating Army Group Centre's preparations for the Kursk offensive, while the previous month had witnessed a joint operation by the Bryansk partisans and the Soviet Air Force against enemy communications. The ranks of the movement swelled; if Soviet accounts are to be believed, in Belorussiya alone more than 96,000 men and women were recruited, and by November the region was sheltering 720 independent detachments, totalling 122,000 men. By the middle of the year, although continually plagued by shortages, the partisans were, in general, better equipped than their enemy. This was due partly to the immense effort put into the guerrilla movement by the Soviet régime, in contrast with the relative neglect of anti-partisan forces by the Germans; and partly to Soviet material supremacy, both in the air and on the ground, which had become a feature of the war. Tanks and mechanised equipment could only be used rarely by the Germans against the partisans, either because they were not available, or because they were unsuited to the terrain in which the guerrillas found refuge. Even in small-arms, the hunter was often inferior; the partisans, relying on heavy firepower to inflict large casualties in a relatively short time, to pin down enemy strongpoints, or to cover their retreat, were equipped with the latest rifles, machine-guns, bazookas, mines, and explosives. Automatic weapons were much used, and artillery, as well as anti-aircraft and anti-tank guns, were not unknown in certain areas. In the Yelnya-Dorogobuzh region, partisans even used Red Army tanks that had been abandoned during the great retreat in 1941. The Germans, on the other hand, equipped most of their anti-guerrilla forces with out-of-date weapons not required for service at the front. Radio, although by no means widespread was regarded as particularly valuable; it not only aided partisan efficiency and morale, but also helped to assert authority over the local population. In mid-1942, only ten per cent of units were in radio contact with the Central Staff but this had risen to forty-five per cent by 1944.

Air power was of great use to the partisans, and represented a major innovation in guerrilla warfare. It played a vital part in transforming the 'little war' into a major instrument of military policy. Fortunately for the Soviets, the Germans proved unable to counter it;[5] by the middle of 1942, German air superiority was on the wane, a situation made worse for the anti-guerrilla forces by the fact that most of the Luftwaffe was employed in the southern part of the Soviet Union, where the Germans were concentrating their efforts, and not in the centre, where the partisans were most active. Like the radio, the aeroplane played an important part in Moscow's continual efforts to dominate the partisan units in the field and to increase the prestige of the guerrillas as representatives of Soviet authority in the opinion of the local inhabitants. Militarily, however, the brigades came to rely on air-drops and air-landings for their existence; in 1941, only about one-tenth of all supplies were delivered by air, but by the middle of 1944 the proportion had risen to nearly one half. In Belorussiya there were twelve partisan airfields, which handled 1,150 tons of supplies in the first six months of 1944. The units became dependent on this mode of communication for certain essential items, such as arms and explosives; by 1943, for example, no fewer than ninety per cent of all mines and high explosive arrived by aircraft, and the increase in attacks on enemy communications was often directly attributed to an increase in such supply. In emergencies, too, air support could prove vital to survival. Temporary food shortages, caused by German action or by seasonal variations, were alleviated, as happened in the Bryansk area and around Vitebsk in 1943; the effects of German counter-guerrilla operations, such as those around the Polisto Lake in late 1942, in the Bryansk region and in northern Belorussiya, were overcome, and new partisan units speedily built up. Tactical air support during operations was important; bombing and strafing raids could be conducted to aid either an attack or a defence, and supplies were flown in to succour units under heavy enemy pressure. On occasions, hostile villages would be bombed at the request of a partisan commander, and trains, derailed by mines, would be shot to pieces. On the other hand, lack of air support could be disastrous. During the winter of 1942–43 in the Crimea, where, owing to complete German air supremacy, it was impossible to aid the bands, partisans were reduced to eating the meat of horses dead since autumn and, according to some reports, to cannibalism, in order to survive. The only disadvantage of air supply was that too great a reliance was placed upon it by both the Central Staff and the guerrilla bands; the Germans, however, proved unable to make use of their enemy's vulnerability.

The year 1943, like 1942, witnessed continued failings in the partisan movement. Well over half German-occupied territory experienced little or no significant guerrilla activity. The Ukraine, the most important sector of the occupied regions, still remained free of partisans, except for certain parts in the north-east. In July, the Germans mounted their last offensive in the East at Kursk, the junction between the central and southern sectors; in Belorussiya, sabotage to the railways had hindered the build-up of supplies for Army Group Centre, but the situation was different in the Ukraine, where Army Group South's preparations proceeded virtually unhindered. On the German failure at Kursk, apparent after only a few days of fighting, came the inevitable Soviet counter-offensive mounted on both Army Groups Centre and South. Constant pressure forced the former back through Bryansk, Smolensk, and, by the end of November, across the Berezina river; but it was to the south where the main effort was placed, and there the Soviets came close to inflicting a decisive defeat on the Germans. By the end of December the invader had been pushed back beyond the Dnepr, and was preparing to meet fresh attacks in the new year, attacks which would reach into Hungary and to the Carpathians by the following April.

Yet in all this activity, the partisans in the Ukraine again played no part, and this despite the fact that, during 1943, the Soviet authorities had spent much effort attempting to build up the guerrilla movement there. Apart from its military importance, the Ukraine was of considerable political interest to the Russian leaders, containing as it did more than one half the economic resources and one half of the population in the occupied territories. Thus, a strong partisan movement in the south would not only weaken the Germans, but it would also strengthen the Soviets in the opinion of the generally hostile Ukrainians. A number of measures were taken: the Ukrainian Staff under Timofei Strokach was withdrawn from the control of the Central Staff in April, and received its orders direct from the Central Committees of the Communist Parties of the Soviet Union and of the Ukraine; arms and supplies were made available whenever required; and, most important of all, roving bands were sent into the open steppe. The results, however, were poor. As the Red Army moved further into the region, the activities of the partisans did increase, but to little avail. In November 1943, for example, Soviet troops met with fierce resistance after capturing Kiev and Zhitomir in the northern Ukraine, and, in an attempt to relieve the pressure, the Ukrainian Staff and Communist Party planned a major partisan offensive against German communications. Little was achieved. According to the Soviets, guerrilla action reduced the capacity of the vital Kovel-Rovno-Shepetovka-Berdichev railway to about one-tenth of normal, and disrupted traffic in other sectors. However, this did not prevent the movement of enemy reserves to the front, and in the second half of November the Germans mounted a counter-offensive on a line Korosten-Zhitomir-Fastov, forcing the Red Army to retreat up to 46 miles. To the south, where partisan activity was negligible, Soviet forces continued to advance, unaided by any dislocation of the German rear. In the Carpathian mountains, the nationalist Ukrainian Insurgent Army kept all Soviet representatives at bay, while, in other parts of western Ukraine, Polish partisan bands proved just as unco-operative. By the end of the year, out of a total of 200,000 partisans, the Soviets claimed only 43,500 operating in the Ukraine, and even this is probably an over-estimate. Official Soviet sources assert that the final total of partisans in the region reached 220,000 men; however, this is a ludicrous exaggeration which probably includes the unarmed partisan reserve and the irregular units parachuted or infiltrated behind the German front line in 1944 when, during its sweeping advances, the Red Army was able to give substantial support to irregular operations.

The activities of the roving bands, heroic though they sometimes may have been, were equally ineffective. At the end of 1942, in order to overcome the problems encountered in establishing partisan units in the Ukraine, and in an attempt to bring dislocation to the German rear in the south, the Central Staff instituted the roving bands. This was a development of a previous practice whereby relatively small units, about 100 men strong, moved through the front lines into the Ukraine with the tasks of 'Terrorisation of the population which was willing to work [for the Germans], especially the Ukrainian auxiliary police and the newly appointed mayors; disturbance of German troops; destruction of railways and important military objectives; liberation of prisoners-of-war; and assembling of scattered partisans and parachutists'.[6] At least one such unit had been sent into the Ukraine in May 1942, but it was unable to achieve much and, having failed to find a safe refuge or to return to Soviet lines, was caught and destroyed midway between Kharkov and Poltava.

More was hoped from the roving bands. They were to operate from the Bryansk forest, an ideal base from which to spread partisan activities to the south, for it occupied a good strategic position close to the northern limit of the east Ukrainian steppe. From there, sheltered by scattered forests, guerrilla units could move from Bryansk to the Dnepr river, and thence into the great forests of north-west Ukraine. On 2 September, the commanders of two of the strongest Ukrainian partisan units, S.A. Kovpak and A.N. Saburov, received their orders to form two roving bands, which were to be strong in numbers, well armed, and supplied largely by air. These bands moved into the region west of the Dnepr river in November 1942 and settled down for the winter in the Pripyat swamps of Belorussiya. In February 1943, a brief raid was made into the northern

Ukraine, around Rovno and Zhitomir. In the spring, Kovpak moved south, again to the Rovno and Zhitomir area, keeping constantly on the move, and was made the supreme partisan authority in the Ukraine west of the Dnepr. His band was followed by more, led by Begma, Fyodorov and others who established themselves in most of the wooded areas of the Ukraine. By the middle of 1943, the north-west forest region had been converted from an area devoid of guerrillas into one of the major centres of the partisan movement. Only in the region around Rovno and Lutsk, where nationalist sympathy was strong, were the Soviets unable to establish themselves.

However, the north-west Ukraine was only a small, economically insignificant area compared with the vast steppes to the south and Galicia to the west, both of which remained free of partisan activity. Therefore, the Ukrainian Staff ordered the roving bands led by Kovpak and M.I. Naumov to undertake two long-range operations during the spring and summer of 1943. They were to take advantage of the disorganisation of the enemy after the débâcle at Stalingrad and the Soviet winter offensive, cut his lines of communication, recruit local Ukrainians to the movement, and disrupt the regional economy. But the experiment ended in disaster. Naumov's band, mounted on horses, having traversed the south-west Ukrainian steppe, was defeated in a wood to the west of Kiev; only 300 survivors escaped to the deep forest on the northern fringe of the Ukraine, where they remained to build up a new band. Naumov was followed by Kovpak, who, leading some 3,000 men, swept over 1,200 miles through the north-west Ukraine, and then turned south into the former Polish region with orders to lay waste the Boryslav-Drohobycz oilfields. Before this was achieved, the band was largely destroyed by German forces. However, by the winter of 1943–44, these and other units safe in the north-western forests constituted a powerful striking force that could be used under Red Army control during the great advances towards the west; their activities were then extended beyond the borders of the Soviet Union, into eastern Poland and even Slovakia. However, apart from their prescence in the north-western Ukraine, the roving bands had been disappointing. Certainly they were of value as propaganda, and they had considerable political influence in indicating to the Ukrainians that Soviet authority was still alive. Militarily, however, they were virtually useless, lacking, as they did, the necessary forest and swamp in which to hide. No partisans could for long fly in the face of the realities of guerrilla existence.

In the western territories – Polish-Belorussiya, the Baltic Republics, the Moldavian Republic, and the western Ukraine – acquired by the USSR in 1939, the Soviet partisans met with almost total failure. Only in Polish-Belorussiya did they succeed in establishing themselves, and then simply because the population lacked any national consciousness (apart from a hatred of Poles) and had no real experience of Soviet rule. In the Baltic Republics, which adjoined regions of vigorous partisan activity and contained much terrain favourable to guerrillas, they failed completely, almost entirely because of the universal hostility of the population. Even by the end of the war there were no more than 9,000 partisans in the region, and these were poorly led and achieved very little. German brutality had, however, resulted in the formation in late 1943 of nationalist bands who fought against both the National Socialists and the Communists with equal vigour, but with little success. In the Moldavian Republic, guerrilla activities were also a failure, though the population, with their long history of incorporation in the Russian Empire, were less antagonistic towards representatives of Soviet authority. The two Moldavian brigades, composed mainly of Russian and Ukrainian personnel, remained hidden in Ukrainian forests some 300 to 500 miles from Moldavia until the Red Army reached the territory.

The western Ukraine was regarded by the Soviets as an area of prime importance: it was the natural gateway to East Europe, a stable economic base for the Germans, and possessed nationalist elements that would be dangerous after the war. Therefore, enormous effort was put into establishing a partisan movement in the area; all to little avail. The Galician Ukrainians, fiercely nationalistic, were unanimous in rejecting the Soviet guerrillas, and the Volhynian Ukrainians were only a little more friendly. As a result, the partisans were able to pass through the western Ukraine only on long-range raids, and it was not until the Red Army was close enough to give them active support that they became anything more than a passing nuisance to the Germans. The greatest service performed by the few Soviet partisans in western Ukraine was an unwitting one: by their existence they caused the nationalists to abandon covert activity and form guerrilla bands in order to counter the Communists and prevent them from gaining the allegiance of all those who wished to fight the Germans. By thus coming out into the open, the nationalists made themselves easier targets for the NKVD and Red Army during the Soviet re-occupation of the area.

With the Germans thrown out of nearly all Soviet territory by the middle of July, 1944 saw the end of partisan operations. On 13 January, in order to make the guerrilla leadership operationally more sensitive to the requirements of the Red Army now that it was surging deep into enemy territory, the Central Staff was abolished, command being exercised by the regional and front staffs. The partisans' main task remained, as before, the sabotage of enemy lines of communication; but, in addition, they took on a new role as the advance-guard of Soviet moves into the

East European countries of Poland, Czechoslovakia, Hungary, and Romania. The guerrillas were not to end fighting when the Red Army had driven the invader from Russian soil; the political goals of the Soviet leaders ensured that they still had a part to play in the class struggle, namely to prevent the re-emergence of bourgeois régimes in Eastern Europe. East Europeans were recruited in increasing numbers by the partisan movement; they were formed into special units which would be supplied on the 'request' of Communist leaders in Czechoslovakia, Hungary, Romania, and Poland. In April 1944, a Polish Staff of the Partisan Movement was instituted, and roving bands were sent to aid the Polish National Guard (Communist-led partisans) and combat the Polish Home Army (guerrillas representing the London-based Polish government). Their achievements, however, appear to have been relatively unimportant. In the Carpatho-Ukraine, which was under the domination of Hungary, some partisans operated with Soviet support, the intention being to use the area as a base from which to extend their activities into Slovakia, Hungary, and Romania. However, the strongly anti-Russian attitude of the peasants made failure certain in all countries except Slovakia, where Soviet efforts successfully transplanted a partisan movement, the core of which consisted of 3,000 Soviet guerrillas. In the other regions, the Red Army was to prove much more effective in establishing Soviet influence. But, however limited the success of the partisans in the future Soviet satellites might have been, their propaganda value was considerable, for they enabled the Communists to contrive a semblance of popular support for military intervention which a regular army alone could never have achieved.

One further weakness of the Soviet partisan movement lay in its composition. During their short history, the bands had gone through many changes. In 1941, they were primarily volunteer, amateur organisations, dependent on Party members, intellectuals, and workers from the cities, men who had always been more influenced by Communism than the peasants; in 1942, new recruits were chiefly stragglers from the Red Army who joined as the only alternative to suffering or death at the hands of the Germans, and men drafted from the civilian population; in 1943, while the influx of draftees continued, and even increased, there was a new wave of volunteers, opportunists, men determined to join the winning side, many of them former collaborators who were regarded by the Soviet authorities as basically unreliable. The number of Party members, as a proportion of the total, fell from around forty per cent in 1941 to ten per cent by the following year; personnel from the Red Army fell from sixty per cent in 1942 to stabilise at around forty per cent by 1943; and peasants, nearly all of whom were drafted against their will,

Reinhard Heydrich, Chief of the Security Police and the SD.

Below left: Erich von dem Bach-Zelewski, Chief of SS Anti-Partisan Formations.

Ernest Kaltenbrunner, Heydrich's successor.

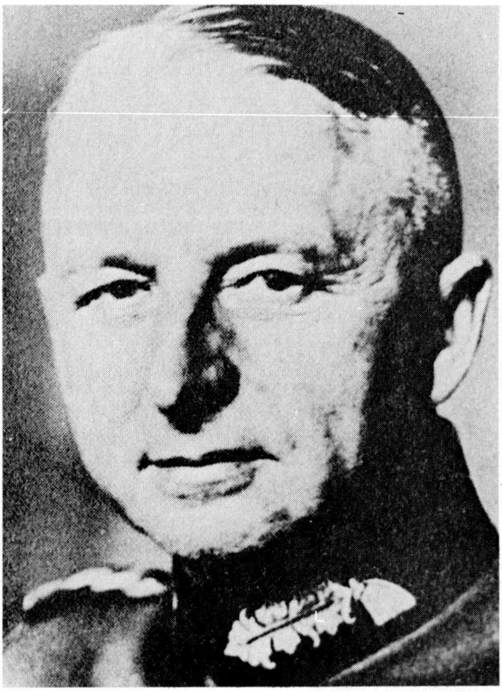

Field-Marshal Erich von Manstein.

Field-Marshal Walter von Reichenau.

Field-Marshal Wilhelm Keitel, Chief of OKW.

General Jodl, Chief of Operations, OKW.

Reich Minister for the Occupied Eastern Territories, Alfred Rosenberg.

Reich Commissar for the Ukraine, Erich Koch.

Reich Commissar for Ostland,
Heinrich Lohse.

General Commissar for Belorussiya,
Wilhelm Kube.

A partisan detachment in Simferopol, Crimea, 1941.

The workings of a German machine-pistol being explained to guerrillas.

A partisan poster showing how to prosecute the struggle against the German invader.

A warning to others hung round a dead partisan's neck. The German version reads: 'We are partisans, and have been shot by German soldiers'.

furnished between forty and sixty per cent. In 1944, former collaborators may have made up as much as between ten and twenty per cent of the total. It would be no exaggeration to say that, after the spring of 1942, at least eighty per cent of Soviet partisans joined either unwillingly or because they had no alternative; enthusiastic volunteers were a rarity.

The Soviets made no pretence about recruitment for the partisan movement. Compulsion was paramount, and served the dual purpose of filling the ranks of the bands and of preventing men being taken by the Germans for forced labour. The following extract from a guerrilla proclamation, addressed to soldiers and citizens in occupied areas, is typical:

> 'All members of the armed forces who escaped . . . and are at home, also all men in the class of 1925 [i.e. born in that year], report to your regular units or join the partisan units. Those who remain in hiding and continue to sit at home in order to save their skins, and those who do not join in the patriotic war to help destroy the German robbers, also those who desert to the Fascist army and help the latter to carry on a robber war against the Soviet people, are traitors to the homeland and will be liquidated by us sooner or later.'[7]

In the spring of 1942, the introduction of the draft as official policy was proclaimed publicly, and straightway partisan units began to put it into practice, either keeping the recruits for themselves or sending them through German lines to the Red Army. South of Bryansk, for example, all men between seventeen and fifty, and childless women fit for military activity, were to be drafted; three-man examining commissions were instituted, lists drawn up, and mass recruitments organised. Methods were crude. Villages were entered by detachments, and the inhabitants called to the square, where they would be told simply that they had been recruited for service for the Motherland. Only those physically unfit were left behind. Sometimes a notice would appear in a village ordering all able-bodied inhabitants to present themselves at a given place on a certain date, warning that failure to do so would incur savage reprisals. On occasions, men would be taken from their homes late at night at gunpoint. One partisan recounted how he was recruited; he, along with fifteen other men, was told: ' "You have now joined the partisans." To the reply that we had been brought by force, he [the partisan leader] answered, "That is not important. Those who do not want to go along can say so." No one answered, as all believed they could count on being shot if they protested. He continued, "You are not to regard yourselves as drafted men, but as voluntary members of a partisan unit which has set itself the task of defending the Motherland." '[8] Such activities were regarded by the Germans as official kidnapping, and there is no doubt that they were deeply resented by the peasants, who, much as they might hate the invaders, had no wish to risk their lives in fighting for the return of what had been to them a similarly abhorrent tyranny. But however arbitrary such drafting was, it was at least preferable to many of the measures undertaken by the Germans. The partisan movement was blessed with the advantage of being the lesser of two evils.

As a result of these changes in the composition of the bands, there grew up a distinct class system within the partisan movement. An 'us' and 'them' attitude was evident between men who were united only by the fact that they fought the Germans. The 'old partisans', those who had become guerrillas within the first year of the war, considered themselves an élite group, above all other late-comers and entitled to special treatment. They especially scorned the 'partisans of 1943', those whom they believed wished to get on to the Soviet band-waggon once German defeat seemed probable. The drafted guerrillas and the Red Army stragglers were treated with suspicion and often given inferior supplies and equipment; former collaborators, especially those who had been in the militia or the police, were regarded with particular contempt. Partisan reports, diaries, and memoirs are full of such instances; typical of the 'old fighter' attitude is this extract from Fyodorov's remembrances:

> 'But there were all kinds of men among the escaped prisoners-of-war. Some had voluntarily surrendered to the Germans. Later, when they had been eaten up by lice in the camps and had become sick and tired of being punched in the jaw, they repented and escaped to join the partisans. Not all of them by any means told us the whole truth. And, of course, very few of them admitted they had surrendered of their own free will.
>
> 'These men joined the partisans only because there was nothing else for them to do. They didn't want to go back to the Germans but, on the other hand, they didn't fight them any too energetically either.
>
> 'Some of the formerly encircled men who joined us had been "hubbies" [stragglers who had married local girls]. These were soldiers who for one reason or another had fallen behind the army. . . . Among the "hubbies" there were specimens who would have been glad to sit out the war behind a woman's skirt, but the Hitlerites would either drive them off to work in Germany or else make them join the police. After turning this over in his mind such a man would come to the conclusion that, after all, joining the partisans was more advantageous.'[9]

But whatever faults Fyodorov might discern, the Red Army men were at least soldiers trained in the art of killing; the peasants, on the other hand, were not only indifferent to the Communist cause, they were usually unskilled in military practice. Thus, partisan leaders often considered them as mere ballast for their units, eminently expendable.

It is not surprising that, under such conditions, the morale of most of the partisans was low. Certainly, the élite were fired by their belief that they were engaged in a heroic struggle for Motherland and Communism, being constantly stimulated by Party propaganda which glamorised their life as partisans and promised them recognition similar to that accorded the Red guerrillas of the Civil War. Their units were given titles of great patriotic distinction – 'The Red Banner', 'Lenin', 'Stalin', 'Alexander Nevsky', 'The People's Avengers', and 'Death to the Fascist'; decorations were awarded freely, the most important brigade commanders becoming 'Heroes of the Soviet Union'; achievements, however minor, were given wide publicity. Exhortations were continually made to induce the partisans to fight harder; guerrillas in the Crimea, for example, had to ascribe to the following:

> 'We, the men and women guerrillas of the detachment Yalta are full of enthusiasm for the appeal of the Highest Soviet, directed to the population of the temporarily occupied districts on the occasion of the 24th Anniversary of the Red Army [23 February 1942]. We have unanimously decided to join the socialist competition. Our aim is to carry out all orders in the best possible manner, to succeed in all actions against the enemy, and to exterminate the invaders to the maximum possible extent.
>
> 'Therefore the detachment Yalta calls on all partisans to take part in this competition using the following methods of scoring:
>
> (i) Each partisan must exterminate at least five (5) fascists or similar traitors.
>
> (ii) He must take part in at least three (3) actions a month.
>
> (iii) Should a fighting comrade or Communist be killed or wounded in action, he must be carried from the battlefield.'[10]

Nevertheless, such 'socialist competition' had little effect on the drafted peasants; their morale was almost uniformly low. A report from the 221st Security Division, dated 15 April 1942, stated: 'Morale is not very good. Only the Red Army stragglers still go along, while those recruited by force are all waiting for an opportunity to escape.'[11] Yet the rate of desertion was not high; as another German report, dated 22 May 1943, noted: 'Morale is low, and during the last days . . . things are hopeless; but, because of fear of their leaders, and also because of punitive measures by the [German] troops, nobody deserts.'[12] The partisan leaders had approached the problem of disaffection with realism. From the beginning, they had noticed that brigades which suffered heavy losses would often be composed of as many as seventy to eighty per cent of inexperienced 'recruits'. In one respect, this was not regarded as too much of handicap, for the form of guerrilla warfare evolved by the Soviets called for large numbers of men as 'cannon-fodder', with a few trained specialists for particular operations. However, there was fear that, with a considerable proportion of inexperienced officers and peasant recruits indifferent to the Communist cause, the bands might become unreliable and lose their military usefulness, and that the defection of just one man might bring about the destruction of an entire band. Suspicion was endemic. Rigorous control was seen as the only solution. The Soviets promoted determined officers and sacrificed the weak; they appointed commissars to instruct guerrillas in Communist ideology and attitude, and instituted NKVD cells to watch for any instance of unreliability. Purges took place whenever deemed necessary, usually aimed against former collaborators. Intensive political indoctrination was undertaken in every unit, although strong appeals were made to patriotism rather than to support of the Communist Party or the Soviet régime. In the partisan oath, for example, there was no reference to Stalin or the Communist creed.

Once recruited, the new partisan went through a probationary period, usually not being given a weapon for about four weeks. His duties were at first menial, tending livestock and such-like, graduating to guard duty without a gun and under the watchful eye of an armed supervisor. All this time, the background of the recruit was being scrutinised by Soviet authorities. Close surveillance was regarded as essential; unreliability was sternly dealt with – usually by death. If a recruit managed to desert, his family were immediately killed. Once successfully through this trial period, the new partisan was given a rifle and told to use it well, being reminded at the same time that from then on he could expect no mercy from the enemy. As a German report of 23 June 1943 noted, 'This procedure is effective. It makes infiltration by our agents difficult, gives sufficient time for screening out undesirables, and places the remaining men in the position of believing themselves to be too deeply involved in partisan activity to risk reprisals from both sides.'[13]

Discipline was strict, summary executions commonplace. The most frequent offences were failing to fight, sleeping or smoking on guard duty, looting, drunkenness, and sexual excess with women; all of these were punishable by the death penalty, although the brigade commander was allowed discretion. In practice, executions were ordered primarily as a means of deterrence, as the following order, dated 2 July 1943, made by the commissar of the Kovpak brigade, S.V. Rudnev, illustrates:

'Recently instances of looting by individual soldiers have been

> noticed in the regiment. After the regiment has passed through the villages, the staff receives complaints about stealing from the peaceful inhabitants. All this helps the enemy to conduct his propaganda against us – the Soviet partisans – and besmirch the honourable calling of the avengers of the people. . . .
>
> 'Because of this, I order: For violation of Order No. 200, concerning robbing and looting, which besmirch the name of the avengers of the people, Semyon Grigoryevich Chibisov and Vasili Yevseyevich Alekseyev are to be shot in front of the assembled regiment.'[14]

Drafted peasants and former collaborators were far more likely to receive a bullet in the neck than were the 'politically reliable' guerrillas. Men who had fallen into disfavour or who were under suspicion could easily be got rid of by assigning them to dangerous missions; others were simply shot without warning by their officers while on patrol or during a minor action with the enemy. Desertion was regarded as the worst of crimes, and resulted in not only the death of the guilty partisan but also the extermination of his family. However, this was not always sufficient, and other measures were required. A report, dated 28 April 1942, from the 221st Infantry Division, notes:

> 'Vetitiyev declared that escape from the partisans is difficult, since guardposts are set up everywhere. If a deserter is captured, he is first tortured and then shot. As a result of the "many" desertions, the partisan officers have become so mistrustful of the partisans who are local men that they have scattered the local men in among the former Red Army soldiers. Consequently, the drafted partisans cannot communicate with each other without being observed. Vetitiyev believes that, if the number of desertions increases, all the partisans who were drafted locally will be shot.'[15]

The partisan was also subject to constant criticism, designed to emphasise his positive and negative characteristics. Every unit had its own wall newspaper, which carried a list of the accomplishments and deficiencies of its members, and at Party and *Komsomol* meetings even the minor failings of partisans were aired. The result of this strict and constant discipline and supervision was that disaffected guerrillas were prevented from deserting in any significant numbers. For example, in the area of the central sector controlled by 3rd Panzer Army, where at any one time some 27,000 guerrillas were believed to be operating, over the period of thirteen months from May 1943 there were only 1,054 desertions to the German forces compared with 12,920 killed and 10,915 captured. Of more significance was the fact that the rate of desertion was far higher during periods of German anti-guerrillas action; in the eight months from September 1943 to April 1944 there were only forty-one desertions, but in the five months from May to August 1943, and during May 1944, when the panzer army was operating against the partisans, there were 1,013. Most of these desertions occurred after the operations had ended, when the guerrilla bands were disorganised, displaced, and spread over a larger area than normal; at these times the supervision usually exerted by the commanders, commissars, and NKVD personnel was lax, and the opportunities available for a man to sneak away undetected were many. But the increase was also indicative of something else. During its anti-partisan operations, the panzer army propagandists emphasised the good treatment that a deserter could expect to receive from their hands. Thus, at the same time as the opportunity to desert presented itself, a number of partisans returned to the old belief, not entirely shattered by events, that the enemy offered something better than the Soviets.

For most of the partisans, however, desertion to the Germans was not a course of action to be entertained for long. By doing so they could not expect to receive better treatment – indeed, instant death might result – nor to find life in the 'safe' areas of the occupied territories particularly secure or rewarding. The effects of National Socialist policies were well known both to the peasants and the Red Army soldiers. Moreover, by 1943 it was evident that to desert to the Germans was probably to desert to the losing side, while to remain with the partisans was to give proof, if not of loyalty to the Soviet régime, at least of non-collaboration with the enemy. German measures and the prospect of the Wehrmacht's defeat had made desertion an unlikely choice even for the discontented guerrillas, of whom there were many.

Chapter 6

The Development of German Security Policy 1942–44

Perhaps we have gone too far
HEINRICH HIMMLER January 1944

In 1941, German reports concerning the partisans had had about them an air of confidence, if not complacency. Severity was seen to be the answer to all problems. If a single sentry were killed, or a length of railway track destroyed, then it was only necessary to execute hostages; far from being a drawback, their innocence was considered to be an advantage. If a partisan were captured, he was to be tortured in order to extract information, and then shot. It was all so simple. As Field-Marshal Gerd von Rundstedt, commander of Army Group South, told his army commanders on 8 December:

> 'The activity of partisans is as good as done with in the 6th Army area [commanded by von Reichenau]. This success is due to the rigorous measures employed by the army. In many cases the threat to the population to take away all their food supplies and to burn down their villages if they do not report in time the location of the partisans, was sufficient.
>
> 'In the course of fighting the partisans, several thousand of them have been hanged publicly or shot in the army area. According to experience, death by hanging has an especially deterring effect. Furthermore the many elements roaming the country without identity papers, behind which hide the agents and the intelligence service of the partisans, were done away with. Since then acts of sabotage have stopped.
>
> 'This experience shows that only such measures, which the population dreads more than the terror of the partisans, will attain their object.
>
> 'The Army Group recommends the taking of corresponding measures whenever necessary.'[1]

Indeed, it appears that, initially at least, the measures which von Rundstedt believed to be so effective were not without success. A Soviet report, dated September 1941, noted: 'There are, however, many elements among the population who sympathize with the partisan movement and the Soviet régime. But, since they fear the consequences, they are using utmost caution in their activities. Thus, it has happened that our agents have received signals to leave a village because the Germans were in it; they were given food . . . and were advised to get out, or be captured by the Germans. . . .'[2] No doubt the writer somewhat over-estimated the devotion of the Russians to the Communist cause and its representatives, but the conclusions about the effect of German measures did coincide with many of the early reports made by the invaders. The reason, if one there be, may lie in the fact that the population, generally so antipathetic to the Soviet system, appreciated that, initially, certain harsh measures by the Germans would be necessary to ensure security in the occupied areas. Provided these were not extreme, and were not accompanied by economic exploitation and abusive treatment, and, even more important, if there remained hope that a large measure of autonomy would soon be given them, the Russian people would tolerate German presence as the lesser of two evils. However, the moment security measures, in line with other German policies, took the nature of racial extermination rather than of pacification, the attitude of the population changed; the harsher and more prolonged the treatment, the more favourable did indigenous opinion become towards the partisans, and the easier was it for the latter to operate. By the middle of 1942, the Provost-Marshal General reported that, in spite of the death penalty and reprisals, people were willing to risk their lives to aid the guerrillas. German measures had proved counter-productive; the question now was: could the military and political leadership understand this, and would they change their policies accordingly?

Alarm was the general reaction among the Germans at the unexpected upsurge of partisan activity in 1942; as a result they tended to exaggerate the threat. Goebbels' diary bears testimony to this; on 6 March he wrote: 'The partisans are in command of large areas in occupied Russia, and are conducting a régime of terror there.' On 16 March, he noted: 'The activity of partisans has increased noticeably in recent weeks. They are conducting a well-organised guerrilla war. It is very difficult to get at them because they are using such terrorist methods in the areas we occupy that the population is afraid of collaborating with us loyally any longer.' And on the 29th, he wrote: 'The danger of the partisans in the occupied areas continues to exist in unmitigated intensity.'[3] The SD reported that the movement was 'steadily growing in all sectors, and gaining new impetus with the advent of the warmer season'; the cares of winter over, the partisans were 'able once again to devote themselves to their proper terror and destruction work'.[4] German newspapers, too, began to carry stories about the guerrilla war; on 13 April, the *Kölnische Zeitung* stated that 'The support provided for the enemy by the civilian population, often in the form of partisan warfare which is particularly cultivated by the Bolsheviks, makes the fight very trying for the German soldiers. These fights, on and behind the front, are extremely severe, imposing all levels of hardship and privations.'[5] Even generals publicly announced the dangers inherent in the situation. On 25 June, General Paul Hasse was reported in the *Hamburger Tageblatt* as saying: 'Guerrilla warfare was used systematically during the winter [1941–42]. Now this partisan warfare is really dangerous and has caused many upsets not only to our rear communications, but also to the rear and flanks of our troops.'[6]

The Germans had some cause for alarm. The nature of guerrilla activity was changing, from attacks on individual soldiers or vehicles to relatively large operations against small units, convoys, and villages. Raids for supplies became incidental; in their place came the blocking of roads, the mining of railway tracks, the destruction of bridges, and raids on army rear services. The Crimean guerrillas wiped out more than 1,000 men of a Jäger infantry division near Salatsk; men from the Moscow region routed a corps headquarters at Ugodsk Zavod; fighters from the area around Smolensk eliminated the garrison at Prigorye station and destroyed all trains there; and Leningrad partisans killed General von Wirtz and his bodyguard. These were just a few of the instances of increased guerrilla action. Despite his gross exaggeration, it was with some justification that Stalin could announce on May Day that 'sabotage in war industries, the blowing up of German depots, the wrecking of German troop trains, the killing of German soldiers and officers have become daily occurrences. All . . . the Soviet areas occupied by the Germans are swept by the flames of partisan warfare.'[7]

As was consistent with their attitude towards the Easterners and the fear that arose out of the realisation of their own lack of strength, the German leaders reacted to the guerrilla threat with a predictable call to increase the ruthlessness of anti-partisan measures – the very step that would stimulate resistance. Any thought of exploiting the weaknesses inherent in the Soviet guerrilla movement, caused by popular hostility and, increasingly, the low morale and reluctance to fight of its members, was dismissed. On 8 August, Hitler told a meeting of his senior military and political aides: 'The struggle we are waging against the partisans resembles very much the struggle in North America against the Red Indians. Victory will go to the strong, and strength is on our side. At all costs we will establish law and order there.'[8] Two months later, the

Führer repeated this theme: 'Only in those instances where the anti-partisan struggle was begun and carried out with ruthless brutality has success not failed to obtain. . . . The struggle against the partisans in the entire East is a life-and-death struggle in which one side or the other must be exterminated.'[9] This contrasted, in part, with the new instructions embodied in War Directive No. 46, dated 18 August 1942, which stipulated: 'The confidence of the local population . . . must be gained by handling them strictly but firmly . . . [their] co-operation . . . is indispensable.' Nonetheless, the people were to be given only 'the minimum requirements of life', and, although rewards for help were to be 'truly attractive, reprisals for action in support of the bandits must be all the more severe'. Moreover, the soldiers and SS men were warned, perhaps needlessly, against 'misplaced confidence in the native population. . . . there are always spies to be reckoned with.'[10]

On 11 November 1942, OKW issued its first directive on anti-guerrilla methods, entitled 'Combat Instructions for Partisan Warfare in the East'. It was, as its author, Generalmajor von Butlar-Brandenfels, admitted, 'written under pressure and without receiving major reports on experience'.[11] He further conceded that it was ineffective, merely a reiteration of previous directives on the subject; it was still left to the ingenuity of individual commanders to determine the nature and method of security operations. Repression continued to be the order of the day, to be achieved by shooting captured partisans and exacting reprisals against civilians. Indeed, even had the OKW generals wished to develop a more rational policy based on the lessons of experience, they would have been prevented from doing so by the Führer's attitude.

On 1 December 1942, Hitler delivered himself of the following thoughts regarding the German conduct of the phantom war: 'Fundamental to anti-partisan operations – and this must be hammered home – is that whatever succeeds is correct. This is basic. If someone does something which is not quite according to regulations, but which can lead to absolute success, or if someone sees that an emergency can only be overcome by the harshest of measures, then those means which bring success are justified. The object must be to annihilate the bands and to restore peace.'[12] Jodl, to his credit, advanced the unfashionable argument that moderation be shown towards civilians, as indiscriminate reprisals would only drive innocent people into the hands of the guerrillas. Hitler, however, would have none of that, and insisted that only the strongest possible measures would destroy the partisan menace. On 16 December 1942, in pursuance of his master's wishes, Keitel issued the following instructions from OKW concerning the conduct of anti-partisan fighting:

'The Führer has received reports that certain members of the

Wehrmacht who took part in fighting against the bands were later called to account for their behaviour while so fighting. In this connection, the Führer ordered: "If the repression of the bands in the East, as well as in the Balkans, is not pursued with the most brutal means, it will not be long before the forces at our disposal will prove insufficient to exterminate this plague.

"The troops therefore have the right and the duty to use, in this fight, any means, even against women and children, provided they are conducive to success. Scruples, of any sort whatsoever, are a crime against the German people and against the front-line soldier who bears the consequences of attacks by bands and who cannot understand why any regard should be shown to them or their associates."

'These principles must serve as a basis for operations against bands in the East. No German participating in action against bands or their associates is to be held responsible for acts of violence either from a disciplinary or a judicial point of view. Commanders of troops engaged in action against the bands are obliged to see to it that all officers of units under their command be immediately and thoroughly notified of this order, that their legal advisers be immediately acquainted therewith, and that no judgements be passed which are in contradiction thereto.'[13]

This firm instruction elaborated on the OKW decree issued on 13 May 1941, and extended by the OKW order of 16 September 1941. It confirmed and strengthened the position established a year and a half previously, and left no room for doubt: no German soldier could be called to account for any action whatsoever, however barbarous, provided he did it in pursuit of anti-guerrilla operations – operations which specifically called for the establishment of a reign of terror in which summary execution, reprisal, and destruction on a wide scale had their officially-approved place.

Thus the relationship between commanders of security forces in the rear areas, even the most junior, and the higher headquarters, extending even to OKH and OKW, was very different from that which pertained at the front. As von dem Bach-Zelewski commented, 'No precise control was possible in individual cases'.[14] Headquarters might decide on an operation and on the movements of troops, but it could do little to regulate the attitude of the soldiers towards the guerrillas or the population, or to limit the number of villages burned to the ground or innocent civilians killed in reprisals, or tortured. The men who undertook the operation were required only to execute tactical moves to the best of their ability and to provide detailed reports on the results; they could not be called to account for their methods. After the war, von dem Bach-Zelewski commented on the effect of this order by providing a specific example: 'A sergeant, on hearing news of an attack upon some comrades on the Shuszk-Bobruysk highway, gathered some of his soldiers together and independently took his revenge. He took four or five civilians from the village nearest the scene of the attack and liquidated them to the applause of watching soldiers. . . . Von Schenkendorff and I carried out court-martial proceedings. In these, all the participants were condemned to death. . . . Von Schenkendorff told me that the sentence was confirmed, but was not proceeded with because of the justified indignation felt by the participants, in accordance with an OKW instruction.'[15]

The destruction that was unleashed on the Russian peoples as a consequence of the directives issued by Hitler and OKW at the end of 1942 outweighed even the brutality that had characterised German occupation policy until then. It was, indeed, a slaughter of the innocents, of which even some of its perpetrators were to grow sick. One eye-witness to an SS anti-guerrilla search in a village, a member of the *Ordnungsdienst* (the collaborationist indigenous police) who had accompanied the SS men on their mission as a guide, was so appalled at what he had seen that he wrote the following report, dated May 1943, to his German commander in the vain hope that something could be done to prevent such outrages in the future. It ran:

> 'We entered the village [believed to be in the Smolensk region] at midday and called for the mayor. The SS officer treated this man abysmally, even though he seemed to be a friend. He was ordered to gather all the people in the square, even the babies, and to take steps to round in all those who might be working in the fields. Guards were posted. By 14.00 all were asssembled. The SS men had meanwhile filled in their time by walking round the village and doing precisely as they pleased. There was at least one rape, and nothing was done about it. To the assembled people, the SS officer, through me, told them that their area was bandit infested, that they must have collaborated with those bandits, and that disciplinary action would be taken against them. There were twenty-three men in the square. Half of them were separated, irrespective of age or health, and taken down a side alley. The SS men seemed to know exactly what to do. Without one word of an order from the officer, automatic firing began, and then the SS men returned, without the peasants. The women became hysterical and had to be beaten into submission. Then the huts

were set on fire, and all food that was found was destroyed. As the flames began to engulf the final row of huts, a man who had obviously been hiding ran out, his clothing partially alight. The SS men were clearly expecting something of the sort, and shot him dead before he had taken five paces. This was the signal for further brutality. The SS officer rounded on the mayor, telling him that he was not merely a collaborator, but a full bandit. He was, therefore, to die like a bandit. But first he would admit where the bandit camp was. The mayor refused, quite probably because he did not know. The SS officer then had one of the young girls brought before them, and told the SS Scharführer [Sergeant] to perform. I find the following incident impossible to recount. The result was that the girl, stripped naked, had one of her breasts cut off. The mayor still refused to talk. The girl was then shot in front of him, and the SS officer fired a few indiscriminate rounds into the group of women, felling two or three. The final refusal to provide the information caused the execution of the mayor by slow hanging and the death by shooting of the rest of the inhabitants. The SS men left, leaving some 70 dead people of all ages behind them. I cannot believe that this is either humane or sensible; action to stop it must be taken.'[16]

In similar vein on 19 July 1943, Herf, a police general in the East, wrote to the Head of the SS Personnel Main Office in great agitation:

> 'You have got to know me well over a number of years and I hope you have a good opinion of me – at least I think you have. I do not know whether I can remain here. Things are going on here which I cannot stomach, to which I am not prepared to subscribe even in the smallest corner of my mind. The problem concerns our official reports.
>
> 'In my opinion, the reports sent out from here to the Reichsführer are "cooked". Long before I arrived people in the Ukraine were saying quite openly that our casualty reports were false. People said that the figures were kept artificially low in order to highlight the "successes". I would not wish even to hint at the reason for this. After I had been here only one day the Head of the Operations Section told me quite openly that things were going on which were not quite right. The ex Chief of Staff (who by the way had been promised my job) told me the same thing. That was on my second day here. I have told both of them that under these circumstances I cannot remain. They advise me to try to get things changed. As you know, I have done so. Yesterday a Gauleiter and General commissar unintentionally and unwitting-

ly broadcast certain secret reports (intended for the Führer!) showing that some 480 rifles were found on 6,000 dead "partisans". Put bluntly, all these men had been shot to swell the figure of enemy losses and highlight our own "heroic deeds". I am under no illusions that, this being the system, the winter 1943–4 will see the beginning of the end in the rear areas and probably at the front as well. The increase in guerrilla warfare is simply and solely due to the way the Russians have been treated.

'I have already on several occasions confided to you my misgivings over the "colonization" process. If, however, we are now going to work on this system, I have no desire to see myself subsequently accused of misleading the Reichsführer-SS, with the files brought forward to prove it. The principle is that dead men there must be, no matter where they come from – otherwise the commander concerned is a bad commander and a bad soldier. What's more he won't get a decoration.

'The Reichsführer-SS "likes" me; I am very distressed by all this because my liking for him is even greater. But . . . Max . . . I am not a crook and I don't intend to become one.

'Yesterday evening I delved into this "6,000/480" problem I mentioned. Answer: "You appear not to know that these bandits destroy their weapons in order to play the innocent and so avoid death." How easy it must be to suppress these guerrillas – when they destroy their weapons!

'My dear Max, I am prepared to serve the country, not some particular person or some pack of lies.

'I am most grateful to you for all the friendship you have shown me, but . . . I must now throw in my hand.

'My reasons I have set out briefly above.

'If you wish, recall me to Berlin and I will gladly come. As you can imagine, this has not been easy to write since it means the end of my career; on that I have no illusions.'[17]

In the light of this, it is easy to accept the testimony before the International Military Tribunal at Nuremberg of Jacob Grigoriev, citizen of the Soviet Union. During the war he lived in the village of Kusnezovo in the Pskov region; his experience, however appalling, was by no means unique. He told the judges:

'On the memorable day of 28 October 1943, German soldiers suddenly raided our village and started murdering the peaceful citizens, shooting them, chasing them into the houses. On that day I was working by the stream with my two sons, Alexei and Nikolai. Suddenly a German soldier came up to us and ordered us to follow him.

'We were led through the village to the last house at the outskirts. There were nineteen of us, all told, in that house. So there we sat in that house. I sat close to the window and looked out of it. I saw my wife and my nine-year-old boy. They were chased right up to the house and then led back again – where I do not know.

'A little later three German machine-gunners came in, accompanied by a fourth carrying a heavy revolver. We were ordered into another room. We went, all nineteen of us, and were lined up against a wall, including my two sons, and they began shooting us with their machine-guns. I stood right up to the wall, bending slightly. After the first volley I fell to the floor, where I lay, too frightened to move. When I came to, I looked round and saw my son Nikolai who had been shot and had fallen, face downwards. Then, when some time had passed, I began to wonder how I could escape. I straightened my legs out from under the man who had fallen on me and began to think out a way of escape. Instead of that, instead of planning my escape, I lost my head and called out, at the top of my voice: "Can I really go now?" At that moment my small son, who had remained alive, recognised me.

'He was wounded in the leg. I calmed him down: "Do not fear, my small son. I shall not leave you here. Somehow or other, we shall get away from here. I shall carry you out." A little later the house began to burn. Then I opened the window and threw myself out of it, carrying my little boy who had been wounded in the leg. So we began to creep out of the house, hiding so that the Germans could not see us, but on our way from the house we suddenly saw a high hedge. We could not move the hedge apart so we began to break it up. At that moment we were noticed by the German soldiers and they began to shoot at us. Then I whispered to my little son to hide while I would run away. I was unable to carry him, and he ran a short distance and hid in the undergrowth, while I ran off. I ran a short distance and then jumped into a building near the burning house. There I sat for a while and then decided to run further on. So I escaped into a nearby forest, not far from our village, where I spent the night. In the morning I met Alexeiev N. from the neighbouring village, who said: "Your son Alexei is alive, he managed to crawl to the next village." Then, on the second day, I met Vitya Kuznetzov, a little boy from the same village who had escaped from Leningrad and was living in our village during the time of the occupation.

'He told me what had happened in the second hut where my

> wife and son had been taken. The German soldiers, having driven the people into the hut, opened the door and began shooting with their machine-guns. According to Vitya's story, people who were still half alive were burning, including my little boy, Petya, who was only nine years old. When he ran out of the hut he saw that Petya was still alive: he was sitting under a bench having covered his ears with his little hands.'

According to Grigoriev, a German soldier had given the following reasons for the punitive expedition:

> 'Do you know the village of Maximovo? (This is the village next to our community village.) I said, "Yes." Then he told me: "This village of Maximovo is *kaput* – the inhabitants are *kaput*, and you, too, will be *kaput* . . . [because] you harboured partisans in your village." But his words were untruthful because we had no partisans in the village and nobody took part in any partisan activities, since there was nobody left. Only old people and small children were left in the village; the village had never seen any partisans and did not know who those partisans were.'

Indeed, the village had only forty-seven inhabitants, of whom the oldest was a woman of 108 and the youngest a baby of four months. There was only one adult man, aged twenty-seven, but he was half-witted and paralysed; the others had gone into the Red Army or joined the partisans. Only the old and very young, the lame, and women were left. But they, together with 350 others in neighbouring villages, fell foul of German counter-guerrilla measures on that day. Grigoriev ended his testimony thus: 'Of my family only I and one of my sons remained alive. They shot my wife, in her sixth month of pregnancy, my son Nikolai, aged sixteen years, my youngest boy, Petya, aged nine years, and my sister-in-law – my brother's wife – with her two infants, Sasha and Tonya'.[18]

The activities of the SS against the partisans had been intensified even before Hitler's pronouncements. On 28 July 1942, Himmler appointed his adjutant, SS Gruppenführer Knoblauch, to the post of Chief of the Reichsführer SS's Command Staff, and gave him special responsibility for the partisan war. Knoblauch was to furnish the SS units necessary for the Higher SS and Police Leaders in the occupied Eastern territories to undertake their tasks, and to guarantee the support of military formations through consultations with OKH and OKW. At the same time, Knoblauch was to arrange for the removal of the families of known partisans to concentration camps in the Reich. Antipathy towards the guerrillas reached such a peak that the SS even introduced semantics into the struggle; on 13 August, an order stated that, henceforth, the word 'partisan' was not to be used, as it was too reminiscent of 'decent', 'civilised' fighters; instead the term 'bandit' was to be employed.[19] Racial extermination still remained the prime aim of SS security measures. This was revealed in a letter, sympathetic to SS intentions, written by Kube, usually no friend of the SS, to Rosenberg, dated 31 July 1942. It opened:

> 'In all the clashes with partisans in Belorussiya, it has been proven that Jewry, in the former Polish section as well as in the former Soviet sections of the District General, together with the Polish movement of resistance in the East and the Red Guards from Moscow, is the main bearer of the partisan movement in the East. In consequence, the treatment of Jewry . . . in view of the endangering of the entire economics, is a matter of political prominence, which should in consequence not be solved only according to an economic, but also according to a political viewpoint. In exhaustive discussions with the SS Brigadier General Zenner and the exceedingly capable Leader of the SD, SS Lieutenant Colonel Dr jur. Strauch, we have liquidated in the last ten weeks about 55,000 Jews. . . .'[20]

SS intentions were further revealed in a letter to Dr Ganzenmuller, State Secretary for Transport, dated 20 January 1943, in which Himmler stated: 'The deportation of suspected partisans and those who may be helping them is an essential prerequisite to the purification of . . . the Russian territories. In this connection, the deportation of Jews is of the first importance.'[21]

Indicative of the attitude taken by the SS security services towards anti-partisan measures, are their reports on specific operations; these, as the police general Herf realised, are in reality nothing other than thinly disguised records of genocide. For example, a report from the commander of the Security Police and SD in Belorussiya dealing with Operation '*Hornung*', which took place between 8 and 26 February 1943 in the Pripyat Marsh area, reveals how low German casualties were in relation to those of the 'partisans', and how few weapons were taken compared to the number of enemy killed or captured. Part of it reads:

> 'Losses of the enemy: 2,219 dead; 7,378 persons who received "special treatment"; 65 prisoners; 3,300 Jews. Our own losses: dead, 2 Germans, 27 non-Germans; wounded: 12 Germans, 26 non-Germans. Booty in weapons and ammunition: 172 rifles; 14 pistols and revolvers; 2 heavy machine-guns; 6 light machine-guns; 5 machine-pistols; 1 gun. . . .'[22]

Representative of the mentality of the SS in the occupied territories was the institution of SS *Sonderkommando* Dirlewanger, a unit composed largely of convicted criminals. In June 1940, SS Sturmführer Oskar Dirlewanger, a Party member since 1923 and formerly a doctor of political science until 1935 when Frankfurt University had deprived him of the title after he had been imprisoned for molesting a minor, was ordered to form a special battalion of prisoners, most of whom had been found guilty of poaching. His first duty was to guard a concentration camp for Jews in Poland, where he and his men earned the disgust even of their SS colleagues. So eager was the Higher SS and Police Leader in Poland, Krüger, to get rid of Dirlewanger's men, that if they had not disappeared from his area within one week, he would put them in prison. Legal proceedings, brought by the SS Judge Advocate, were dropped only on the interference of senior SS officials in Berlin, and Dirlewanger's unit was transferred to Belorussiya to hunt partisans. There, its brutality would be a distinct advantage, so the SS authorities thought. Indeed, the unit lived up to expectations, and was reinforced to the strength of a brigade. Himmler was delighted. To assembled Gauleiters at a conference in August 1944, he recounted proudly:

> 'In 1941 I organised a "poachers' regiment" under Dirlewanger . . . a good Swabian fellow, wounded ten times, a real character – bit of an oddity, I suppose. I obtained permission from the Führer to collect from every prison in Germany all the poachers who had used firearms and not, of course, traps, in their poaching days – about 2,000 in all. Alas, only 400 of these "upstanding and worthy characters" remain today. I have kept replenishing this regiment with people on SS probation, for in the SS we really have far too strict a system of justice . . . when these did not suffice, I said to Dirlewanger . . . "Now, why not look for suitable candidates among the villains, the real criminals, in the concentration camps?"
>
> 'The atmosphere in the regiment is often somewhat medieval in the use of corporal punishment and so on . . . if someone pulls a face when asked whether we will win the war or not he will slump down from the table . . . dead, because the others will have shot him out of hand.'[23]

The convicted murderers, former concentration camp 'block leaders', stool-pigeons, and the like, went on what can only be described as an orgy of destruction in the East. Wherever they operated, indiscriminate beatings, slaughter, and looting were rife; rape and corruption formed an every-day part of life. When they were moved to Warsaw in August 1944 to help to crush the uprising, their activities shocked all who came in contact with them. Himmler, however, recommended Dirlewanger for the Knight's Cross. Such were the standards by which the SS leaders conducted themselves in the phantom war.

The conduct of the German security troops was not helped by the conditions under which they had to fight. Fear and suspicion were endemic. As the Soviets boasted: 'the German troops . . . can never be sure that an innocent-looking clump of bushes does not conceal a machine-gun or that a simple farm girl is not carrying a hand-grenade with her in her market-basket.'[24] The invaders felt particularly vulnerable, as Field-Marshal von Küchler, one-time commander of Army Group North, commented: 'It was an extremely one-sided type of warfare, because the German soldier was easily recognisable, and the partisan fighter, because he wore civilian clothes, was not.'[25] Women and children were suspected equally with men; even small school-children acted on behalf of the partisans. When German soldiers were captured by the guerrillas, they were often abominably treated; it was not unusual for the Soviets to torture their prisoners and then hang them up, sometimes with their genitals stuffed in their mouths, as a warning to others. Furthermore, the natural environment of forest and swamp in which the German forces had to operate was not conducive to contentment among the troops, nor to respect of those whose activities caused them to be there. Combat in such places was generally regarded as the most dangerous, and certainly the most unpleasant, of all types of warfare, favouring the hunted rather than the hunter. General Halder wrote:

> 'It was our experience that Russian forces, once they were driven into wooded and swampy areas, were extremely difficult to attack by normal means and could hardly ever be completely destroyed. On countless occasions, we were confronted with the fact that the Russian was able to move about in these impenetrable forests and treacherous swamps with the certain instinct and sense of security of an animal, whereas any soldier reared and trained in a civilized country of the West was severely restricted in his movements and thereby placed at a disadvantage. There are no effective tactical remedies to compensate for this disadvantage. Even the most thorough training applied to troops from the West cannot replace the natural instinct peculiar to eastern Europeans who were born and raised in a region of forests and swamps.'[26]

Fighting in swamps, especially, put the German troops under exceptionally severe handicaps. In the summer, they had to live in constant moisture: boots and uniforms rotted; myriads of mosquitoes were a continual curse; epidemics of diarrhoea, jaundice, dysentery, and even typhoid spread like wildfire; good drinking water was a precious commodity; and proper body hygiene was impossible. Many of the local huts which might have been expected to provide cosy refuge to the tired guerrilla hunter were, instead, breeding grounds for vermin such as bedbugs, fleas, head- and body-lice. Flies were everywhere and tormented the men without respite. One officer from a security division wrote: 'It is the continual plague of flies and mosquitoes which gives me more pain and anguish than do the partisans. Oh to be rid of them, but even mosquito nets do not afford complete protection. The faces of some men are swollen beyond belief.'[27] Of particular concern to commanders was the typhus plague, which affected particularly those who had contact with the civilian population; during the autumn and winter the infestation of troops with lice reached serious proportions, and whole companies often had to be withdrawn from operations and quarantined. For the troops, continuous delousing became as much a feature of anti-partisan warfare as did the security tasks themselves.

Anti-partisan operations were often immensely frustrating; much effort and discomfort were expended for little or no return. This is revealed in the following report from a German lieutenant, dated 24 February 1942; it provides a good insight into anti-partisan operations:

> 'With a patrol composed of one officer, two NCOs, nine men, and thirteen *Ordnungsdienst* – OD – men, I left Kletnya at 1230 to clean out this partisan nest. The patrol was guided by a captured partisan under guard. At the beginning we marched along fairly good sled trails. . . . Scattered blood stains on the snow indicated that we were on the right trail. After one hour we reached the end of the sled tracks.
>
> From there on faint footprints were observed which followed winding forest paths. Here and there more blood stains appeared. Frequently, secondary tracks led off into the forest, obviously made to confuse pursuers. Zigzagging back and forth in the forest I lost my sense of direction, but I think we went in a generally north-westerly direction. At 1400 . . . we came to a clearing. . . . According to the prisoner we were still about two miles from the camp. Knee-high snow made movement difficult. . . .
>
> After another twenty minutes' march we came to another small clearing where one track branched off to the left. We had all gone on past, when an OD man who had followed that track called our attention to a man standing in a fir thicket sixty to

seventy yards away. He had already opened fire on us. Splinters of birch twigs fell around me. We returned the fire as the man turned and ran. I sent several men [to cut him off].

With the OD men and three or four of our men, I formed a skirmish line and moved forward through the forest. The fleeing man, of whom we caught occasional glimpses through the trees, fired on us several more times. After we had moved on another 500 yards or so, I suddenly found myself in a clump of scattered fir trees. Catching sight of horses' hooves hanging out of the trees [carcasses hung there for storage], I thought I had come upon the dugout we were looking for. As I circled the spot, I was fired upon from nearby. I took cover and noticed for the first time an excellently camouflaged bunker-like structure about thirty yards away. I ordered hand grenades thrown into the bunker. . . . It was empty. . . .'[28]

It is easy to imagine the fear and frustration of the hunter resulting in the maltreatment, even the execution, of innocent civilians in the neighbourhood, civilians whom the soldier feared might in fact be guerrillas, or at least sympathetic to them.

The Germans were also subjected to continual measures aimed at undermining their morale and discipline. Perhaps the most successful of all partisan operations, these did not take the form of propaganda appeals to the 'good sense' and basic proletarian instincts of the ordinary German soldier so as to induce him to desert to the Soviet side; such efforts would have been futile and, probably, none too desirable because of the difficulties of guarding and feeding the deserters. Only in the very first and last months of the war on Russian soil did the partisans appeal directly to German troops by means of leaflets, posters, or newspapers, and then they achieved nothing worthy of note. Instead, the guerrillas aimed at creating impossible conditions for the enemy in the rear by engendering fear, uncertainty, and even panic among the soldiers and civilian administrators. The belief that partisans could strike suddenly, without warning, against a single sentry or a whole motor convoy hundreds of miles behind the front line was bound to promote a state of nervousness and insecurity among the occupation troops and officials.

Attacks on German units were rare, but not so on individual sentries and collaborators. The guerrillas were told:

'Hunting a German is similar to hunting partridges. One creeps up to a partridge whilst it is singing, and one sits in hiding when it looks round. The same method applies to a German sentry. Armed with a hatchet one creeps up to him in the dark. If he is walking to and fro or looking around, stand still. If he stands deep

> in thought, one slinks near to him step by step. When you are close enough to grasp him, you suddenly give him a blow on his skull with the hatchet with all your strength. Do it so swiftly that he has no time to cry out.'[29]

Terror and assassination were designed to lower the morale of the occupation forces and their collaborators as well as to deter Russian civilians from aiding the enemy. Thousands of collaborators, and even civilians who accepted the demands placed upon them by German authorities, were executed in the central and northern sectors; in some areas the killing of indigenous officials and the deterrence of would-be collaborators ensured the disruption and paralysis of the entire local administration. German officials were favourite targets, and, if captured, were often maltreated quite hideously. The greatest success was the assassination of Wilhelm Kube, General Commissar of Belorussiya, on 22 September 1943, by the placing of a mine in his bed by one of his 'intimate' serving girls. Of this event, Goebbels wrote: 'This shows what dangers leading National Socialists must face, especially in the occupied territories of the East. To remain alive in the present crisis one cannot be too careful.'[30]

The psychological effect of such partisan activity spread among all ranks of the German soldiery and officialdom; no one was immune. Senior officers were particularly worried, as they possessed the unsettling knowledge of the dire shortage of security troops available for service in the rear. The general atmosphere in large parts of occupied Russia was typified by the following rhyme:

Vorne Russen	Russians ahead
Hintern Russen	Russians behind
Und dazwischen	And in between
Wird geschüssen	Shooting

Fear among Germans behind the central and, to a lesser extent, the northern fronts was endemic, so that they would not walk alone even in the most strongly garrisoned towns; the feeling of isolation and imminent danger was always present, especially among the soldiers posted to outlying areas. As a result, the Germans often over-estimated the strength of the partisan movement, and over-reacted in their reprisals against innocent civilians, thereby providing the Russians with a further stimulus to oppose the invader. Moreover, partisan activity contributed to the feeling among both German and Russian alike that the Third Reich had lost the war, and that it was only a matter of time before Soviet rule was re-established.

Special attention was directed against the Axis troops who operated against the partisans, notably the Romanians, Italians, Hungarians, and Slovaks, together with a few French and Croatians. The Germans were largely written off as entrenched Nazis unsusceptible to persuasion, whereas the Axis troops were rightly considered to be of different calibre. Usually they were much inferior to their ally in leadership, training, and morale; they were often resentful of German domination; and, after 1942, they were fearful of the consequence of defeat. Against such a background, Soviet propaganda was bound to have some effect, although to what extent is difficult to assess. Upon capture by the guerrillas, Axis troops were usually well treated, and often asked to join the fight against their former masters, which some did. In their dealings with them, the partisans themselves followed the simple axiom: 'As soldiers, you must be ruthless avengers; as captors, you must teach the prisoners the truth.'[31] It did not take long before the Axis soldiers became aware that, should they be taken by the guerrillas in action, they would be accorded good treatment provided they co-operated with their captors, a factor which must have affected their steadfastness under fire. On one occasion, a secret arrangement was concluded between a Slovak unit and a partisan band under Sidor Kovpak, whereby they would not fight each other. On another, the Slovak garrison of Buinovichi surrendered without a fight to the Saburov band after prolonged negotiations.

The partisans were well aware of the important psychological impact their operations could have on the enemy. As early as July 1941, one Soviet command advised that 'sudden short raids from ambush on live targets . . . engender panic in his ranks, induce him to flight, and create confusion among his units and sub-divisions, whereby his further movement is held up and serious losses are inflicted on men and material'.[32] Another order, also made in 1941, permitted guerrillas to wear German dress so as 'to exploit rumours regarding the activity of partisans in German uniforms, to arouse mistrust among individual soldiers, and to undermine their morale'.[33] As expected by the Soviets, the Germans, in their turn, reacted harshly. It was inconceivable that, given the contemporary view about rule in the East, harassing German personnel would not be returned in kind by ruthless retaliation against the only Russians available – innocent civilians. Reprisals, which often amounted to the destruction of entire communities, had the effect of further alienating the population while doing nothing to eradicate the partisan movement; instead it only furthered its aims.

As well as reinforcing the reign of terror throughout the battle areas of the occupied East, Hitler also ordered certain changes of direction in the anti-partisan effort. On 18 August 1942, he issued his War Directive No. 46, entitled 'Instructions for Intensified Action against the Bands in the

East'.[34] It opened with the words: 'In recent months, banditry in the East has assumed intolerable proportions, and threatens to become a serious danger to supplies for the front and to the economic exploitation of the country.' It was a matter of urgency, the Führer continued, that the partisans should be substantially eliminated by the winter, and to achieve this, all economic, political and propaganda measures had to be concentrated, and the forces of the Armed Forces, the SS, and the Police coordinated against the threat. Hitler made the Reichsführer SS 'the central authority for the collection and evaluation of all information concerning action against bandits' and gave him the 'sole responsibility' for anti-partisan operations in the Reich Commissariats, the Wehrmacht commanders having to support the Higher SS and Police Leaders when required. In the operational areas, where the Army remained supreme, the Chief of the General Staff was made solely responsible for anti-partisan measures, the argument being that 'the fight against banditry is as much a matter of strategy as the fight against the enemy at the front. It will, therefore, be organised and carried out by the same staffs.' This meant that control of security was taken from the Quartermaster's Department and transferred to the Operations Branch of OKH and the operations staffs of armies and army groups, although military government still remained Wagner's responsibility. Additional forces were allocated to the partisan fight, mainly from reserve formations, and the number of indigenous militia units was increased. Matters were to be so much improved that 'There must be no German in the area threatened by bandits who is not engaged, actively or passively, in the fight against them'.

Hitler's directive, containing much verbal thunder, in fact amounted to very little. Nothing of substance had changed. Overall control of the fight against guerrillas was still denied to any one body, the SS having only the task of collecting all relevant information, and resources were still divided between the operational areas and the Reich Commissariats. Despite the good relations usually enjoyed between the military and the SS, there still remained a dire need for unification and standardisation of effort, resources, and techniques based on the experience gained during the past fifteen months. However, these were provided neither by the Führer's War Directive nor by the subsequent OKW Directive which followed in December 1942.[35]

On 23 October 1942, in pursuance of his newly found responsibilities, Himmler appointed the Higher SS and Police Leader for Central Russia, SS Obergruppenführer und General der Polizei Erich von dem Bach-Zelewski, to the post of *Bevollmächtigte für die Bandenbekampfung im Osten* (Plenipotentiary for the Combating of Partisans in the East). In December a special staff was established under his command, with the approval of OKW, designed primarily to liaise between OKW, OKH, and the SS. Von dem Bach-Zelewski had no authority to issue commands, control over SS troops remaining with the Reichsführer SS's Command Staff, which, from spring 1943 to the end of the war, was under Generalmajor der Waffen SS und Polizei Ernst Rode. He could only prepare reports for the Reichsführer SS and propose courses of action; command in the field still lay with the relevant SS and military authorities.

Von dem Bach-Zelewski, despite his half-Slav descent, was a man for whom Hitler had high regard. In December 1942, the Führer called him 'one of the cleverest persons', whom he used for 'the most difficult tasks'. Certainly, his National Socialist pedigree was good; after a commendable war record, he joined the Free Corps in 1919 and the Party and the SS in 1930; he was elected to the Reichstag in 1932 as National Socialist representative for Breslau, a position he was to hold until 1944. His SS career, too, was out of the ordinary; by 1934, at the age of thirty-five, he had gained the rank of SS Gruppenführer and the command of the SS *Oberabschnitt* (the largest SS administrative division) of East Prussia and Silesia. In 1941 he was promoted to the rank of SS Obergruppenführer und General der Polizei, commensurate with his new position as the Higher SS and Police Leader in charge of security in Central Russia. However, his duties, chief among which was the extermination of Jews, proved too much for him, and in the spring of 1942 he was admitted to an SS hospital suffering from a nervous breakdown and congestion of the liver. The Head SS doctor, Dr Grawitz, reported to Himmler that 'He is suffering particularly from hallucinations connected with the shooting of Jews, which he himself carried out, and with other grievous experiences in the East'.[36] Von dem Bach-Zelewski even asked the Reichsführer SS whether the extermination of Jews in the East could not be brought to an end, but received a sharp reply warning him to stop interfering. Hearing of Hitler's war directive, he suggested to Himmler that he should be appointed to oversee the conduct of anti-partisan warfare. The Reichsführer, although he did not give him the control he desired, nevertheless made him Plenipotentiary.

Von dem Bach-Zelweski had not to wait long before receiving further elevation; early in 1943, he was made *Chef der Bandenkampfverbände* (Chief of Anti-Partisan Formations). However, grand though his title might be, he still lacked any right of overall command, his responsibility being limited to training matters, the compilation of records and the publication of manuals. Only when he undertook the leadership of specific anti-partisan operations, as he did on one occasion in the autumn of 1943, did he possess any direct control over activities in the field. This was to remain the situation until the end of the war; division of responsibility and diversity of aim were to continue as the distinctive features of German anti-partisan operations.

Just as anti-partisan warfare was used to further Hitler's racial policies, so too was it seen as an economic measure to aid the Reich's war effort. On 26 October 1942, the Plenipotentiary for the Four Year Plan, Herman Göring, issued the following decree:

> 'Simultaneously with the intensified combating of guerrilla activity ordered by the Führer and the cleaning up of the area behind the lines, in particular that behind the Army Group Centre, I request that the following points be taken into consideration and the conclusions drawn therefrom be put into practice:
>
> 1. Simultaneously with the combating of the underground forces and the combing out of the areas contaminated by them, all available livestock must be driven off to safe areas. Similarly, food supplies are to be removed and brought into safety, so that they will no longer be available to the guerrillas.
> 2. All male and female labour suitable for any kind of employment must be forcibly recruited and allocated to the General-Plenipotentiary for Manpower, who will then employ them in safe areas behind the lines or in the Reich. Separate camps must be organised behind the lines for the children.'[37]

Later that year, on 30 December, Himmler introduced the practice whereby Higher SS and Police Leaders could transport partisan helpers and suspects to concentration camps in Germany for hard labour. OKH proposed a similar scheme, but suggested that the deportees should be sent to prison camps or training centres in their own areas instead; OKW, however, disagreed with this, saying that it 'does not take sufficient account of the severity required and leads to a comparison with the treatment meted out to the "peaceful population" called upon to work'.[38] On 14 March 1943, therefore, OKW ordered that partisan helpers and suspects who were not to be executed were to be handed over to a Higher SS and Police Leader for transport to concentration camps within the Reich.

Such measures only further increased resistance, although in their practice some Germans saw a solution to the guerrilla menace. What would be more effective, it was argued, than to depopulate completely the partisan-infested areas and so deprive the bands of their support? Moreover, civilian-free territory would make the hunting of the partisans much easier, while those removed could be employed fruitfully in German factories and fields. In a directive dated 10 July 1943 and sent to the Higher SS and Police Leaders in Russia, Himmler announced: 'The Führer has decided that the whole population has to be evacuated from the partisan-ridden territories of the northern Ukraine and the central Russian sector.'[39] All males fit for work and most of the females were to be handed over to the Reich Plenipotentiary for the Allocation of Manpower for use as required; their conditions would be those of prisoners-of-war. The evacuated areas would be administered by the SS, and as much agricultural use as possible made of them. This, the Reichsführer SS believed, was the supreme solution. It was however unreal. The size of the areas and numbers of people involved, the difficulty of the terrain, and the strength of the partisans themselves made such a policy impossible; its attempt, however, further alienated the population from the Germans.

The policy of ruthless oppression was not without its critics. Although it was powerless against Hitler's will, the Army High Command admitted in August 1942: 'Time after time the population [in this case, of the Ukraine] shows itself grateful for every instance when it is dealt with humanely on the basis of equality, and reacts strongly against contemptuous treatment.'[40] Terror was found to be counter-productive; the chief of staff to 2nd Army noted in May 1942: 'We can master the wide Russian expanse which we have conquered only with the Russians and Ukrainians who live in it, never against their will.'[41] Even some politicians came to disapprove of severe security measures. In early 1943, Rosenberg wrote to Himmler complaining of the indiscriminate burning of Ukrainian and Belorussiyan villages that was providing the enemy with excellent propaganda material. After an anti-partisan operation code-named 'Cottbus', which took place from 3 to 23 June 1943 in the area of Polotsk, Borisov, and Lepel under the command of the SS, and which included also Army and Luftwaffe units, the commander, SS Brigadeführer und Generalmajor der Polizei von Gottberg, reported 4,500 partisans and 5,000 suspects killed for the loss of fifty-nine Germans. As Wilhelm Kube pointed out in a report:

> 'The figures mentioned above indicate that again a heavy destruction of the population must be expected. If only 492 rifles are taken from 4,500 enemy dead, this discrepancy shows that among these enemy dead were numerous peasants from the country. The Battalion Dirlewanger especially has a reputation for destroying many human lives. Among the 5,000 people suspected of belonging to bands, there were numerous women and children. The political effect of this large-scale operation upon the peaceful populations is simply dreadful in view of the many shootings of

> women and children. In December, the town of Begomie was evacuated by the armed forces and the police. At that time, the population of Begomie was preponderantly on our side. In the course of the fighting, Begomie, which was built up as a strong point by the partisans, has been destroyed by German air attacks.'[42]

Lohse, bemoaning the fact that many of the killed would have been suitable for forced-labour in the Reich, wrote to Rosenberg enclosing Kube's report and stating:

> 'It should not be ignored in this connection that in view of the difficulties of making oneself understood, as generally in such clean-up operations, it is very hard to distinguish friend from foe. Nevertheless, it should be possible to avoid atrocities and to bury those who have been liquidated. To lock men, women, and children into barns and to set fire to these, does not appear to be a suitable method of combating bands, even if it is desired to exterminate the population. This method is not worthy of the German cause and hurts our reputation severely. I am asking that you take the necessary action.'[43]

The Reich Commissar's request, however, went unheeded.

A number of attempts were made to get official policy altered, but to little avail. General von Schenkendorff made numerous reports suggesting that more control over anti-partisan warfare be given to senior commanders, implying by this that the OKW order of 13 May 1941, which had been reinforced by the orders of 16 September 1941 and 16 December 1942, be revoked.[44] The Quartermaster-General, Wagner, attempted to have rigid lines of conduct imposed on the troops, but he, too, failed. If von dem Bach-Zelewski's claims in the witness box at Nuremberg after the war are to be believed, he also wanted to see introduced a series of regulations which would have placed emphasis on better treatment of the population and captured partisans. Indeed, he and von Schenkendorff worked out a directive on these lines which argued, among other things, that captured partisans and suspects were of more use to the Reich alive, as forced workers, than dead. However, the 'Regulations for the Conduct of Partisan Warfare', prepared by February 1943, were never published, and work was begun on another series, eventually to emerge in May 1944.

Unofficially, a number of military commanders pursued the dictates of their own conscience, reason, and experience, and acted against both the spirit and the letter of military policy. In evidence at Nuremberg, General Röttiger wrote of the danger that the methods of the SS units posed to the troops: 'they assumed such proportions as to threaten the security of the Army in its combat areas because of the infuriated civilian populace.'[45] For this reason, Field-Marshal von Kluge, commander of Army Group Centre from December 1941 to October 1943, had to order SD units out of the front-line areas. Hitler was contemptuous of what he considered to be his soldiers' temerity, and on one occasion accused OKH of wanting 'to turn professional soldiers into clergymen'.[46] In conversation with Mussolini in October 1942, Göring made reference to the reluctance of the soldiers in the field to commit themselves wholeheartedly to the policy of mass slaughter advocated by some of their leaders, both political and military. Describing the methods adopted in anti-guerrilla operations, the Reichsmarschall asserted: 'Whenever attacks occurred, the entire male population of the villages was lined up on one side and the women on the other. The women were told that all the men would be shot unless they [the women] pointed out which men did not belong to the village. In order to save their men, the women always pointed out the non-residents. Germany had found that, generally speaking, it was not easy to get soldiers to carry out such measures. Members of the Party discharged this task much more harshly. . . .'[47]

The soldiers' reluctance was clearly revealed in the treatment of partisans after capture. Instead of ordering the summary execution as officially required, some commanders ensured that the guerrillas were made prisoners-of-war. Others were concerned also to treat the civilian population with justice. In March 1943, for example, the commander of the rear of 9th Army laid down the following guidelines:

> 'It is absolutely imperative to realise that we need the Russians more than ever before, not only as helpers in the rebuilding of the country, but also as collaborators in the fight against the partisan menace. It is not the Russian people but Bolshevism which is our opponent. Just and fair treatment . . . must be basic conduct for every soldier. Animals and all property which belong to the people, who are without any doubt not partisans, are either to be left or to be returned. It is not the task of the troops to loot the country; the objective is to win the trust of the population and secure their basic standard of living.'[48]

General Röttiger recalled that, when he was chief of staff to 4th Army from May 1942 to June 1943, his commander, Generaloberst Gotthard Heinrici, 'instructed his troops many times not to wage war against the partisans more severely than was required at the time. . . . This struggle should only be pushed to the annihilation of the enemy after all attempts to bring about a surrender failed. Apart from humanitarian reasons, we necessarily had an interest in taking prisoners, since very many of them could well be used as members of native volunteer units against the partisans.' The 4th Army also made much use of propaganda, aimed at both the partisans and the population 'with the object of causing them by peaceful means to give up partisan activities . . . the women, too, were continually urged to get their men back from the forests or to keep them by other means from joining the partisans, and this propaganda had good results. In the spring of 1943, the area of 4th Army was as good as cleared of partisans'.[49]

The effects that enlightened security measures and administration may have had are well illustrated by the German occupation of the Caucasus. Despite the fact that partisan bands had been organised by the Soviets in the region a full year before it was seized, the invader suffered little from their activities. This was remarkable because, in the southern part of the area occupied by the Germans, the rapidly varying and often difficult terrain of the foothills and mountains of the Greater Caucasus range provided guerrillas with an excellent refuge. In a large area extending from the Black Sea to the Caspian, they could have comparative safety from the invaders, albeit often at the price of considerable hardship. Even in the northern foothills, with their thick forests and nearby mountains, they would have found effective cover as well as protection from the frosts, isolation, and hunger that were to be found in the higher ridges to the south. But, with all these advantages, the Soviet partisans in the North Caucasus achieved very little, and the Central Staff, forced to recognise the near certainty of defeat once the Germans had occupied the region for a short time, paid them little attention. There were several reasons for the failure: the absence of Red Army stragglers to reinforce the bands; the rapidity of the German advance which induced a certain paralysis amongst those wishing to resist; and the remoteness of the partisan areas from centres of population, and therefore of recruitment. But, above all, the failure was due to the policy adopted by the Germans. This, despite its inadequacies, was sufficient not only to keep the indigenous population from joining or aiding the guerrillas, but also to rouse them to take active measures against the representatives of Soviet authority. Thus, unlike their Belorussiyan counterparts, the Caucasian bands were to suffer as much from lack of men and the antipathy of the local population as from active German counter-measures.

The lesson to be learnt from German policy in the Caucasus was well summed up by Dr Otto Bräutigam. While criticising the failure to win popular support in the occupied areas of the East, he noted:

'How easy it would have been to win [the support of] the

> population was illustrated in the administration of the North Caucasus territory where Army Group A co-ordinated its measures with the Ministry for the Occupied Eastern Territories. The speedier implementation of the agrarian reform, the prohibition of measures of compulsion in the recruitment of labour, and a humane treatment of the population led to a simply enthusiastic co-operation of the peoples of the North Caucasus. This resulted in the utter absence of a partisan movement, even though it is precisely the Caucasus that might have provided the best [geographic] basis for it; in thousands volunteering for the police and the army; in higher quotas of economic procurement; and in a stronger refugee movement when the German troops withdrew. . . .'[50]

The policy adopted during the German occupation of the North Caucasus, which lasted from August 1942 to February 1943, differed considerably from that in the other regions of the Soviet Union. It represented, at least for a time, the triumph of the 'realist' approach towards the conquered Eastern peoples, and resulted in an almost complete absence of partisan activity. It was fortunate for both the inhabitants and the security forces that the Caucasus was not intended to become a German settlement; instead, it was to be used only as a springboard for German operations in the Near and Middle East and to supply the Reich with adequate oil and fuel. Moreover, the Caucasians themselves were not considered Slavs; in large part they were 'Aryans', and this, coupled with Hitler's policy of preserving friendly relations with Turkey, which possessed an interest in the Turkic-Moslem peoples such as the Azerbaijanis, and in the Caucasus as a whole, ensured that a relatively relaxed attitude would be taken towards the indigenous population. Furthermore, although it was intended that the Caucasus should have a civilian administration, the Reich Commissariat, under the pedant Arno Schickedanz, was never established; instead, because the region was occupied for only a short period, the Army authorities, influenced by some of the more astute diplomats and members of the *Ostministerium*, never relinquished control. This was possible only because Hitler's attitude, always crucial, was remarkably *laissez-faire* towards the Caucasus; although he recognised its vital importance as a source of oil, he nevertheless did not believe that annexation was necessary. With his approval, the propaganda aimed at the Caucasians was liberal to a point undreamt of in the other occupied regions; its theme was: 'Under the Germans, you shall live as you please.'[51] Rosenberg's views, for once, were similar to his Führer's, envisaging the creation of a federation of four states: North Caucasus, Georgia, Armenia, and Azerbaijan, with Germany as the protecting power.

The Army took immediate advantage of Hitler's unusually liberal attitude. General Wagner, armed with a number of reports stressing the value of co-operation with the indigenous population, urged the Führer to make a public declaration concerning German intentions in the Caucasus; in response, on 8 September, Hitler issued a directive which authorised the encouragement of puppet régimes among the various nationalities in the Caucasus, and placed the commander of Army Group A occupying the northern region, Field-Marshal Wilhelm List, in control of the area, subject to co-operation with Rosenberg and Göring (the latter in his capacity as Chief of the Four Year Plan – the economic development of the Reich). As his representative, Rosenberg appointed Bräutigam, a career diplomat with a good understanding of Soviet affairs and one who favoured an enlightened policy towards the Eastern peoples. Claus von Stauffenberg, at OKH, was delighted with the way matters had turned out, and managed to get the Russian-born General Köstring appointed Inspector of Caucasian collaborator troops, with the aim of one day establishing him as governor-general of the region, in place of Schikedanz. At the same time, Dr Otto Schiller, a specialist in Soviet agriculture, was appointed to reform the agricultural system in the Caucasus. These men were of a very different calibre from such as Koch, Lohse, and their minions.

Following Hitler's directive of 8 September, von Stauffenberg, Bräutigam, and Schmid von Attenstadt, chief of the Military Government Section in the Quartermaster-General's office, worked out a detailed policy for the Caucasus. Bräutigam was helped by the far-sighted instructions he had been given by his master, the Reichsminister:

> 'The Caucasus is a region of unique ethnic multiplicity. For this reason, if for no other, the representative [of the Reich] will be expected to evince an utmost measure of sensitivity, tact, and ability to adjust. The geopolitical role of the Caucasus as a bridge to the Near East points in the same direction. This suggests the style of administration which – unlike the Ukraine, the Central, and Northern sectors – combines greater discretion with careful observation [and] far-reaching responsible use of an indigenous population devoted to the Reich, under German supervision.'[52]

Between them, the three men decided that terms like 'freedom', 'independence', and 'co-operation' were to be used in German appeals to the Caucasians, and that no forced labour was to be recruited from the region. Thus, an enlightened approach towards the civilian population became, at last, official German policy in the East; the irony was that it applied only to one relatively small area which was to be occupied for just six months.

SS men in a wood during operations.

A Russian hut burning during Operation *Cottbus*.

An SS anti-partisan operation: attacking a barn, searching for hidden weapons, interrogating suspects, and lining-up those captured before shooting them.

Searching for partisans; a German soldier enters a barn.

Opposite: A guard-post at a river crossing in the Pripyat region.

Men of an SS *Einsatzgruppe*.

Above and opposite: The SS Cavalry Brigade Fegelein (later the 8th SS Cavalry Division 'Florian Geyer') in camp and on patrol. These men earnt a formidable reputation as brutal partisan hunters.

SS and Hungarian troops plan an anti-partisan operation, 1943.

Guerrillas, immediately after capture, being treated with circumspection by SS troops.

The German troops who invaded the Caucasus were given specific instructions as to how to deal with the inhabitants. They were ordered by List:

> '1. To treat the Caucasus population as friendly peoples, except when they show themselves to be anti-German.
> 2. To lay no obstacles in the path of the aspirations of Mountaineers striving to abolish the collective farm system.
> 3. To permit the reopening of places of worship of all denominations and the conduct of religious services, customs, and ceremonies.
> 4. To respect private property and to pay for requisitioned goods.
> 5. To win the confidence of the population by model conduct. . . .
> 6. To give reasons for all harsh military measures toward the population.
> 7. To respect especially the honour of the Caucasus women.'[53]

General von Roques, then commander of the rear area of Army Group A, declared that the 'unlimited co-operation of the population' was to be 'a major goal requiring special "psychological" treatment by all German agencies'.[54] The two army commanders, Generals Ewald von Kleist of 1st Panzer Army and Richard Ruoff of 17th Army, also adopted this attitude. Von Kleist asserted: 'The Commanding General [List] based himself on the Führer's order that the German Armed Forces shall make the population into their friend. . . . The best propaganda, inward and outward, is a satisfied and hopeful population who know that it faces a better future than under the rule of Tsars and Stalin. The people must know that we are trying to do our best even if we cannot give it everything it wishes . . . that we are of good will. . . .'[55]

Ruoff appealed to the population thus: 'We bring you the right to own property, freedom from the *kolkhoz* system, freedom of labour, freedom to develop natural culture, and freedom of religion. . . . Thousands of volunteers, sons of the peoples of the Caucasus, are fighting on our side for the honour and liberation of the entire Caucasus.'[56] He told his soldiers: 'An important means of preventing personal and material support of the partisans by the population lies in the proper treatment of the population. He who plunders, steals cattle, and threatens and thrashes the population is driving it into the hands of the bands.'[57]

Official directives apart, the Caucasians fared substantially better under German rule than did the other Eastern peoples. The actions of the SD were circumscribed to a greater extent than those of their counterparts further north had been. For example, in their liquidation of the Jews they were forced by Army Group A to stop their persecution of the Tats, or 'Mountain Jews' – a people who had for long been considered a fully indigenous element of the Caucasian population. In particular, the reopening by the Germans of the Orthodox churches, Moslem mosques, and Buddhist temples, and of local schools teaching indigenous language and traditions was welcomed by the population. The desired agricultural reform, of which the abolition of the collective farms was the first step, was too little and came too late, but its promise, which met popular aspirations still further, was earnestly meant and proved of some propaganda value. In terms of autonomous government, the Germans achieved much. Hitler had agreed to the 'furtherance of the national, cultural, and economic development of the Caucasian peoples'[58] and, as a result, Army Group A decided that, after the harvest of 1942, self-government would be established in each ethnic area. In the Karachai region, the Moslem 'Mountaineers' formed a National Committee and an autonomous region was set up. In the Kabardino-Balkar area, the Mountaineers instituted a regional committee, and south of Rostov the Cossacks formed an autonomous area. Such reforms, and the promise of more to come, met with considerable popular approval.

With these policies, the Germans won the general co-operation of the Caucasians. Even before the invaders had reached the region, popular revolts had broken out in the Mountaineer regions, particularly in the Moslem areas among the Chechens and Karachai; these were symbolic of the dissatisfaction felt with the Soviet régime, despite the fact that the inhabitants had been dealt with comparatively leniently since the Revolution. When the Germans arrived, only the Karbardins, Osetins, and Cherkess (Circassians) – who had been more assimilated by the Greater Russians and contained a large percentage of Christians – were not 'natural' collaborators; they were, however, passive in their reactions to the invader. On the other hand, the Balkans, Chechens, and, especially, the Karachai were ready supporters of the Germans. As a result, the Soviet partisans fared badly; of their complete destruction in Karachai, a German field-gendarmerie report noted: 'the co-operation of the [local] militia and the population must be particularly stressed.'[59] On 25 November, 1st Panzer Army reported that 'the population had little interest in engaging in partisan warfare against the German Armed Forces because a part of their old prerogatives had been restored'.[60] But even more than that, the Caucasians were willing to work actively against the guerrillas. Another report produced by 1st Panzer Army contained the following: 'In view of the largely positive attitude of the population of the Caucasus toward the German occupation authorities, the intelligence activities of Soviet agents meet with difficulties. The same is true of partisan activity. Thanks to the active assistance of the population, it proved possible to destroy small partisan groups while they were in process of organization or soon after, since without leadership they had no cohesion, and suffered from a lack of food.'[61]

Yet in spite of their successes, the Germans proved incapable of learning the obvious lesson: that brutality does not pay when waging anti-guerrilla warfare. Even in the Caucasus, looting, indiscriminate violence, economic exploitation, and racial persecution were not unknown. Towards the close of 1942, pro-German feeling began to ebb, and as the spectre of a return of Soviet forces became ever closer, collaboration decreased. It was only because the period of occupation was not long enough for disillusionment to develop into antipathy, as it had done elsewhere in the East, that hostile action did not result. Food shortages and a deterioration in the standard of living were noticeable from October onwards, at the time when the German advance to the south had lost its impetus. Moreover, delays in implementing agrarian reform, and the inevitable failure of a conquering power to fulfil the expectations of the conquered peoples, even when they were regarded more as allies than enemies, brought their own frustrations. Matters were not helped by Hitler's dismissal of List on 9 September and his assumption of command of Army Group A, which he directed from Vinnitsa – almost 1,000 miles from the troops in the field – until 22 November, when he handed it over to von Kleist. As defeat at the front appeared imminent, and as the population's coldness grew, German attitudes hardened. By December, suspects of partisan activity were being liquidated in hundreds, SD commandos were increasing their activity, and forced labour began. In January and February 1942, during its retreat, the Army gave up all its liberality and evacuated and liquidated, requisitioned and demolished with abandon. In the Kuban bridgehead, held by 17th Army, where the Germans retained a foothold on Caucasian soil until September 1943, repression was endemic. A policy of reprisals for guerrilla action was instituted, and the V Corps, in charge of anti-partisan warfare, established a régime of terror by decreeing 'Popular fear of harsh measures must be greater than the terror of the bands'. Such was the fear felt by the Germans for Soviet guerrillas that in August the army commander promised three weeks' leave to every soldier who apprehended a partisan or an agent. But despite all security measures, the Kuban guerrillas continued to make the exposed position of the bridgehead even more unpleasant for the invaders. In defeat also, the policy of repression was a failure.

Finally, with time, even Hitler became aware of the limitations of his policies, and sought to reverse at least some of them. As early as May 1942, he had been forced to revoke his order whereby every political official with the Red Army would be summarily executed upon capture, recognising that commissars should be spared 'in order to strengthen the inclination of the encircled Russian forces to desert and surrender'.[62] As with front-line troops so, ultimately, with guerrillas. In the late summer of 1942, the Führer authorised a propaganda campaign which promised that the lives of partisans would be spared if they defected to the Germans; special prisoner-of-war compounds were even built in the rear area of Army Group Centre for guerrilla defectors. These provisions were incorporated into the OKW instructions for fighting guerrillas, issued in November. However, they achieved very little; the damage had been done. In Operation 'Fire at Will', for example, undertaken in May and June of 1943 in the Bryansk area, only five partisans surrendered after more than half a million leaflets, promising good treatment to all those who defected to the Germans, had been scattered. It was, indeed, a poor response. At about that same time, OKW told Fritz Sauckel, the Plenipotentiary-General for the Allocation of Manpower, that all partisans captured after 5 July 1943 were not to be shot but instead taken prisoners-of-war and sent to work in the industries of the Reich. This was confirmed in an OKW order dated 18 August.

However, not until May 1944, only a few weeks before the Germans finally left Russian soil, was this policy embodied in strict instructions issued from the highest authority. On 6 May, OKW published a directive entitled 'The Fight Against the Partisan Bands', the result of careful consultation with officers from many departments within the Army, the SS, and the Luftwaffe. It was the first, and last, effort by the German Armed Forces to organise and standardise their anti-partisan warfare, and to deal with the subject in its own right, not as an adjunct to political, racial, or even economic policies. For practical reasons, brutality was abandoned in favour of a more civilised approach. In paragraph 70, it was stated: 'The interrogation of prisoners is one of the best sources of information. It is therefore wrong to shoot captured bandits at once.' In paragraph 163, it was laid down that captured guerrillas were to be treated as prisoners-of-war:

> 'All guerrillas captured in enemy uniform or civilian clothing or surrendering during combat are to be treated, on principle, as prisoners-of-war. The same applies to all persons encountered in the immediate fighting area who are to be considered as guerrilla accomplices, even when no acts of combat can be proved against them. Guerrillas in German uniform or in the uniform of an allied armed force are to be shot, after careful interrogation. . . . Deserters – even if they are dressed in German uniform – are, on principle, to be well treated. The guerrillas must hear of this.'[63]

Moreover, the previous orders issued by Hitler and OKW, which had given individual soldiers unlimited freedom to kill and destroy at will in the conduct of anti-guerrilla operations, were, by implication, revoked; the OKW directive stipulated: 'collective measures to be taken against the inhabitants of entire villages ... are to be ordered exclusively by the division commanders or the leaders of the SS troops and police.'[64] The attitude of the population was, at long last, regarded as crucial. Wisdom, derived from bitter experience, lay in the following direction:

> 'The attitude of the population is of great importance in the fight against bands. Bands cannot for any length of time continue in existence in the midst of a population which entertains good relations with us.... The administration has to see to it, by just treatment, planned and energetic government, and thorough and purposeful enlightenment, that the population is brought into the right relation to ourselves.
>
> 'The aim must be: The peasants themselves should defend their property against the band, in which task they can be supplied by us with weapons and technical help, if they have proved their reliability....'[65]

But wisdom came too late; the fight for the few remaining German-occupied territories in the East was as good as over.

Chapter 7

'Untermensch' with Iron Crosses

We shall never build a Russian army;
that is a phantom of the first order.
ADOLF HITLER June 1943

Had the war in the East been won in a matter of months, as the German planners anticipated, there would have been little need, for military purposes, to take account of the hopes and feelings of the Russian peoples; but, as soon as the outcome was brought into doubt, as it was for the senior military commanders during the autumn of 1941, the attitude of the multitudes of Russian civilians and prisoners-of-war in the occupied territories became a matter of prime importance. This was so for two reasons: first, it was necessary to ensure not only the pacification of the rear areas, but also the co-operation of the population in economic matters; and, second, it was possible to exploit the intense anti-Communist and pro-national feelings of large sections of the occupied regions in order to induce them to fight against their former Soviet masters, both at the front and in the rear. As General von Schenkendorff wrote in March 1942, with special reference to the growing guerrilla menace:

> 'The prerequisite of effective anti-partisan warfare is the willingness of the Russian population to be friends. If this is not achieved or maintained by the German troops, the partisans will have the population's support in recruitment and supplies. In spite of severe [German] economic measures . . . the majority of the population is loyal . . . [but] thus far we have done little to win its sympathy. *One must put goals before their eyes*, goals which they understand and for which it is worth fighting. These are (1) the establishment of a national Russia free from Bolshevism, closely dependent on Germany, under a *national government* "for peace and freedom". Its western borders will be determined by our settlement plans. Even a sham government should have a strong propaganda effect. . . . The Russian will not adjust to a

> Russia reduced to a German colony.... (2) an agrarian reform dissolving the collective farms.... (3) religious freedom....'[1]

This found considerable favour with Halder, Wagner, and von Kluge, and expressed forcefully sentiments which had been felt for some months. As early as August 1941, a military report from the East had noted that 'it was possible to organise with very minor concessions a population which can be very useful. If this is not done, there is the danger that the peasants... will fall prey to Communist propaganda and support the partisan movement.'[2]

By the autumn of 1942, the majority of senior officers in the German Army had come to reject the policies of unenlightened colonialism and brutality practised by their political counterparts. Colonel Henning von Tresckow, the operations officer of Army Group Centre, who, in 1944, was to die for his opposition to Hitler, wrote a summary of his experiences of, and recommendations for, the occupation of the East. It was dated 25 December 1942. He was unequivocal that the Germans had squandered an excellent opportunity to win the co-operation of the Russian peoples in the fight against the Soviets. As a consequence, opposition to German rule was rife. 'What are the causes of this deterioration?' he asked. His own reply provided four main reasons: '(a)... the economic situation of the people has worsened...; (b) unwise treatment by the troops, e.g. reckless terror, wild requisitioning, burning of villages, etc. drive the population into the arms of the partisans; (c) conscription of labour for service in Germany...; (d) partisan counter-terror, combined with persuasive [Soviet] propaganda... and therewith a withering of faith in the staying power of the German Armed Forces....' Underlying all these was 'the lack of a uniform political approach to the treatment of the Russian people.'[3] Von Tresckow, like so many other military men, saw that to ensure the collaboration of the people and, thereby, the extinction of the guerrillas, it was necessary to recognise the natural human needs of the Russians and, at the same time, to grant them a large measure of self-government. His memorandum appeared in December 1942; two months later Field-Marshal von Kleist, commander of Army Group A in the south, ensured that the population under his control would benefit from a more liberal policy by issuing a fifteen-point directive on the treatment of civilians in the operations area. A week later, Field-Marshal von Manstein, commander of Army Group South, produced a similar order, with as its basis the argument that 'The population of the occupied Eastern territories... is to be treated as an ally'. Reforms in administration social welfare, education, agriculture, and religious life were introduced. Henceforth, a Russian who collaborated in any way with the Germans was to be regarded not as an enemy but as a 'fellow fighter and fellow worker in the struggle against the world foe'.[4]

The military were almost alone in their advocacy of such policies, which they dubbed 'political warfare'. Their reasons varied from political idealism to military necessity. Foremost in the drive for an enlightened *Ostpolitik* were General Wagner, his administrators, and the military commandants, mainly prompted by the growth of the partisan menace to the proper supply of the front-line forces. The *Abwehr*, the OKW intelligence service under Admiral Wilhelm Canaris, the *Fremde Heere Ost* (Foreign Armies East) intelligence branch of the General Staff, under Generalmajor Reinhard Gehlen, together with Nikolas von Grote and Wilfried Strik-Strikfeldt and others of the special staff for Soviet affairs at the OKW Propaganda Department were particularly active in this field, as was Count Claus von Stauffenberg, Chief of the section in the OKH Organisation Branch concerned with the establishment of new army units. Such men were the breed of which resistors are made, and Wagner, Canaris, and Stauffenberg were to die as a result of the abortive coup against Hitler in June 1944.

By the spring of 1943, 'realist' policy had reached its peak. General Harteneck, chief of staff to 2nd Army, in a directive dated 11 May, summed up the reason that lay behind the new attitude of the soldiers: 'We can master the wide Russian expanse which we have conquered only with the Russians and Ukrainians who live in it, never against their will.'[5] The military situation in the East was by then such that few officers could ignore the danger signs; defeat at the front, dislocation in the rear, and personnel shortages in the Armed Forces were daily growing greater and did not augur well. It was clear for all to see that the Germans simply had insufficient manpower and material resources to defeat the Red Army as well as the partisans. This was a situation that had long existed. An OKH report, dated 30 March 1942, had revealed that of a total of 162 divisions facing the Red Army, only eight were strong enough to be used in an offensive; because of the high casualties suffered in the East, there were 359,000 fewer men available at the time of the opening of the 1942 summer campaign than there had been the previous year. A year later, after the disaster at Stalingrad, the situation had worsened considerably; by March 1943 the Army in the East was 470,000 men below establishment, and even if this shortage had been made good, it would still have left the generals with too few soldiers for their tasks. The Third Reich was bankrupt of reserves of manpower; the only answer lay in the recruitment of Russians to serve against their former Communist masters. Thus, a policy designed to satisfy the population in the occupied territories would not only help in their pacification, but would also provide badly needed men to fight both the Red Army and the partisan movement.

An example of the potential that lay within German grasp may be found in the history of the Kaminski brigade. At the end of 1941, the 2nd Panzer Army, under Generaloberst Rudolf Schmidt, was halted in its advance south of Moscow and forced to fall back on a line Zhizdra-Orel-Kursk. The rear area was soon infested with partisans who posed a constant threat to the army's two inadequately guarded supply lines – the railway Minsk-Orsha-Unetcha-Bryansk-Karachev-Orel, and the road Smolensk-Roslavl-Bryansk-Orel. Part of Schmidt's solution to this problem was ingenious. With the approval of both Army Group Centre and the *Ostministerium*, he instituted a virtually autonomous province, Lokot, in the Orel-Kursk region south of Bryansk. A Russian engineer called Voskoboinik was appointed governor and was authorised to act independently of the Germans, appoint his own officials, and organise the government and the economy of the area. He was to be responsible only to Schmidt. A small liaison staff was the only German presence. The fiercely anti-Communist inhabitants, divesting themselves of the hated collective farm system, thrived, and provided the Germans with the stipulated quantities of food at regular intervals.

In the early spring of 1942, Voskoboinik was killed in a partisan ambush, and was replaced by Bronislav Kaminski, a gifted, unscrupulous middle-aged man of Polish-Russian origin, who was also possibly Jewish. Under his leadership, the Autonomous Administrative District of Lokot flourished, both economically and militarily, and he gradually extended the area under his control to include 1,700,000 people defended from the partisans by a militia 10,000 men strong. Kaminski's force, known as a brigade, assumed the title of *Russkaia Osvoboditelnaia Narodnaia Armiia*, RONA (Russian National Liberation Army). Divided into five infantry regiments, RONA, unassisted by the Germans, equipped itself with a tank unit of twenty-four Soviet T34s, an artillery battalion, and numerous heavy weapons, machine-guns etc. Kaminski's men proved themselves quite capable of eliminating the Soviet guerrillas in their midst, and even launched counter-raids against enemy strongholds outside their region. In the spring of 1943, they took part in a major anti-partisan operation, code-named 'Robber Baron', mounted by the Army, significantly widening their area of control and further easing the burden on the German security forces. Kaminski also assisted in the forming of railway security units attached to the German Army in the Bryansk region.

But co-operation with the Germans was not entirely beneficial to RONA. Even though the Lokot region was free from the brutal activities of the SS, in late 1942 Kaminski was forced to warn the Germans that the mood of his people might change should the invaders not cease their anti-Slav policies elsewhere. What would have happened in the end must remain open to conjecture, for, before disillusion set in completely, the

Red Army had reoccupied the region and Kaminski's men, taking with them their families, a total of some 50,000 people, had moved westwards with the retreating Germans. For a short period, Kube's successor as the General Commissar of Belorussiya, von Gottberg (who was also HSSPF of Central Russia in place of von dem Bach-Zelewski) employed the unit in anti-partisan operations around Lepel. In May 1944, Himmler, impressed by the way RONA had acquitted itself, granted Kaminski the rank of SS Oberführer and incorporated his unit into the Waffen SS, giving it the title of 'People's Army Brigade' and then, in June, 'SS Assault Brigade RONA'. Its days as an anti-partisan unit over, it was employed against the Polish patriots in Warsaw in August, where its men earned a reputation for brutality. For some reason, which remains a mystery, the SS charged Kaminski with looting jewellery and executed him. His men, by now thoroughly disillusioned by the treatment they had received since leaving their homes, resisted the attempts to reform them into an SS division and were disbanded.

From the German point of view, sad though the end of RONA was, in its heyday it had been an unqualified success, and the Lokot region had supplied all that was required of it: food at regular intervals and freedom from guerrilla activity. The exploits of the Kaminski Brigade revealed how effective indigenous units could be in the fight against the partisans, for the native Russians possessed advantages that the Germans lacked – familiarity with the people, language, customs, and terrain of the country – and they also proved themselves hardy and skilful fighters in the dark forests and treacherous swamps that were the natural home of the guerrilla.

From the very beginning of the war in the East, before the 'realist' approach was put into practice, use had been made by the Army of those Russians willing to combat the Soviet régime. The Eastern recruits, all voluntary, were known as *Osttruppen* (Eastern troops), and by the end of the war their total number approached one million. They began with the unofficial recruiting of Red Army deserters who, glad to have the opportunity of avoiding the prison camps, served their German masters well. Before long, most Army units had their own helpers, known as *Hilfswillige*, or Hiwis, employed as ammunition carriers, batmen, cooks, drivers, and horse grooms. Although they were not listed in Army reports or statistics, and were without formal rights or duties, by June 1943 their numbers had grown to around 320,000, of whom only twenty to thirty per cent were engaged in combat. In some German units as many as twenty per cent of the personnel were Hiwis. With many proving themselves tough and reliable under fire and implacable in their hatred of the Soviet régime, the impression soon gained hold among front-line troops that, whenever the Hiwis were treated as equals, they were prepared to do anything for the Germans and their cause.

The most significant development in the history of the Eastern volunteers as guerrilla fighters came in November 1941 with the formation by Army Group Centre of six independent battalions of former Ukrainian and Belorussiyan Red Army soldiers to act as construction and pioneer troops. Soon, however, the demands of rear-area security ensured that the German-led Russians were armed and employed in anti-partisan operations, the forerunners of the 'independent' *Osttruppen* which, by the beginning of 1943, composed 176 battalions and 38 companies – some 150,000 men – usually formed into various separate national units. The size of unit, however, was rigorously controlled. Hitler and the two High Commands possessed an inordinate fear that large groupings of Eastern Volunteers would constitute a danger. As a result, the largest unit permitted was a single regiment; the rest, either independent battalions or companies, were separated from each other and scattered throughout the occupied territories. Moreover, initially at least, the Russian volunteers received inferior rations and billets compared with their German counterparts, and until the end of the war their leadership was firmly in German hands. At the same time *Hilfswachmannschaften*, or Hiwa (guard units) were created to combat Soviet guerrillas and to undertake intelligence missions. German mistrust, however, ensured that these were poorly equipped with captured material, and issued with only a limited number of rounds of ammunition, 90, to each man. Russians were restricted to the lowest ranks and units were kept small, no bigger than 200 men. By the middle of 1943 there were some 60,000 volunteers in such units.

Despite all prejudice and obstacles, the 'independent' *Osttruppen* were able to exert some influence on the course of the phantom war. In August 1942, Hitler acknowledged their usefulness in combating the increased guerrilla warfare in the German rear, and in his Directive No. 46 he provided for their maintenance and expansion. They were, however, only to be used against the partisans. The Führer then allowed OKH to provide the Eastern troops with better rations, pay, and rewards; discrimination, although it remained, became less. On 15 December 1942, an Inspectorate of Eastern Troops was instituted at the Army High Command under Generalleutnant Heinz Hellmich, whose supervisory role gave the *Osttruppen* some official standing. Although his performance was ineffective, causing him to be replaced by General der Kavallerie Ernst Köstring after a year, his championing of their worth was unequivocal. Hellmich stated in a secret memorandum dated 23 March 1943:

> 'Relation between space and the available forces necessarily led to self-help by the troops; thus were created the *Hilfswillige* and later on the *Osttruppen*. This improvisation, undesirable in itself, |was| brought about by lack of manpower.... To renounce... the units would only have been possible if at the right time sufficient German forces had been available.... Consequently, the population's readiness to help had to be exploited as far as possible in order to (a) fill the empty positions in German units, (b) pacify and secure the undefended areas (partisan combat, etc.), (c) reconnaissance and information activity before the front....'
>
> 'The use of indigenous units so far had had the following advantages. (1) The appearance at the front of indigenous units increases the incentive for the Russian soldier to "go over to his countrymen". (2) The German soldier receives an ally trained in battle who is well acquainted with the terrain and way of fighting of the enemy and speaks the latter's language. (3) The fact that their own husbands and sons are fighting on our side also obliges the civilian population to favour our cause. (4) The use of indigenous units saves German forces and German blood.'[6]

Thus, in attempting to secure the rear areas, the Germans were able to rely heavily on the Eastern volunteers, thereby allowing the movement of the better trained and equipped German fighting troops to the front line. In February 1943, the *Osttruppen* were collectively christened the *Russkaia Osvoboditelnaia Armiia*, *ROA* (Russian Liberation Army), a move designed to foster a sense of community, but which did not betoken their grouping into units any larger than battalion strength. Hellmich's command was renamed 'Inspectorate of Volunteer Formations'.

Of considerable value to the Germans were the V-men (*Vertrauensleute* – literally 'confidential people'), sometimes known as K-men; undercover agents recruited from among the most reliable of collaborators after an exhaustive examination. One German report noted: 'In the Ukraine, a general revival of Communist activity has taken place. The development of the formation of Communist cells is being carefully watched by the ... SD. Thanks to the immediate "placing" of V-men, the Security Police is thoroughly informed about the state of the organisation.'[7] The V-men were specially trained and sent into partisan-occupied areas to join with the brigades, where they would send back information to the Army as to the whereabouts of guerrilla bases, future operations, strengths of bands, names of local sympathisers, and the like. Strict security surrounded their use; their identity remained a closely guarded secret, and only the very few German officers concerned with their work were in contact with them. The screening processes adopted by the partisans made it extremely important that the V-men were provided with cast-iron backgrounds immune to detection. However, because of the highly dangerous nature of their work, the Germans were forced to induce them to operate with rewards of generous grants of land, the size and quality depending on the value of the information received. By the spring of 1943, by which time it was clear that Germany was going to lose the war in the East, recruiting of V-men became difficult, despite a significant increase in the range of rewards. Instead, the military authorities were forced to organise small bands of Russian-speaking German soldiers who, posing as civilians, infiltrated the partisan areas on intelligence missions. Their task was one of the most dangerous that any serving soldier could be called on to undertake, but they generally performed it with an efficiency and a bravery which earned the respect even of the guerrillas.

The Cossacks were particularly favoured by the Germans. Their soldierly qualities appealed to the Army, and their antecedents, which proved that they were not Slavs at all but descendants of the Ostrogoths and therefore Germanic, allowed the politicians to tolerate them. Directives continually stressed that the Cossacks of the Don and the Kuban were to be treated as friends. As early as 16 November 1941, OKH sanctioned the use of Cossack units, known as *Sotni* (literally 'hundreds'), attached to the security divisions. These were the first of many. In October 1942, an autonomous Cossack region was established in the Kuban under Ataman Domanov; it was successful, but, owing to the Red Army's reoccupation of the area in the early spring of 1943, short-lived. However, the mounted Cossacks, some of regimental strength, moved back with the German forces, often being employed in counter-guerrilla operations in which they delighted. Hitler was particularly pleased with them in this role, and on 15 April 1942 had specifically assigned them to this type of warfare, although they increasingly took part in operations at the front as well. By Easter 1943, some 12,000 Cossacks had been assembled and were moved to Mlawa in Poland, there to be formed into brigades and, later, into two divisions for service at the front under the overall charge of Generalmajor Helmuth von Pannwitz, an excellent horseman and admirer of the Cossacks. Their anti-partisan days, however, were over.

Other, non-Slavic, nationalities were also favoured by Hitler and the military authorities. On 15 November 1941, OKW allowed the recruitment of Turkmenians under German command, and, on 30 December, OKW ordered four 'legions' to be formed: Turkestan (of Turkmenians, Uzbeks, Kazakhs, Kirghizs, Karakalpaks and Tadziks), Caucasian-Mohammedan (of Azerbaijanis, Daghestans, Ingushes, Lezghins, and

Chechens), Georgian, and Armenian. In August 1943, a Turkestan Division was formed and sent to the Balkans. The SS also came to recruit Eastern volunteers; however these, along with the Army legions, took little or no part in anti-guerrilla operations inside the Soviet Union.

Of importance to the German counter-partisan struggle were the auxiliary police units known by a variety of names such as *Schutzmannschaften*, *Selbstschutz*, *Bürgerwehr*, *Ordnungsdienst*, *Miliz*, and *Ortsmiliz*. They came under the control of the SS, and consisted of ethnic Germans, former members of the Soviet militia, and collaborators in general. By October 1941, the SS Hauptamt realised that, with the increasing shortage of manpower, the German police units being sent into occupied areas would be insufficient to ensure the pacification of the Easterners; it was, therefore, decided that local inhabitants who were reliable and sympathetic to German rule would be recruited as auxiliary policemen. On 6 November, Himmler gave the order that all indigenous auxiliaries were to be formed into units known as *Schutzmannschaften* (Protection Squads) – abbreviated to Schuma. Btl. – and placed at the disposal of the Higher SS and Police Leaders and German Order Police commanders. Latvians, Lithuanians, Estonians, Belorussiyans, and Ukrainians, clad in German uniforms and armed with Russian small-arms, were recruited for periods of six months, to be retained if performance proved satisfactory. A poor record could easily lead to a bullet in the nape of the neck.

By the autumn of 1942, there were some 48,000 Russians in the auxiliary police, almost all of whom were concerned with the fight against partisans. The *Schuma* were divided into two major types: the *Wachtbataillonen* (Guard Battalions), which served as local security units, and the *Front Bataillonen* (Front Battalions), which were used actively to search and destroy the Soviet guerrillas. The militia, too, had a role to play. In the Ukraine, the Popular Self-Defence Corps (UNS) was created and reached a strength of 180,000 men; in Belorussiya, the Self-Defence Corps (BNS) and, later, the Security Corps (BKA) reached a total of six battalions. In 1944, the local guard units were used to create a series of armed villages (*Wehrdorfer*) in threatened areas, in communication with each other and with German forces by means of radio. These proved successful and, at least until German defeat seemed inevitable, the indigenous police and many of the militia served their masters well. On the German retreat, a number of units were integrated into the Waffen SS. Particularly successful in combating the partisans were the 3,000 men of the *Tartaren Selbstschutz Kompanien* (Tartar Self-Defence Companies) who were recruited at the beginning of 1942 by SD officers touring the prisoner-of-war camps. They received the same pay as their

German counterparts, and, whenever possible, were well equipped and armed.

Eastern volunteers, whether *Osttruppen* or auxiliary police, were of inestimable value to German counter-partisan activities, often amounting to more than half the units involved. During the war, around one million Russians passed through their ranks. Not only did they help solve the crucial problem of lack of manpower, but they also often added a qualitative advantage to the anti-guerrilla forces by providing an intimate knowledge of, and familiarity with, the people and terrain of the partisan areas. However, the potential that lay in a policy of treating the Eastern peoples as equals in the fight against the Soviet régime was never recognised by those in whose hands the destiny of the Reich lay. The soldiers might understand the realities of the situation, but their advice counted for naught in Hitler's Germany during the Second World War. Just as it was incomprehensible to the Führer that the Russians were to be anything other than the slaves of Greater Germany, so it was unthinkable that they should bear arms in the German cause. This principle he applied throughout occupied Europe. 'If we ever give any one of the conquered provinces', he declared 'the right to build up its own army or air force, our rule is over'.[8] Of the eastern territories, he was particularly specific. To assembled generals on 16 July 1941, he announced: 'It must always remain a cast-iron principle that none but Germans shall be allowed to bear arms. Even if it seems easier at first to enlist subject peoples to carry arms, it is wrong to do so. Some day they are bound to turn against us. Only the German people shall bear arms, not the Slavs, not the Czechs, not the Cossacks, and not the Ukrainians.'[9] In June 1943, he reaffirmed this principle, declaring: 'We shall never build a Russian army: that is a phantom of the first order.' To do so would be to forfeit Germany's war aims. Moreover, he declared: 'I do not need a Russian Army.'[10] In the autumn of 1941, when a proposal by Army Group Centre to form a Russian 'army of liberation' was forwarded to Field-Marshal von Brauchitsch, who considered the matter 'decisive' for the prosecution of the war, it appears that the Führer rejected it out of hand. The following January, he similarly dismissed Field-Marshal von Reichenau's attempts to urge him to permit the establishment of Ukrainian and Belorussiyan divisions. Hitler was supported by men like Bormann, Koch, Lohse, and, for much of the time, Himmler. Against such opposition, the proponents of a 'Russian liberation army', even under German control, stood little chance. The lesson that the Kaminski brigade represented was never learnt.

This attitude on the part of Germany's leaders, which was an inevitable result of their racial dogma, meant that the full potential that lay in the arming of the Easterners remained far from being realised. The opportunity of forming a fully fledged 'Russian liberation army', composed of units up to divisional strength, well armed, and under the leadership of a 'Russian de Gaulle', an idea proposed in late 1942 by the former Red Army General, Andrei Vlasov, was never taken. It was not until November 1944, after the last German soldier had left Soviet soil, that the embryo of such an organisation, the Committee for the Liberation of the Peoples of Russia (*Komitet Osvobozhdeniia Narodov Rossii*, KONR), was instituted, and it was the following February, only three months before the demise of the Third Reich, before even a battalion of the half-formed army of KONR saw action – in Silesia.

The recruitment of Eastern volunteers suffered greatly. Not until defeat at the front and the rise of the partisan movement in the rear forced Hitler to realise that he had under-estimated Soviet strength and over-estimated his own, did the Führer sanction any arming of collaborator units. Beginning as an expedient, it continued as such until the end of the war; never was the use of *Osttruppen* elevated to the status of a principle founded on a coherent, well-conceived plan. As the *Ostministerium* noted somewhat tartly in October 1942: 'Only in the last few weeks, under the pressure of danger from partisans, was the formation of native units allowed, and that only for combat with the bandits.'[11] Hitler continually interfered with the development of the *Osttruppen*: on 10 February 1942, he prohibited the creation of new units, the circumvention of which order led him to reiterate it in stronger form in June, adding that the *Osttruppen* were not to be employed in front-line combat, an instruction he repeated in August; in June 1943, he declared that there be no further expansion of native units; and in October 1943, on being informed by the SS that many *Osttruppen* were deserting to the enemy, he ordered that unreliable units be disbanded and the rest transferred to the West and South-East. The latter move would have had disastrous effects on German rear-area security, for the Führer was advocating the dispersal of battalions amounting to the equivalent of thirty divisions – some 427,000 men. The Army resisted, and a compromise was arrived at whereby only those units whose unreliability was proven would be disbanded; the others would be transferred to other theatres of war as soon as possible. In the event, only some 5,000 *Osttruppen* were disarmed and a number of units remained in the East until the end. However, many were transferred to the Balkans, western Europe, and Italy, where they either fought the resistance or garrisoned fortifications. Their only reason for existence – to fight against the Communists – gone, their morale, together with their effectiveness, dropped to a low level. Indeed, German commanders in the West believed that the drain on scarce resources caused by the *Osttruppen* under their command was greater than their value to the armies in the field.

The disillusion with the Eastern volunteers experienced by Hitler and the High Commands was forcibly expressed by Jodl in a speech given on 7 November 1943:

> 'The use of foreign peoples as soldiers must be regarded with the greatest scepticism. There was a time when something approaching a psychosis radiated from the Eastern front under the slogan, "Russia can be beaten only by Russians". In many heads there was the ghostly idea of a giant Vlasov army. We then established over 160 battalions. Experiences were good so long as we were victoriously advancing. They became bad when the situation changed and we were compelled to retreat. Today there are only about 100 Eastern battalions in existence, and almost none of them is in the East.'[12]

Just a month earlier, Halder's successor as Chief of the General Staff, Kurt Zeitzler, had noted: 'The *Osttruppen* are becoming more and more unreliable. . . . It is better to have no security units in the rear areas than to have unreliable elements who in a crisis desert to the partisans together with their weapons. Unreliable indigenous battalions must be dissolved in the shortest possible time. . . . Independently, the exchange of reliable formations for German security battalions will continue. . . .'[13]

But the Germans had only themselves to blame for the deterioration in the reliability of the Eastern volunteers. The Russian collaborators, whether military or police, were exposed to a high degree of psychological warfare and retaliation against their families by the Soviets. Because of German policy towards Russians in general, and collaborators in particular, the propaganda had considerable appeal, especially as the war proceeded and the defeat of the Third Reich appeared imminent. Collaborators usually fell into three groups: those who sought to escape suffering in prisoner-of-war camps; those who, initially convinced of German victory, wished to affiliate themselves to the winning side and thereby gain prestige and status; and those who, out of a deeply held hatred for the Soviet régime, fought for a better society. However, the German attitude towards the *Untermensch*, the limited prospects for advancement under German rule, and the continued refusal to acknowledge the autonomous and nationalist desires of many Russians, led to disillusion which, when coupled with the prospect of defeat, turned to fear and a belief that rule by the Soviets might be better than the abuses of the invaders. The Germans, while giving the Eastern volunteers the material necessities for life, failed to provide them with spiritual succour. As Hellmich noted in March 1943:

> 'The [German] troops were able to supply the *Osttruppen* with food, clothing, and arms, but they could not provide them with a lasting purpose. In the beginning, in order to ask their bloody sacrifice, there was hardly any need for a stronger incentive than to be on the side of the victor. The critical winter months of 1942–43 have shown that the anti-Bolshevik spirit of the Eastern troops suffices to keep these units together, but it has no longer any power for the recruiting of new ones. The thesis "We know whom we are fighting but we do not know what we are fighting for" is no longer sufficient. . . . A political purpose is necessary for carrying through the total war.'[14]

With the knowledge that Stalin had declared an amnesty for collaborators, and that partisan units were ready to accept them into their own ranks to fight their former masters, many *Osttruppen* and auxiliary policemen were persuaded by Soviet propaganda and common-sense to desert to the guerrillas. Whole units would sometimes go over to the Soviets, the rank and file being led, often with no advance knowledge, to the partisan strongholds by their leaders. This had the result of making the Germans even more suspicious and restrictive, which in turn caused more defections. The vicious circle once begun, it was possible to break it only by a complete reversal of National Socialist policy. This was not forthcoming. The Soviets were further helped by the fact that German mistrust would not allow collaborator units, apart from a handful of non-Slavic 'legions', to be greater than battalion strength; it was far easier to arrange for the defection of just a few hundred isolated men than of a whole regiment or division.

The Germans often misused the Eastern units which served them, even those which performed well. Two examples of such behaviour are to be found in the histories of the *Graukopf* and the *Druzhina* organisations. At the end of 1941, the *Abwehr* instituted a special unit of former Red Army men designed to undertake special operations behind enemy lines. The organisation, commanded by an emigré, Colonel Sakharov, was based at Osintorf, a large industrial area north-east of Orsha, and entitled Experimental Organisation (*Versuchsverband*) Osintorf (or Mitte). Because of the grey hair of its commander, it soon became known as the *Graukopf* (Grey-head) battalion. At the time of its formation it numbered between 350–400 men; in July 1942, when 3,000 strong, it was retitled the Russian National People's Army (*Russkaia Natsionalnaia Narodnaia Armia*, RNNA). Officered entirely by Russians, it wore a variant of Red Army uniform and was unusually well equipped with captured weapons. It fought many successful actions against partisans, and the Germans were very content with its performance. However, they failed to understand how to handle its personnel; friction developed between German officials and RNNA officers, some of whom were replaced as a result. In December 1942, while inspecting the unit, Field-Marshal von Kluge, commander of Army Group Centre, said that he was so much impressed with the way it had conducted itself that he intended to separate its battalions among German front-line units. The commander, who was then Vladimir Boiarsky, a former Red Army Guards officer, and his second in command, G.N. Zhilenkhov, previously a high official in the Communist Party, were dismayed that their dream of an army of liberation was to be shattered. So, too, were their men, who by then numbered some 10,000. But von Kluge would hear no remonstrance, and, as 300 of its members had defected to the partisans on hearing the news, the RNNA was dispersed not to front-line units as intended but to four security divisions in the rear. Thus came to an end one of the most effective anti-partisan units possessed by the Germans.

The history of *Druzhina* was similar. From March to June 1942, the SD undertook an operation, known as 'Zeppelin', aimed at the creation of Russian units to serve the German war effort. As in the case of the *Abwehr* with the *Graukopf* brigade, SS men visited prisoner-of-war camps to recruit large numbers of former Red Army men for special operations behind Soviet lines. However, because of the lack of aircraft in which to transport the men, and because of fears that the Russians would defect to the Soviets as soon as they were out of the German-held areas, the 'Zeppelin' men were not so used; instead, the majority were turned over to anti-partisan operations. The organisation was divided into *Druzhina* I and *Druzhina* II, the former being composed of those soldiers considered unsuitable for subversive activities, while the latter was retained for special operations. The name *Druzhina* was a romantic Russian term associated with an élite order of knights and bodyguards.

Druzhina I, a battalion strong, was under the command of a Kuban Cossack, V.V. Gil, who adopted the *nom de guerre* of Rodinov. It was transferred to Nevel, north-east of Polotsk, and thrown into the front line to help to contain a Red Army breakthrough. After this action, *Druzhina* I was included in the anti-partisan units available to the Higher SS and Police Leader for Central Russia. In the spring of 1943, it was assigned to the area of Gluboko, which it administered as an autonomous region similar to the Lokot province. Under Rodinov's leadership, the SS *Verband Druzhina*, as it was called, grew to a strength of over 2,000 well-armed men clad in SS uniform; they formed self-defence units among the local population, and generally established friendly relations with the inhabitants. In March 1943, *Druzhina* II was merged with Rodinov's men. However, despite their successes against the guerrillas, relations between *Druzhina* and the German authorities were less than cordial,

Rodinov and his men being resented because of their incursion into an area previously administered exclusively by the invader. During the night of 24–25 November 1942, sixty-three men deserted to the partisans at Kolitschenko, killing five Germans in the process. However, despite such signs of discontent, *Druzhina* continued to act decisively against the Soviet guerrillas, in the summer of 1943 taking part in 'Cottbus', one of the largest anti-partisan operations held in Belorussiya. Nevertheless, German suspicions and political ineptitude finally destroyed what had been, for them, a highly successful partnership. There was talk of incorporating *Druzhina* into Vlasov's Russian Army of Liberation, but Rodinov and his men would have none of that; to them, their autonomy was precious. They, after all, had taken to themselves the motto 'Fight for a New Russia'. Tensions with the Germans, especially with the SS, had, by that time, reached a high level; disillusion with the Third Reich and its policy toward the East had set in; contact was made with the partisans. On 18 August 1943, Rodinov and most of his men, taking with them all their arms, went over to the guerrillas, killing in the process ninety Germans and most of the officers and men who remained loyal to the invader. Under its new flag, *Druzhina*, renamed the 1st Anti-Fascist Brigade, proceeded to fight their former masters with considerable success, although some men redefected back to the Germans. Not until April 1944 did the Germans have their revenge, when, during Operation 'Spring Feast', Rodinov and most of his men were killed. The deaths, however, were a hollow victory for the Germans; poor recompense for their inability to maintain the loyalty of *Druzhina* and to realise the potential that lay in their grasp. It is a story which epitomises German failure.

Chapter 8

'Passive' Security – The Success

It is simply a waiting game.
SS OBERGRUPPENFÜHRER VON DEM BACH-ZELEWSKI
Chief of SS Anti-Partisan Units, January 1944

The military aims of the Soviet partisan movement were set out succinctly in the basic directive for guerrilla warfare issued by the Central Committee of the Communist Party, dated 18 July 1941. 'Its task is to create unbearable conditions for the German invaders, to disorganise their lines of communications, supply, and military units, to paralyse all their measures, to destroy the hoarders and collaborators . . . to spread the wide network of our Bolshevik organisation in order to carry out all measures against the Fascist occupiers.'[1] The guerrillas, it was understood, had no hope of defeating the Germans by their own efforts; instead, their activities were to be directed towards aiding the Red Army to gain victory at the front. This was to be achieved by the disruption of rail, road, and telegraphic communications; the dislocation of supplies and troop movements; the gathering of information that would be of use to the Red Army; the diversion of German effort from the front line to security tasks in the rear area; and the creation of an atmosphere of suspicion, fear, and uncertainty in the occupied regions, which would lower the morale, and therefore the effectiveness, of enemy forces.

With the exception of gathering information, these military tasks were largely interdependent. An attack on a road convoy, for example, would disrupt communications, destroy supplies and manpower, contribute to the need to withdraw troops from the front to increase security precautions, and, at the same time, heighten the fear and uncertainty in the enemy rear. Similarly, with the death of even a single German sentry, the Reich's war effort would suffer, and the Soviet forces gain by this weakening of their opponent. On some occasions, the partisans co-operated directly with the Red Army. Perhaps the most famous example took place during the Soviet offensive on the central front in the summer of 1944; on 20 June, Moscow ordered the partisans in the Vitebsk-

Bobruysk area to intensify their activities without regard for the consequences even to the civilian population. On the night of the 21st, just a few hours before the Red Army attacked, the guerrillas made more than 10,000 raids aimed at cutting the enemy's communications with the front. The operation was successful, and the progress of the offensive was helped by the enemy's inability to co-ordinate his defensive reactions. The mopping-up of the last centres of resistance was left to the partisans, who performed the task with relish; they took few prisoners. However, such actions were rare. A cardinal principle of guerrillas was to avoid open combat as far as possible, for the superior training of regular troops would usually prove too much for them. Moreover, operations usually took place either at night, or at dawn or dusk, when the partisans were able to take full advantage of the poor visibility. Surprise, speed, and the avoidance of trouble were basic rules of partisan warfare.

Of all the military tasks of the guerrillas, by far the most important was the dislocation of communications. To any army, the ability to send supplies and reinforcements to the fighters at the front, and to move units as and when the occasion demands, is vital to its continued operation in the field. As a partisan instruction to local inhabitants in the Bryansk area put it:

> 'The technically well-equipped German Army requires an uninterrupted and secure connection with the rear area to supply its troops with fuel, ammunition, food, and spare parts. Slight damage to a road suffices to create a traffic jam in a very short time. As a result large quantities of technical material could become an excellent target for our air force or artillery within a short time. . . . All this illustrates how important it is to cause destruction to the supply lines and routes of retreat. All highways and railways must be destroyed. . . .'[2]

Of all targets, the railways were at once both the most important and the most vulnerable. Important, because without the men and supplies that were transported over them to the front, the armies would very soon have been defeated by their own material exhaustion; and vulnerable because of the immense length of track, the innumerable bridges and installations, many of them in forested country, which had to be guarded. Security could never be total, but it was essential; the nature of communications in Russia, together with the woefully inadequate state of motorisation within the German Army, made dependence on the railways inescapable. Indeed, it was impossible for infantry divisions to operate effectively more than sixty miles away from the nearest railhead. The proposed zone of German operations, which was to end on the line Archangel-Astrakhan, was one million square miles; within this vast space, the total road-network was estimated to be only some 40,000 miles, and, of this, just one highway, 700 miles long, was made to European standards. Most of the other roads were unpaved and became rivers of mud during the spring thaw and autumn rains, while those few that had been given some form of hard surface were thinly-surfaced and narrow, and so totally unsuited for heavy military use. The dust of summer, which clogged engines, and the extreme cold of winter, which froze them, further limited mobility.

Before the war, the Chief of Army Administration and Supply had recognised that the train should take priority over the truck and had stated that 'As distance from the border increases, the railroads become increasingly more important for the purpose of supply. . . . The great distances, lack of highways, and the wide-meshed rail net increases the value of the few existing stretches.'[3] This truth became strikingly evident during the first months of 'Barbarossa'; by late July the high rate of mechanical breakdown caused by the appalling roads, together with loss through enemy action, had reduced motor transport units in the East to almost half-strength. By January 1942, the Russian railways had been converted to the European gauge, and, by the summer, trucks were used only to carry men and munitions from the stations to the battle lines; in the interior, all other transport concerned with the armies at the front, whether it was for supplies, soldiers on leave, reinforcements, or the movement of divisions, was undertaken almost exclusively by rail.

The Soviet guerrillas were aware of the signal importance of railways to the German forces, and that their disruption would be the most effective way of aiding the Red Army. They were helped by the inadequacy of the rail system available to the invaders. In 1941, the Soviet Union possessed only 67,000 miles of railway, most of which were located in European Russia. Of these, only one-quarter were double-tracked, and almost all were based on poor-quality beds, with primitive technical equipment. This, together with the contortions necessary to negotiate the numerous gullies, streams, and rivers that characterised the terrain from the southern edge of the Pripyat marshes to the Gulf of Finland, limited train speeds in most areas of western Russia to about twenty miles an hour. Thus, the partisans were offered the German invaders' life-line on a plate; the opportunities for dislocation could not have been greater.

Yet, in view of the immense difficulties with which they were faced, it was the Germans and not the partisans who emerged the victors in the battle for the railways. Not that it was a complete victory, for acts of sabotage were never eliminated, and dislocation of the system became an everyday fact of life for the invader. Nevertheless, German countermeasures succeeded in preventing the partisans from gaining their prime goal: the cutting of the strategic supply lines, a goal which would have ensured the destruction of the German armies in the East.

Attacks on the rail system in 1941 were few, and their results insignificant. By the autumn, German intelligence reports indicated that the partisans were more concerned with the construction of their winter quarters than with sabotage. During the battle for Moscow in November and December, the Germans recorded only four cases of rail sabotage in the crucial central sector; over the same period in the north, sabotage dropped from sixteen breakages of lines in November to one in December. In the first two months of 1942, the German authorities expressed more concern at the effect on communications of snow and floods than of guerrilla action. Compared with what was to come, sabotage of the railways was minimal.

In March 1942 came the first significant partisan attacks. In the central sector, five bridges were blown up, and over one-quarter of a mile of track was torn up. This was followed in April by thirty-nine sabotage attempts. Goebbels wrote in his diary for 29 April: 'The danger of the partisans in the occupied areas continues to exist in unmitigated intensity. They have caused us very great difficulties during the winter, and these by no means ceased with the beginning of spring. Partisans have blasted the railway tracks in the central front between Bryansk and Roslavl at five points – a further proof of their extremely discomforting activity.'[4] In May, attacks intensified, and by the end of the month there had been ninety-four attempts at dislocating the railway lines, most of them successful. For the first time, the War Diary of the Wehrmacht High Command contains a note of such action. The problem was made greater by the preparations for the summer offensive aimed at Stalingrad and the Caucasus; although this was to take place in the south, where partisan activity was almost non-existent, a not insignificant part of the personnel and supplies necessary for the attack had to pass through Belorussiya, where successful sabotage attacks against the railways had risen to 102 by June and were to reach 235 by September. In comparison, the figures for the decisive southern sector were negligible. Kruschev had urged the partisans to strike heavy blows against enemy communications and not to let any trains with soldiers, military equipment, and munitions pass to the front. Guerrilla reinforcements were even sent from the Bryansk forests into the Ukraine. Despite this, results remained extremely poor; during June and July, when the German armies were beginning their advances towards the Volga river and into the Caucasus, instances of rail sabotage had amounted to only eight and thirteen respectively. In August, after Kruschev's exhortation and with the beginning of the crucial battle for Stalingrad, there were fourteen instances of sabotage to the railways, rising to twenty-one in October when the fight for the city was reaching its crucial phase. In November, when the Red Army counter-attacked to surround the German 6th Army in Stalingrad, rail sabotage in the Ukraine reached its peak – twenty-two instances – but dropped to only nine the following month, when the Germans were making strenuous efforts to relieve the encircled defenders. Such activity in the decisive southern sector cannot be regarded as anything more than a minor irritant for the Germans.

The methods used by the partisans varied. To ambush or derail trains, obstructions were placed on the lines, preferably at points where the driver's vision was obscured by a bend or a natural obstacle; joints were loosened; and pressure- and vibration-detonated mines were placed under the tracks. Sometimes guerrillas simply fired on locomotives and trucks with small arms, anti-tank rifles, or bazookas. To destroy particularly valuable supply trains, such as those carrying petrol, partisans employed mines with fuses detonated by wires operated by remote control. Magnetic mines equipped with time-delay fuses were also used, being placed on trains in workshops or stations. Sometimes mines would simply be thrown in front of an oncoming train, thus making it impossible for guards to detect them beforehand. A directive contained in a partisan newspaper, *Krasnajo Sviesda*, enumerated a number of rules to be observed when operating against the railways:

> 'The Wehrmacht, relying on its technical equipment, requirès non-interrupted lines of communication with the rear area in order to supply the troops with fuel, ammunition, food, and spare parts. . . . For this reason, it is absolutely necessary to carry out demolitions along their supply routes and escape routes. In order to cause the steel girders of a bridge to collapse, the two longitudinal rails both on top and below must be broken by explosives. In the case of wooden bridges, the main job consists in undermining the supports and in burning, if possible, the other parts of the structure.
>
> 'The demolition of railway tracks is most fruitful at those points where maintenance work is particularly difficult, e.g. at bends, in cuttings, or on high embankments. The explosives must be arranged in such a way that the track will be pierced at three points. In order to cause the derailment of a train, it is advisable to loosen the joining pieces and to remove the rivets, as these measures – in contrast to blasting the track – cannot be noticed from the train. . . .'[5]

German reports contain detailed descriptions of partisan operations aimed at cutting railway communications. One, dated 23 July 1943, made by 707th Infantry Division, provides an analysis of small, covert actions in the Dyatkovo-Bryansk area:

> 'The [destruction] groups are employed for demolitions. Each group has for this purpose two to three demolition experts who were brought in by air. Mines and explosives are also brought in by air. For the blowing-up of railways old Russian ammunition boxes (zinc) are used. . . . These boxes are buried under the tracks. Through its pressure the moving train sets off the explosion. The partisans leave two to three scouts behind who report on the results of the demolition. Mines with electric ignition are also used. In such cases, several groups are lying in ambush to the left and right of the railway and open fire from machine guns after the demolition. Current observations have shown that the partisans generally plant mines during the late evening hours up to 2300 hrs.'[6]

To meet the partisan threat to their communications, the Germans stepped up their security measures. This was not easy, for manpower was stretched to the limit. In October of the previous year, the Germans had instituted a system for protecting railway lines, stations, and other facilities. Security battalions were assigned to areas especially threatened, and each was made responsible for 62 miles of track. Four soldiers were to guard one and a quarter miles, and the rest of the battalion was to constitute the reserve, available for counter-action or routine patrolling. At water-towers, signal-boxes, point-switches, stations, and the like, special garrisons were quartered. Only those Russians who were performing labour service were allowed near the lines, and then under armed guard. In the spring of 1942, however, these precautions were found to be quite inadequate against determined partisan attack, and it was realised that new security precautions would have to be introduced. At the beginning of May, therefore, a series of directives laid down new measures on how to prevent and counter guerrilla attacks on the railways.

In forested regions, the land on both sides of the tracks was cleared for distances ranging up to nine miles; anything, including buildings, which could conceal partisans was removed, and a no-man's-land created in which only guards and a few pass-carrying civilians were allowed. Along the lines in certain areas, strongpoints were constructed within sight or sound of each other, between which German units could ambush the partisans. Patrols were mounted regularly, and guards placed in villages close to the tracks. Watch-towers equipped with searchlights were erected at all railway facilities, and stations were turned into forts surrounded by barbed wire, mines, and high timber stockades designed for defence against rifle and bazooka fire. Special protection was afforded to water-towers, so essential for the operation of locomotives, and guard detachments with heavy weapons were posted at all major rail bridges. For emergencies, engineer units were located at various points, to be quickly dispatched to wherever sabotage had taken place. All German personnel were issued with weapons, and guard dogs were used in large numbers. A strict watch was kept on all Russian civilians working on the railways, amounting to some 110,000 in the central sector alone. Other Russians were recruited to serve as voice-alarm sentries; posted at intervals along the line, they were to warn the nearest German guard-post by shouting whenever they spotted partisans, and then take cover. Theirs was an unenviable position, for they and their families were subject to reprisals by the partisans if they did their job well, and to rigorous punishment by the Germans if they did not.

Measures were also taken to protect the trains themselves. Each supply train was provided with a guard detachment of some forty men, and at least one truck was equipped with an elevated machine-gun platform which provided good observation and fields of fire. During the day, trains usually moved in convoy, and at night speeds were reduced to ten miles an hour; on some lines traffic was discontinued altogether. Armoured trains would patrol certain tracks, but their numbers were few. Flatcars full of rocks, and in some special cases a whole train of empty trucks, would be placed in front of the locomotives to detonate any mines. Later, special crewless clearing devices were designed to detonate mines by subjecting the track to constant vibration.

The security of troop trains was also a problem, and when they traversed partisan-infested areas they had to be organised as combat units. A soldier sent on leave would have to carry his weapon until he reached a designated station, where he left it until his return journey. The transport commander of each truck was also made combat commander. In case of a surprise attack, or on a specific signal, the occupants of all coaches were instructed to jump out – those in even-numbered coaches to the left, and odd-numbered to the right – and repel the attack. A few assault detachments and a small reserve remained at the disposal of the transport commander in case of a special emergency. Typical of the problems with which troop movements had to cope took place in November 1942, when 6th Panzer Division was transported to the area south of Stalingrad after its rehabilitation in Brittany. The division was loaded on seventy-eight trains, each of approximately fifty coaches and trucks, and organised for combat. Numerous raids and surprise attacks occurred during the trip through the marshy forests, and only a few trains got through the Pripyat region without incident. Most of the attacks were directed against the trains hauling tanks and artillery, and fierce fighting broke out in each instance. The trains were greatly delayed, and many of them had to be rerouted, with the result that during the ten-day trip they were mixed up, arriving at their destination out of order and long overdue. A special problem was created by the fact that the trains loaded with artillery and tanks arrived last because twenty of them were attacked by partisans, some repeatedly. From the time the first train unloaded at Kotelnikovo, the division was under Russian artillery fire and the railway station was attacked by dismounted cavalry. To secure and enlarge the detraining area required more fighting, because, the German front not being continuous in this area after the encirclement of Stalingrad, the division had to detrain where the enemy was assembling his forces. It was only because of enemy hesitation that the newly arrived units, lacking the support of heavy weapons, did not get into serious trouble and that the division was not destroyed.

In retaliation against German measures, the partisans improved their methods of sabotage. Remote-control mines were used more frequently, as also were those with time-delay fuses, both of which made it possible to blow up the locomotives despite the protective cars placed in front of them. In order to escape the mine detectors, which located the presence of metal, nearly all mines were made in wooden containers and their construction was primitive; some of them consisted of no more than a small package of explosives with a safety fuse. In October 1942, the Germans noted the first use of chain demolitions, whereby charges were placed along the tracks at short intervals and detonated simultaneously, either by pressure, vibration, or remote control. Damage to track could be considerable, and by the use of remote-control it was possible to blow up a whole train with one push of a button. Whereas damage caused by single mines could usually be repaired quickly, that caused by chain demolition took longer, with the added difficulty that there was not always sufficient spare track to replace the destroyed rails. Another tactical method devised by the guerrillas involved the use of civilians, willing or unwilling. If, for example, the partisans wished to destroy a bridge, they would send a long column of old men, women, and children towards it; the German guards, presuming them to be refugees, took no action. But behind the column crept the guerrillas, who opened fire when the leading civilians had reached the bridge, killed the sentries, and pinned down any further resistance until the charges had been placed on the target. The civilians had to look after themselves as best they could.

Bitterly fought though the 1942 campaign for the railways was, the Germans, learning fast, began to defeat the partisans. In the last seven months of the year, the rear communications in the central sector, though often seriously damaged, were seldom out of service, even temporarily. The number of attacks declined from a peak of 384 in October to 307 in December, and in the latter month the 147 which were successful were fewer than at any time since July. This was partly owing to the fact that the onset of winter had reduced partisan activity, but mainly to the improvement in German security methods. In June, successful sabotage acts against the railways had been almost twice as many as those prevented by the Germans (102 and 56 respectively); in December, however, more were prevented than were successful (160 compared with 147). By the end of the year, the network of strongpoints in the central sector was complete, and ski-equipped patrols were being employed by the Germans along all the major supply routes. A large proportion of mines were found before the trains reached them, and a number of partisan attacks were frustrated merely by the close proximity of German personnel.

In accordance with previous developments, 1943 began with much activity. In January, there were 397 attacks in all three sectors, of which half were successfully repulsed, resulting in the damage of 112 locomotives, one-third of them seriously, and 22 bridges, none beyond repair. February saw a similar amount of sabotage. The onset of spring was the signal for a further increase in activity; emerging from their winter quarters, the Soviet guerrillas were ordered to do all in their power to frustrate the forthcoming German offensive at Kursk, which was to take place at the junction of Army Groups Centre and South. At that time, the partisans were developing a new technique against the lines of communication: the direct assault by large groups. This took the form of an attack on the strongpoints guarding the lines of communication, which temporarily pinned down the enemy while demolition groups placed their explosives and then retired. The Germans first experienced such attacks in the late autumn of 1942, and they grew in frequency as the partisan movement became stronger. Probably the most spectacular operation of this kind was the attack that seriously disrupted the operation of the railway line running to the vital Orel salient, from which Army Group Centre was to launch one of the two thrusts into the area around Kursk. The break occurred about fifteen miles south-west of Bryansk, where a double-span railway bridge crossed the Desna river. The paramount importance of this bridge had been impressed upon the local commander who had, therefore, assigned a security platoon with anti-tank weapons to guard it. But one of the German relief units failed to take the proper precautions; its officers neglected to assign their men before nightfall to their individual defensive positions, and this omission was observed by guerrillas in the woods. At dawn, the partisans, under the command of an explosives expert from Moscow, made a feint assault from the west. Once they had succeeded in distracting the attention of the security unit, a group of 200 to 300 men attacked the bridge from the east; the guards were overrun; the bridge was blown up. The main line was thus blocked to all traffic.

All available railway engineer and maintenance forces were immediately put to work to deal with this emergency; they constructed crib piers of railway ties to a height of sixty feet. It took five days before this improvised structure was usable for single freight wagons, which had to be moved across by hand, and after a little more than a week, the bridge was capable of supporting entire trains, but without their locomotives. Each train had to be pushed onto the bridge from one side and pulled off from the other. During the same night in which the bridge was destroyed, other partisan forces disabled the relief line running from Krichev to Unecha by cutting it in ninety places over a total length of about sixty miles. This was the first occasion on which a major German line of communication had been broken for any significant length of time. As a result, security precautions at all other major bridges were immediately improved, and for the rest of the war no other partisan attack on such a vital installation was to be so successful.

During the spring and early summer of 1943, attacks on the railways in the central sector increased steadily, rising from 626 in April to 841 in June. In the latter month, partisans derailed 296 of the 1,822 trains going through the area. Such activity preceding the Kursk offensive inevitably made the systematic movement of men and supplies more difficult, and only by the extensive re-routing of trains could transport to the front be kept to an adequate level. But German efforts were prodigious. Despite all difficulties, the build-up of the attacking force went according to plan, and there was no postponement of the offensive because of supply difficulties. However, on 5 July, as soon as the offensive was launched, sabotage increased to such an extent that the movement of trains by night had to be stopped completely. By the 12th, the German attack had come to a halt – for reasons other than transport difficulties – and the Red Army counter-attacked. To aid their comrades in the front line, the partisans mounted a number of operations to prevent the enemy from moving up reinforcements to the threatened area. On the night of the 21st, for example, a total of 430 demolitions were set off simultaneously on the main railway running south of Bryansk, and the line was blocked for two days. By the end of July, no fewer than 1,114 attacks on the railways in the central sector had been reported by the Germans, an average of thirty-six a day. On the 25th, there were sixty separate rail demolitions. During the month, the Germans suffered damage to 358 locomotives and to 1,295 trucks out of the 2,282 trains sent through the sector, while the affected stretches of line were blocked for a total of 2,688 hours. But partisan action was to increase further. In August, while the Germans were being forced to retreat to the Dnepr, there began the two-month partisan campaign known as the 'Battle of the Rails'. The plan had been completed by the Central Staff in July, and envisaged the total disorganisation of rail

Soldiers of the Waffen SS and Army with partisan suspect during an operation, 1943.

Peasants supplying bread to guerrillas, Leningrad district, 1941 (*Novosti Press Agency*).

A guerrilla 'destruction battalion' on the move, Southern Front, 1941 (*Novosti Press Agency*).

Death by hanging for hostages.

Guerrillas about to be hanged.

A repair gang on the railways, guarded by an armoured train.

A demolition of a railway line.

Men of the Reich Labour Service searching a cave for partisans.

Russian Militia men with partisans they have just captured.

Above left: Luftwaffe soldiers on a 'partridge shoot'. *Below left:* Hunting partisans in the Crimea. *Above:* A Hungarian soldier participating in the guerrilla struggle.

Andrei Vlassov with one of his men.

Bronislav Kaminski.

communication in the German rear by making large numbers of lines, bridges, and stations unusable and by rendering quick repair impossible. The Central Staff required the destruction of 213,000 rails, mostly in the central sector, in the month of August alone; 167 bands were to be used, totalling more than 95,000 men, of whom 74,000 were in Belorussiya. On the night of 3 August, the operation began.

The campaign undoubtedly had great effect on German movements by rail. The monthly report of the chief of transport in Army Group Centre, covering the period from 1 to 31 August, contained the following information:

> 'Despite the employment of special alert units for the protection of the railway, partisan activity increased by twenty-five per cent during August 1943 and reached a record of 1,392 incidents as compared with 1,114 for July. The daily average amounted to forty-five demolitions. In 364 of them, rails were cut simultaneously in more than ten places. Individual demolition points amounted to 20,505, while 4,528 mines were removed. During the night from 2 to 3 August, the partisans began to put into effect a program of large-scale destruction. Numerous demolitions were carried out which caused a serious curtailment of all railway traffic and a considerable loss of railway material. Within two nights, the six to seven thousand miles of track in the area were cut in 8,422 places, while another 2,478 mines were detected and removed prior to exploding. Several lines could not be put back into operation for a considerable time.
>
> 'Another major handicap in the operation of the railways was the increasing number of sabotage acts, committed chiefly by native workers under partisan orders. These acts resulted chiefly in a severe shortage of locomotives. In many instances, the so-called Eastern volunteer units, employed to protect the railways, made common cause with the partisans and took German weapons along with them. In one case, for instance, an entire Russian security detachment of 600 men went over to the partisans. On 17 August, this force attacked the Krulevshchizna railway station. Using the machine-guns, mortars, and anti-tank guns which they had taken with them at the time of their desertion, the Russians caused considerable damage. German losses in that engagement amounted to 240 dead and 491 wounded. Altogether, partisan activities from 1 to 31 August 1943 resulted in damage to 266 locomotives and 1,373 coaches and trucks; about 160 miles of track were rendered unserviceable.'[7]

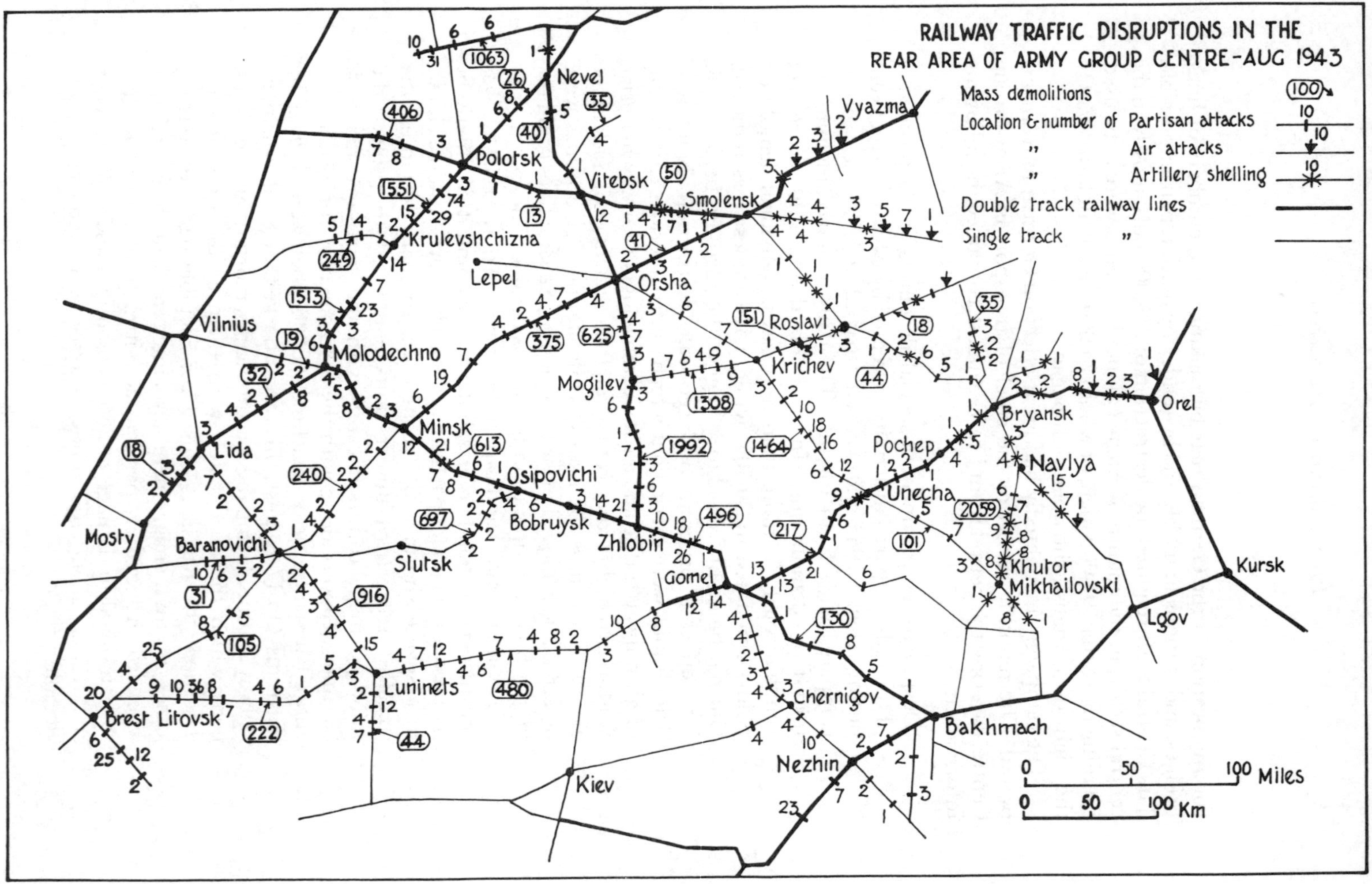
RAILWAY TRAFFIC DISRUPTIONS IN THE
REAR AREA OF ARMY GROUP CENTRE-AUG 1943
Mass demolitions
Location & number of Partisan attacks
" Air attacks
" Artillery shelling
Double track railway lines
Single track "
Nevel
Polotsk
Vitebsk
Smolensk
Vyazma
Krulevshchizna
Lepel
Orsha
Vilnius
Molodechno
Roslavl
Krichev
Mogilev
Lida
Minsk
Osipovichi
Bobruysk
Zhlobin
Mosty
Baranovichi
Slutsk
Gomel
Bryansk
Orel
Pochep
Unecha
Navlya
Khutor Mikhailovski
Kursk
Lgov
Luninets
Brest Litovsk
Chernigov
Bakhmach
Nezhin
Kiev
0 50 100 Miles
0 50 100 Km

During August, stations, supply depots, switches and water towers were struck to a greater extent than ever before. Extensive stocks of railway construction and maintenance material were destroyed. In view of the long sections of track blown up by chain demolitions, this loss made the job of the German repair crews even more difficult. In order to get rails to mend a line, one set of tracks in a double-tracked line often had to be torn up. The Soviets gauged the effectiveness of their operations by the number of rails demolished; for August they claimed a record number – 171,000 in occupied territory. The Germans, however, stated at the time that only some 30,000 lines were destroyed, and admitted to the damage of 266 locomotives and 1,378 trucks and coaches in the central sector alone, out of a total of 2,159 trains sent through the area. The second part of the 'Battle of the Rails' opened on 1 September, and continued until 1 November. Partisans in the Baltic States and the Crimea took part; the number of bands involved was 193, totalling 120,000 men. The plan envisaged the destruction of no fewer than 272,000 rails; in the event, the Soviets claimed only 148,500 destroyed, and the Germans some 32,000. However, 281 locomotives out of the 1,552 trains which passed through the central sector were damaged in September, a higher proportion than in the previous month.

The 'Battle of the Rails' undoubtedly caused problems for the Germans in their withdrawal to the Dnepr, but not even the Soviets claimed that the campaign had any great impact on the situation at the front. A third similar operation, although planned, was cancelled, probably because the immense effort involved was not worth the outcome. The vast majority of guerrilla attacks had taken place in the centre, but it was to the south, in the Ukraine, that the most important fighting at the front was taking place. There, throughout the month of August, the number of rails destroyed amounted to only seventeen per cent of the total for all occupied Russia. Indeed, throughout the latter half of 1943, sabotage attacks in the southern sector were abysmally low, averaging twenty-one a month, reaching their lowest, ten, in July during the Kursk battles, and their highest, thirty-six, in September. According to the Germans, none of these involved chain demolitions. In the north, too, the number of rail dislocations was extremely low, the partisans there being poor at sabotage. On their part, the Germans had exhibited considerable energy and resourcefulness in repairing track and re-routing trains, thereby managing to keep open their lines of supply and evacuation in all parts of the East. Their armies at the front suffered from other, far greater, disabilities than those inflicted on them by the partisans.

In the last three months of 1943, the number of partisan attacks on the railways fell considerably, reaching a low of 795 in December. Two factors were mainly responsible: a large reduction in the area occupied by the Germans, and a shortage of mines and explosives – the latter caused by the bad weather that prevented the Soviet Air Force from flying in sufficient supplies. Nevertheless, the efficiency of the partisans had dramatically increased, as is revealed by the fact that, although the numbers of rolling stock damaged decreased considerably, the numbers of locomotives damaged actually rose to 326 in October, 353 in November, and 323 in December. Moreover, the extent of the damage became greater; during December there were no fewer than 493 rail breaks which took twelve hours to repair, and forty-six which took twenty-four hours. This was no doubt the result of the use of a new type of mine with an electrical clock mechanism which, buried deep under the tracks, could be set to explode minutes, hours, or even weeks later. To counter this new threat, the Germans began using dogs trained to locate the buried mines; the partisans retaliated by spreading gunpowder along the tracks, thus causing the dogs to lose their scent.

In 1944, the German armies continued to retreat. Although the central front remained relatively stable until June, the northern and southern fronts moved back quite considerably. But there the partisans were of little use, being effective only when trains for the north or south had to pass through the central sector. In late January, the Red Army broke the siege of Leningrad, and the German forces stationed in the north began withdrawing to the west and south, into the Baltic States as well as into the central sector. Within the Baltic States, partisan activity during the first half of 1944 was confined almost exclusively to the eastern border regions. Here, attacks on railways averaged about fifty a month, but demolition techniques were poor and chain demolitions seldom used. As a result, damage was slight and German security patrols removed most of the mines. In the Ukraine, the only partisan activity reported by the Germans during the first months of 1944 was in the northern, forested areas of the republic. Here, too, rail attacks were few in number and involved no chain demolitions. In March, the Russians began their spring offensive along the entire Ukrainian front and, by the middle of April, the Red Army had penetrated into Romania, with little help from the guerrillas.

In the central sector, however, the partisans continued to ravage the German rail system. Attacks increased from 841 in January to 1,052 in May, although the number of locomotives damaged was fewer than in the previous year. During the first two months, the Germans reported many instances of guerrillas using anti-tank rifles to explode locomotive boilers. If the last train of a convoy could be stopped or derailed, partisans would then attack, plunder, and burn it. The Germans attempted to counter these actions by providing more and better-armed train guards, although the general shortage of personnel made this difficult. During

January and February, the partisans also tried to lay siege to Kovel, a major German rail centre and strongpoint on the southern flank of the central sector; units operating in the forests and swamps around Pinsk greatly hindered the movement of supplies and reinforcements into the city and slowed down, but did not prevent, its eventual evacuation by the Germans. In March, partisan activity in the central sector was mainly directed against the Brest-Litovsk-Baranovichi railway – the key to the whole sector – blocking the line for a total of 143 hours and limiting it to one-way traffic for 227 hours. During the following month, attacks on railways were mainly concentrated around Minsk. In May, the guerrillas shifted their operations westward, more than doubling their attacks in the area around Bialystock.

From March to May there was a reduction in rail demolitions, especially of the chain-type, in order to conserve explosives for the greatest partisan attack of the war. This took place during the night of 19–20 June and set the stage for the Soviet Belorussiyan offensive which was to begin on the 23rd, the third anniversary of the German invasion of Russia. During that night, the partisans brought all railway traffic in the central sector to a complete standstill, and demolition attacks continued during the next two nights. After the offensive, the Germans estimated that there had been at least 10,500 demolitions along the railways during the nights of 19, 20, and 21 June, and approximately 3,500 mines were discovered and removed. As an immediate result, all double-track lines were blocked for a period of twenty-four hours, while the operation of single-track lines was interrupted for more than forty-eight hours. Although there were no demolitions during the night preceding the attack, the damage already done was great enough to prevent the Germans from bringing in any reinforcements from other areas. The main effort had been directed against the supply lines that served the 3rd Panzer Army, the German unit that was to bear the brunt of the first heavy attack by the Red Army. Here, for the first time, the partisans had a direct effect on the outcome of a major battle, but it hardly seems likely that they altered either the strategic balance or the outcome. The forces facing the Germans were, at that stage of the war, simply too overwhelming.

Partisan activity against road communications was much more limited than against the railways. There were two reasons for this: first, the damage done to roads could nearly always be easily repaired, and secondly, from early 1942 it was the railways, not the roads, that carried the main burden of men and supplies to the front, motor traffic being restricted to army operational areas. Bridges were prime targets for sabotage, as they were the sole means by which a road could be cut for more than a few hours. Apart from mining, the main guerrilla tactic employed against the roads consisted of direct attacks on enemy vehicles and convoys. These generally followed the same pattern. A German convoy travelling through a forest would meet a log barrier placed at a blind spot on the road; on coming to a halt, or attempting to turn, they would be exposed to devastating fire from all sides. If any vehicle managed to escape, it would be caught and destroyed by another roadblock set up in the rear. Single snipers were also used, especially during the early days of the war, and, as the partisans became stronger, infantry-type assaults were made on convoys which had been brought to a halt; these usually ended with the destruction of the vehicles, the capture of their crews, and the seizure of their contents. Another method consisted of raids on villages situated on the main roads, as the prevention of the local population from undertaking road maintenance and repair work at the behest of the German authorities was considered important.

To counter guerrilla attacks, the Germans took a number of precautions. Machine-guns were mounted on the platforms of half-ton and one-ton trucks, and the relief driver was made to watch out for signs of ambush or roadblock. Later on in the war, truck cabs were reinforced with light armour-plate, and drivers were required to wear steel helmets at all times. Soldiers returning from leave would be employed as escort personnel for convoys. Strongpoints were established along major routes, especially at bridges, and trucks were forbidden to travel alone through many areas, being instead required to join escorted convoys of between ten and thirty vehicles according to the degree of danger. When in convoy, the trucks had to keep at a distance of 100 metres from each other. Regular patrolling of the roads was instituted; this proved most successful, with no fewer than two-thirds of all mines sown by the partisans being discovered.

Other partisan activity consisted of attacks on supply depots, the cutting of telephone lines, and the gathering of intelligence for the Red Army. German precautions included the fortification of supply dumps, the placing in telegraph poles of explosive charges designed to detonate when anyone attempted to cut them down, and strict supervision of all Russian civilians working on, or near, military installations. The latter task was of considerable importance; the famous partisan leader, Kovpak, recorded:

> 'Every guerrilla band had its agents who worked . . . in normal civilian occupations. Women and girls, employed as washerwomen and servants, had the mission to get in touch with German officers and NCOs in order to obtain information.

> Russian doctors and nurses, taken on by the Germans for work in German hospitals, interpreters, railwaymen, and voluntary members of the labour companies, members of the provost service, industrial workers and a host of others worked as part-time agents for the partisans. Even beggars were recruited for this job; they made the rounds at army installations. Children frequently acted as agents.'[8]

In addition, the partisans occasionally provided direct aid for the Red Army; this usually took the form of attacking German-held bridges, power-plants, and factories immediately before an offensive, and even, on occasions, of liberating towns and villages. Such action, however, was not particularly common, and took place mainly during the final year of the phantom war, by which time Soviet front-line strength was overwhelming. The partisans were usually strongly reinforced by regular units infiltrated through the German lines especially for the purpose. Other help consisted of preparing roads and communications on the Red Army's line of advance and, in one instance at least, in building twenty-five special under-water bridges across the Dnepr, Desna, and Pripyat rivers to aid the general offensive in the autumn of 1943. During the winter counter-offensive of 1941–42, partisans helped Red Army units to hold salients at Kirov and Vitebsk, and during the German attack at Zhitomir in November 1943 they acted as a shield for the withdrawal of Soviet forces by covering their right flank from the forests and swamps of the southern Pripyat region. The following year, the activities of guerrillas, reinforced by troops who had been infiltrated through German lines, reached such proportions west of the Narva river that the left wing of III SS Panzer Corps had to be withdrawn to form a shorter, more easily protected line. However, the guerrilla bands were neither trained nor equipped for open confrontation with the enemy; they usually suffered heavily in such actions, and, as a consequence, engaged in them only rarely.

The non-military activities of the partisans were primarily the dissemination of propaganda, the re-establishment of Soviet agencies in partisan-controlled territory, and the disruption of the economy in the German-occupied regions. This last was regarded as extremely important, for it was designed to stop the enemy from fully exploiting the rich potential that lay in the East. Food was a prime target; by mid-1942 partisans had succeeded in preventing the collection of food quotas by the Germans in most areas of the northern and central sectors. However, this mattered little, for the nature of the ground was such that it could have produced only a very small percentage of German requirements. In the Ukraine, where good farmland was far more plentiful, the enemy was free of such interference until the end of the occupation, the exception being in the northern Ukraine, which came under the control of the roving bands and where, by mid-1943, the partisans controlled sixty per cent of cultivated land. In other spheres of economic activity, especially in the valuable coal, iron, and manganese areas of the Ukraine, disruption was limited to the occasional sabotage attempt and, in the central sector, to attacks on shipments by road or rail. Only in lumber production did the guerrillas succeed in preventing any significant German exploitation. They controlled some eighty per cent of the forest area of Belorussiya and the northern Ukraine and in 1943, for example, they reduced logging operations by about thirty-five per cent and sawing by forty-two per cent. This, in turn, had some effect on coal production, for the mines of Donbass could not be operated without a plentiful supply of pit props. However, further German occupation of the area was to last for such a short time that this problem was of only a minor nature.

In conclusion, it must be said that partisan efforts to cut German supply lines and disrupt the economy were a failure. While the Germans assert victory in the railway war, the Soviets are vague in their claims of success, and have never said that partisan activity resulted in the collapse of parts of the enemy front. Throughout the war in the East, rail and road traffic in the northern and southern sectors was near normal, and it was the latter which, from 1942, was the single most important region of military operations. In the central sector, there was no threat to communications until May 1942, and this did not become serious until February 1943, when chain demolitions were first used extensively. Even then, German energy and improvisation succeeded in overcoming many of the difficulties posed by the attacks. The strength of the Transport Command in the central sector alone was 51,000 men, and large numbers of Russian civilians were used to repair damage or serve as sentries. Most of the mines laid on the lines were discovered by German security patrols, and clever re-routing, together with an efficient and speedy maintenance and repair service, ensured that supply trains usually reached their destination with the minimum of delay. Certainly, the situation at the front was seldom affected by guerrilla activity, and on those few occasions, such as the Belorussiyan offensive in June 1944, when German operations were hampered by sabotage, the outcome of the battle was, in any case, never in doubt.

Chapter 9

'Active' Security – The Failure

With enough good troops, anything is possible.

GENERAL VON SCHENKENDORFF Commander, Rear Area, Army Group Centre, October, 1942

Ruthlessness and lack of resources were the greatest drawbacks under which the Germans had to labour in their conduct of the phantom war. Both, to a certain extent, were dependent on one another. The brutality practised by the invaders in the East required large security forces to deal with its consequence – guerrilla activity; on the other hand, the Germans believed that only harsh measures could compensate for their lack of men and material to pursue the partisans. As an OKW order put it:

> 'In view of the vast size of the occupied areas in the East, forces available for establishing security will be sufficient only if all resistance is punished, not by legal prosecution of the guilty, but by spreading such terror as is alone appropriate to eradicate every inclination to resist.
>
> 'The respective Commanders are to be held responsible for maintaining peace. The Commanders must find the means of keeping order within the regions where security is their responsibility, not by demanding more forces, but by applying suitable draconian measures.'[1]

That this was a vicious circle went unrecognised by the Führer and his advisers until too late. Once begun, only sufficient troops made available for security could break the pattern, and although Hitler and the military and SS authorities came to understand the necessity of assigning considerable forces to secure the rear area, they were never able to make them available.

Throughout the war, and increasingly towards the end, Germany experienced a severe shortage of men and material; in March 1943, for example, the German Field Army was 700,000 men below establishment, and its 240-odd divisions were far too few to carry out adequate offensive and defensive operations in all four corners of Europe, still less to provide full security in the many occupied areas. Apart from the Army, by mid-1943 the Waffen SS could provide only a further eleven divisions and the Luftwaffe twenty-two. Moreover the grand total of 273 field divisions was achieved only by decreasing the combat strengths of individual divisions, resulting in a wasteful inflation in the ratio of administrative to fighting soldiers, and a consequent deterioration in the quality of those formations. The future gave no hope of improvement, only of further degeneration. For example, by April 1944 Army Group Centre could deploy only one division of about 2,000 men to every sixteen miles of its 650-mile-long front. Against this background, it is not surprising that the German High Commands allocated only a relatively few divisions and assorted units to the security of the rear areas, and even these were of low quality. Failure to pacify the occupied territories by other means meant that force was the only solution, and of force the Germans had not enough.

The situation in the rear area of Army Group Centre under Generalleutnant von Schenkendorff was particularly bad. For the security of 90,000 square miles, much of it covered in thick forest and swamp, von Schenkendorff, at the beginning of 1942, had three security divisions based respectively on Gomel, Orsha, and Bobruysk; by the end of the year, which had seen a considerable growth in partisan activity, he had been given only one additional security division, based on Vitebsk. All these formations were low in strength, with, at most, only 9,000 soldiers each (only 36,000 men between them, but usually less), and often the more battle-worthy elements among them were used at the front against the Red Army. As a reserve, von Schenkendorff had at his disposal a further 20,000 men: a cavalry regiment, a cycle regiment, a tank battalion, a Cossack battalion, and the *Graukopf* Brigade, of four battalions of former Red Army men. To supplement these, he had to rely heavily on indigenous militia units, the SS and Police, the *Geheime Feldpolizei* (Secret Field Police), and troops belonging to the rear area services. The number of men of all types available for security duties in the centre was some 60,000 – just two men to three square miles. They were opposed by roughly the same number of partisans – men who had the resources of the Soviet Union behind them.

There was little improvement during 1942. For specific anti-partisan operations lasting over a period of days or weeks, it became necessary for the Germans to employ divisions, sometimes even corps, taken from the front line. In October, field-replacement divisions and reserve divisions moved into the occupied territories to take up security duties in accordance with Hitler's War Directive No. 46. These divisions were essentially training formations, ill-equipped, low in manpower (averaging between 4,000–5,000 men), and quite unsuited to offensive operations. However, they were to prove of use in passive security tasks, such as guarding railway lines, and they eased the burden on the security divisions. Of the five field-replacement divisions assigned to the East, two went to Army Group Centre, two to Army Group North, and one to Army Group South; the four reserve divisions were divided between the two Reich Commissariats. The addition of these troops meant that some 80,000 soldiers were available to the vital rear area of Army Group Centre, where, by the autumn of 1942, German casualties in the fight against partisans had reached between fifty and sixty men a day. This, however, was not to last, and in the late summer of 1943, two security divisions, together with battle-worthy elements of the field-replacement divisions, were sent to the front lines where Soviet pressure was daily becoming greater. At most, the German soldiers available in the East for military security duties, whether in the rear areas or in the Reich Commissariats, amounted to some 180,000, together with, at their peak, some 420,000 *Osttruppen* under military control. To these must be added three groups of men under the control of the Higher SS and Police Leaders, the *Einsatzgruppen*, the *Ordnungspolizei*, and a selection of independent units ranging from Waffen SS divisions, who might occasionally find themselves engaged in anti-guerrilla operations, to special units, such as the *Sonderkommando* Dirlewanger, used solely for fighting partisans. After the invasion had taken place, and the front stabilised, the *Einsatzgruppen* settled down and instituted a static territorial organisation. The commanders of *Einsatzgruppen* A and C (in the Reich Commissariats Ostland and Ukraine) became known as commanders of Security Police and SD (*Befehlshaber der Sipo und des SD* – BdS), and under their control came a number of local commanders (*Kommandeure der Sipo und der SD* – KdS). Their aims remained similar. By the end of 1942, these, together with the five regiments of *Ordnungspolizei*, the *Sonderkommando* Dirlewanger, and the indigenous militia, amounted to 15,000 Germans and 238,000 auxiliaries engaged in SS security duties.

The forces made available by the Reich's allies in the East – in Hungary, Romania, and Italy – were of limited use. Hungary provided five infantry divisions, of which only one, with 5,000 men, was considered by the Germans to be battle-worthy. This latter formation was given the task of rail security, while the others were so badly trained and equipped that they were assigned to only minor tasks. Romania gave two divisions for security purposes, but their value, too, was limited as they were to be assigned only to the near partisan-free south-western Ukraine, next to the Romanian-occupied Transniestria. The Italian units, which were badly beaten at the front along the Don River in early 1943, proved so feeble as fighters that the Germans decided to send them back to Italy rather than employ them in a security role. When other military elements not specifically assigned to security tasks in the occupied areas, such as supply troops, construction troops, and the Reich Labour Service, are taken into account, the total manpower of the security forces in the East at any one time can have been no more than 900,000, well over one half being Eastern volunteers, and all of whom were of vastly differing, but usually low, quality.

The German refusal to divert front-line units for permanent security duty in the rear, although rendering successful 'active' security measures impossible, did however ensure the substantial failure of the partisans' aim of diverting enemy formations away from fighting the Red Army. After the war, the Soviets claimed that their efforts had ensured that the equivalent of forty German divisions was employed to safeguard supplies and communications and to mount counter-operations, but this was somewhat of an exaggeration. At no time did the number of German troops and SS men on security duty even equal those stationed in Norway (372,000 in 1944); never did it exceed 250,000, and for most of the time there were far fewer, usually about 190,000. Of these men, some twenty-five per cent belonged to units stationed in the East in order to be available for guard duties while completing their military training; a further sixty per cent, including many in SS formations, were either too old or else physically below standard for front-line service. Thus, at most, only fifteen per cent of the Germans permanently garrisoned in the occupied areas were suitable for the front – some 37,000 men, or three divisions' worth. Moreover, the equipment with which they were provided was generally of a lower quality than that required in combat with the Red Army, most of it being either captured from the Russians and former enemy forces, or obsolescent German stock. Seldom were armoured vehicles or heavy artillery employed, except by front-line units allocated for specific operations. The satellite troops that took part in anti-partisan warfare were generally of such poor quality that their use in conventional combat would have been a liability, while the indigenous militia units and *Osttruppen*, however good, were prevented from being anything more than of limited value at the front because of Hitler's reluctance to use them. Moreover, those German army units that were temporarily taken from the front to engage in specific anti-partisan operations were never withdrawn at the expense of the fight against the Red Army and were always returned within a short space of time, usually having suffered very few casualties. Indeed, this was true of all units who participated in fighting the partisans; because the guerrillas avoided open conflict whenever possible, and because German training was generally superior to that of their opponents, those killed probably did not exceed 45,000, of which only half were German.

Shortages were not simply confined to troops. Airpower was, to the Germans, a highly effective method of waging the phantom war. Unlike the Soviets, however, they had not enough aeroplanes or pilots to guarantee command of the air over their armies at the front, still less to mount anti-guerrilla operations in the rear. But from the limited experience of the Germans in this field of activity, it was clear that if the identification and harassment of partisan bands and, above all, the interception of their air support, upon which they were so reliant, had been undertaken extensively and continuously, it would have had considerable effect on the course of the struggle. This was quite apart from the advantages which came from any ability to communicate with, and supply, their own troops during anti-partisan operations. The disruption of the guerrillas' air support was especially important, as the following German report, dated June 1942, indicates:

> 'According to the observations of the 221st Security Division, the partisans receive weapons and ammunition as well as officers and commissars by planes. Recent observations have led to the conclusion that newly organized bands are led by officers and commissars brought in by plane, rather than by those recruited from the local population. Because the forces available to the security division are very weak, the bands cannot be destroyed at this time. In order to decrease the strength and combat worthiness of the bands, or to prevent the formation of new ones, it is most important that the air traffic be interrupted.'[2]

However, this disruption was never achieved; a few Red Air Force aeroplanes were shot down, fake airfields and drop areas were occasionally set up, and guerrilla airfields were bombed, but with little success. There was no substantial reduction in the trained personnel, equipment, and supplies sent from the 'Great Land' to the partisan bands. Indeed, the willingness of the Soviet High Command to allocate so many aeroplanes to the guerrilla struggle was largely due to the extremely low losses inflicted on them by the Gemans.

Although, by the end of 1941, Army commanders were coming to realise that airpower would be valuable in the fight against the partisans, it was not until the spring of 1942 that the first systematic use of aeroplanes in anti-guerrilla operations took place. On 11 March, a special anti-partisan squadron of out-of-date reconnaissance, fighter, and light bomber aircraft was formed under the command of VIII Air Corps, and based at Bobruysk. The commander of the rear area of Army Group

Centre stated: 'Its assignment is anti-partisan warfare, when possible in co-operation with operations of the ground forces. Since the squadron is the only one available in the entire area of the army group, its employment can be considered only against especially important and promising targets.'[3] Operation Munich, the counter-guerrilla operation in the Yelnya-Dorogobuzh area which took place in March 1942, was the first large-scale action in which the Luftwaffe participated, and in practically all subsequent operations air support was forthcoming. The number of aeroplanes taking part was between three and fifteen, and each usually flew several missions. Reports on the results of bombing and strafing were almost uniformly favourable, as the following from the 221st Security Division, dated June 1943, indicates: 'During operations, the employment of armed reconnaissance planes offers special advantages. Enemy units which have been surrounded and are hiding in trackless swamps can be attacked with bombs and machine-guns. Enemy preparations inside a pocket for mass break-outs can be discovered [so that] reserves can be moved in time to the spot selected for the break-out. Enemy units which succeed in breaking out can be pursued and scattered, and heavy casualties [inflicted].'[4]

The partisans were extremely sensitive to air raids, which often caused them to move in panic when the best course of action would have been to remain where they were. More often than not material damage was slight, but because of the limited experience, training, and discipline of the guerrillas, many of whom had been 'conscripted' against their will, morale was badly shaken. The effect on the morale of German troops was quite the opposite; the psychological impact on second-rate soldiers of seeing their own aeroplanes destroying partisan strongpoints and cutting escape routes was particularly uplifting in the general atmosphere of a demoralising form of warfare in which they were continually outclassed in military equipment. On some occasions, however, the activity of the Luftwaffe could be a mixed blessing for the German soldiers; communications between air and ground proved very difficult, and it was not uncommon for aeroplanes to bomb villages already occupied by their own troops.

Reconnaissance was a particularly valuable use of air power. The security forces were usually based in small towns and, with outposts in villages and along the lines of communication, far from the centres of partisan activity. Information was, therefore, hard to obtain. Few were the informers prepared to co-operate with the Germans, and few also the spies, known as V-men, willing to infiltrate enemy areas. Periodic patrols might skirt the most dangerous partisan-infested areas, but otherwise information would come only from the interrogation of captured guerrillas, defectors, or from air reconnaissance. It was often stated that success in anti-partisan operations was owed in large measure to effective reconnaissance missions beforehand; these had to be skilfully undertaken, for a sudden increase in flights over a partisan area served as an excellent warning of forthcoming action. A report from 221st Security Division in the western part of the Bryansk forests, dated 21 June 1943, noted:

> 'Considering the large size of each security [division] area and the resulting incomplete coverage in guarding the area by strongpoints and informants, keeping the entire area under constant supervision (by ground troops) is impossible. Only through the continual employment of reconnaissance planes is it possible to carry out constant reconnaissance of the whole area and to obtain an accurate enemy situation report, especially for areas temporarily not accessible to the troops. . . . In addition there is the factor of speed; reconnaissance can be initiated in a few minutes and the findings reach the troop commanders with equal speed (ground-aeroplane radio communications, message drops). In partisan warfare especially, because the enemy situation changes constantly, such timely and speedy reconnaissance acquires great significance. Operations undertaken after time-consuming ground reconnaissance and reports by informants and other inhabitants frequently fail because the enemy situation has undergone basic changes in the meantime.'[5]

The division was fortunate in that it was allocated a reconnaissance flight of three Focke Wulf 189s (a twin-fuselage fighter-bomber/reconnaissance aeroplane), a facility granted to few other such formations. However, the Luftwaffe made every effort to provide air reconnaissance whenever it was vitally needed.

In addition to the reconnaissance of partisan-held areas, the Luftwaffe also undertook missions which were a cross between harassment raids and strategic bombing. Villages, camps, and installations were bombed and strafed without reference to any complementary operation on the ground, and an effort was made to spread destruction and confusion in the 'safe' guerrilla strongholds. In 1943 and 1944, such attacks increased in intensity, and were concentrated on those areas that the Germans had not entered for months, or even years. Training of bomber crews was often undertaken in this manner; it was not without danger, as the partisans were liable to respond by mass small-arms fire and even 20mm anti-aircraft guns. The guerrillas were aided in their endeavours by the fact that on such missions the Luftwaffe usually employed obsolete aeroplanes, which were relatively slow and vulnerable to the increasingly heavy fire that was encountered. However, the results of the raids were such that the

Germans found it worthwhile to continue them. As with tactical missions during anti-partisan ground operations, the material effect on the guerrillas was usually far less than the impact on their morale. The passage overhead of enemy aeroplanes laden with bombs served as a useful reminder to Soviet fighter and citizen alike in the 'Little Land' that German power was not dead, and was capable of inflicting heavy damage on them. The dropping of propaganda leaflets over the areas had a similar, though less destructive, effect. However, as the resources that the Luftwaffe was able to commit to the prosecution of the phantom war were limited, the actual result of their bombing and strafing had a nuisance value rather than a strategic effect, and it was never able to reach its full potential.

The effect that the shortage of troops and resources had on German security is well illustrated by the history of anti-partisan operations around Bryansk. The Bryansk area was the best known, and possibly the most important, of the partisan regions in the East. Two hundred miles south-west of Moscow, it occupied a crucial strategic position, on the border between Army Group Centre and South, in the rear of 2nd Panzer Army. Here, when they were most numerous, some 16,000 partisans operated in an area of 4,000 square miles. The town of Bryansk itself was the junction of three major railway lines and one highway, and was a vital staging-post on the main line of communications to the front around Orel, in an area which became important in mid-1943 during the Kursk offensive and the subsequent Soviet counter-attack. Because of its thickly wooded terrain, it was prime refuge for guerrillas, and its central position made it a perfect base for partisan bands from many parts of the occupied territories. There the guerrillas could find shelter from German anti-partisan operations mounted elsewhere; in the thick forests, they were able to regroup and prepare themselves for future operations, being well supplied by air from the 'Great Land'. The forest which stretched for about 50 miles south of Bryansk was also important as a staging-post for the roving bands that were sent into the Ukraine. The Germans, therefore, had cause to worry about the threat to their rear posed by the Bryansk partisans, a threat which they spent much time and energy in attempting to overcome.

From the beginning, the Germans were hampered by their lack of troops. At first, the Bryansk region was occupied by only one security division and two guard and police battalions, reinforced, from October to December 1941, by one regiment from the 56th Infantry Division, units which were responsible also for a far greater area besides. Even the following year, when a further security division was allocated to the region, the forces still proved insufficient and were still unable to devote

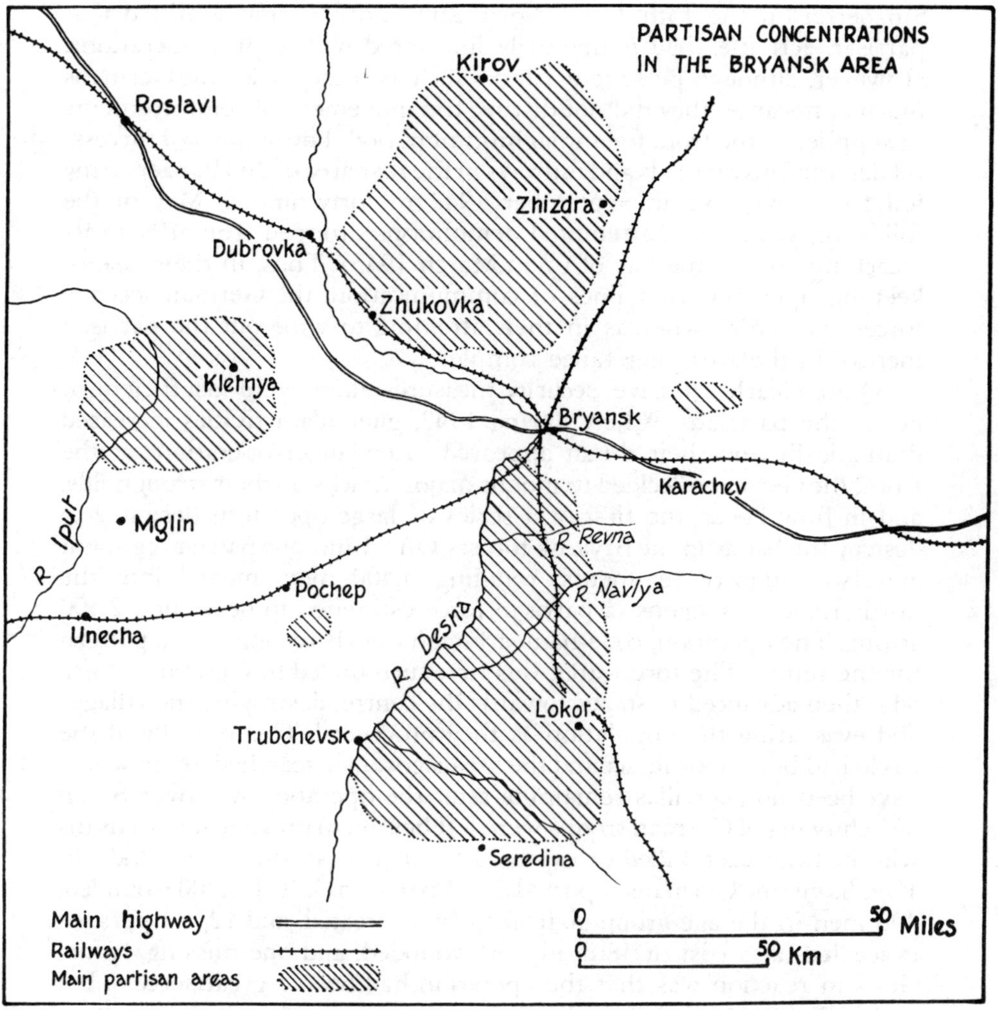

all their attention to the Bryansk guerrillas. Security, therefore, could only be 'passive', limited to safeguarding major supply routes and towns; strongpoints were established at regular intervals and small patrols organised to prevent partisans from operating effectively. By September 1942, guerrilla activity against German communications had become a major threat, with 199 demolition attacks mounted in that month alone; of these, sixty-five were successful. Perhaps the most spectacular success was in March 1943, when two important bridges were destroyed, the Desna bridge near Vygonichi on the 7th and the Revna bridge near

Sinzoertei on the 13th. On 1 April, 2nd Panzer Army admitted that partisan activities had temporarily interfered with supply operations. However, although persistent attacks such as these caused the Germans much annoyance, they did not disrupt the movement of reinforcements or supplies to the front for any significant period. The number of successful demolitions on roads and railways in the rear area of 2nd Panzer Army fell from sixty-five in September 1942 to forty-nine in May of the following year, while attempted demolitions dropped from 199 to 97 (reaching an all-time low of 67 in March 1943). Thus, in their task of keeping open the vital lines of communication, the German security forces succeeded; whereas in their attempts to wipe out the partisan menace in the area, they failed completely.

Quite clearly, 'passive' security measures alone were insufficient to defeat the partisans. When, during 1942, guerrilla activities increased dramatically and their threat appeared to endanger operations at the front, the Germans decided to mount major attacks on their strongholds, and in June began the first of a series of large operatons designed to destroy the bands in the Bryansk forests. On 5 June, one panzer regiment and two infantry regiments, totalling 5,500 men, moved into the northern forests against a partisan force estimated to be around 2,500 strong. The operation, code-named *Vogelsang* (Birdsong), set a pattern for the future. The forest area was first surrounded by German troops, who then advanced in stages towards the centre, destroying the villages and evacuating the population as they proceeded. Theoretically, if the circle had been kept intact and the area rigorously searched, there would have been no guerrillas remaining after the operation was over. Small detachments of German troops were left behind to prevent any partisans who had not been killed or captured from reorganising their bands. In *Vogelsang*, the Germans reported 1,193 partisans killed, 1,400 wounded, 498 men in the age-group sixteen to fifty arrested, and 12,531 persons evacuated, at a cost of 58 dead, 130 wounded, and one missing. Initial German reaction was that the operation had been a great success, but within a short period guerrilla activity was renewed.

In the Bryansk area, *Vogelsang* was followed by six other major anti-partisan operations. In the northern region a further operation proved necessary, for, by October 1942, the strength of the guerrillas there was estimated to be as high as 2,000, despite all German attempts to keep the forests free of their activities. By May of the following year, the number had risen to 3,000. Between 21 and 30 May, Operation *Freischutz* (Fire-at-Will) was launched, with two divisions and two regimental combat teams taking part, supported by two formations of light bombers and fighters. Although some 2,000 partisans were either killed or captured, the bands were not destroyed, and by mid-June the number of partisans in the northern forests was again estimated at 2,000.

In the western region of Bryansk, around Kletnya-Mamayerka, anti-partisan measures were also a failure. In October 1942, an operation conducted by a force of 1,600 men against an estimated 4,000 partisans was unsuccessful – only forty-three guerrillas were killed and two captured, the rest escaping from the encirclement. By the end of the month, the number of guerrillas had risen to 6,000. Another German attempt, *Klette* II, mounted between 15 January and 9 February 1943, was also a failure; only 745 men were lost by the partisans, most of whom had succeeded in either breaking out of, or eluding, the encirclement. By May, total partisan strength in the forest was believed to be around 8,000 men. In a final effort, Operation *Nachbarhilfe* (Good Neighbour) was mounted between 19 May and 19 June by two task-forces each the size of a division. The Germans were fairly satisfied with the results; the bands were indeed broken up, but only 864 partisans were killed or captured, although 16,900 'suspects' were evacuated. But again, the guerrillas soon returned.

In the southern area, two major anti-partisan operations were conducted: *Dreieck und Viereck* (Triangle and Quadrangle) between 16 and 30 September 1942, followed from 16 May to 6 June 1943 by *Zigeunerbaron* (Robber Baron), the largest operation in the Bryansk area. The first resulted in the death or capture of 2,244 partisans, but not the extinction of the guerrilla movement, for by December 1942 some 6,000 partisans were reported to be in the area. The second involved six German divisions, of which one was armoured, together with supporting aircraft that dropped no fewer than 840,000 surrender leaflets, killed 1,584 partisans, captured 1,568, took in 869 deserters, and evacuated 15,812 civilians; 207 camps were destroyed, and the booty taken included three tanks and twenty-one heavy guns. However, the number of estimated partisans in the area a short time after the end of the operation was still as high as 4,000–4,500.

In their seven major anti-partisan operations in the Bryansk area, the Germans had, according to their own estimates, killed or captured some 13,000 Soviet guerrillas (many of whom, no doubt, were in fact civilians); however, at any given time in 1943, until the region was reoccupied by the Red Army in July, there were between 12,000 and 16,000 partisans in the area. The cause of the German failure was both easy to analyse and impossible to rectify; it was, simply, lack of troops. Time and time again, the guerrillas and their commanders were able to break out of the lightly held encirclements. On completion of their operations, by which time few, if any, partisans remained in the area, the Germans were unable to occupy the forests in sufficient strength to prevent any recurrence of guerrilla activity. Once the operation was over, they withdrew, leaving the partisans to reassemble their bands in their old areas. As the rear area commander of 2nd Panzer Army noted after the conclusion of *Vogelsang*: 'The success did not measure up to expectations. The partisans continued their old tactics of evasion, withdrawing into the forests, or moving in larger groups in the areas south and south-west. . . .'[6] Rear area commanders complained continually about the lack of troops, which prevented them from engaging the partisans in continuous combat and thereby destroying them. As the 221st Security Division reported in 1943, without permanent occupation of 'pacified' areas and pursuit of escaped bands 'the partisans had the opportunity . . . of reoccupying their former areas and thus making the success of these operations illusory. . . . Any removal of troops or a temporary withdrawal of troops from pacified areas resulted in reoccupation by partisans.'[7] Equally annoying to the German commanders was the continuous movement of the units under their command, which prevented the troops from getting to know the terrain. Furthermore, front-line units were often allocated to anti-partisan operations only for a particular period of time, often too short to complete the operation satisfactorily. For this reason, the encirclement of Operation *Freischutz* had to be less comprehensive and proceed at a faster pace than was desirable, with the result that enemy breakthroughs were made possible. Finally, German reports made mention of the high average age, 35 years, of the security forces, and of their insufficient training and obsolescent equipment, both of which diminished the combat capabilities of the limited number of troops available.

Except for the Bryansk forests, the Polotsk Lowland was the most important area of partisan activity behind the German front line. There, too, the Germans were to prove quite unable to crush the movement, despite making numerous efforts, employing, at peak strength, some 50,000 men, of whom 27,000 were Russian collaborators, against 40,000 guerrillas.

The Polotsk Lowland, covering some 14,500 square miles, comprised about one-fifth of Belorussiya and contained one-seventh (1,100,000) of its total population. Strategically placed in the middle of the central sector of occupation, the region contained several major lines of communication, notably the Warsaw-Minsk-Smolensk-Moscow and the Leningrad-Kiev railways and highways. This, together with the fact that some thirty per cent of the area was covered with thick forest and swamp, ensured that the Lowland would become a major centre for partisan activity. By November 1942, the guerrillas were in full control of forty-five per cent of the region and exercised considerable influence over a further twenty-two per cent, though this was entered occasionally by German units. The invader was confined to only one-third of the

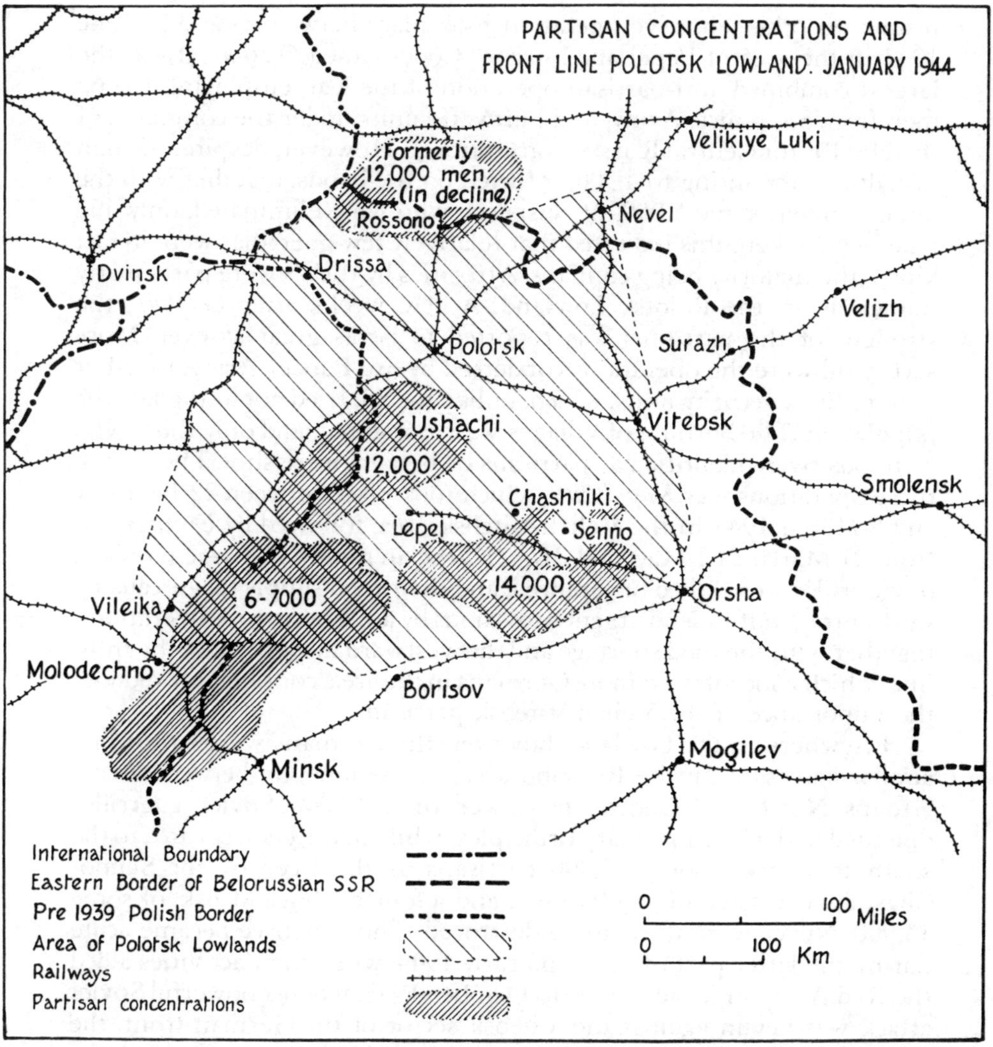

Lowland, including the cities of Vitebsk and Polotsk, and the territory close to the railways and major roads. The situation became increasingly serious when, in late 1942, Soviet advances brought the front line to within a short distance of the lowland guerrillas, who were thus able to threaten the rear of 3rd Panzer Army. Major operations to destroy the partisan strongholds began in the late autumn of 1942, when a combat formation, 12th Panzer Division, was sent to clear the area between Nevel and Polotsk. This unit, however, failed to achieve any significant results. Another abortive operation took place between 3 and 23 June 1943 in the area of Lepel and Borisov. Code-named *Cottbus*, it was the largest combined anti-partisan operation of the war, employing 16,662 men from SS, police, Army, and Luftwaffe units under the command of the HSSPF for Central Russia, von Gottberg. However, despite the high casualties, amounting to 4,500, inflicted on the bands, together with the large number, some 5,000, of 'suspects' who were eliminated, only 492 rifles were taken; this indicated that relatively few guerrillas were in fact killed, the majority being civilians. Atrocities by the SS were particularly numerous in the Polotsk Lowland. A few weeks after *Cottbus*, the strength of the partisans was reported to be as great as ever. More successful were the operations conducted by 3rd Panzer Army, together with military security units, which, unlike the SS, tried not to alienate the population. The burning of villages was prohibited, and only those who were positively identified as partisans or helpers were shot. The first of these operations was *Kugelblitz*, which took place between 22 February and 8 March 1943 in the Velizh-Vitebsk area, followed by *Donnerkeil*, from 21 March to 2 May, and *Maigewitter*, in mid-May. Large numbers of guerrillas were killed or captured, and their food supply taken, causing the Central Staff to send urgent provisions by air. These three operations, together with the food shortage and the westward movement of the front line, which concentrated more Germans in the area, considerably reduced the importance of the Velizh-Vitebsk partisans.

Elsewhere in the Lowland, however, the Germans were to gain no similar successes. In the Rossono area, at the junction between Army Groups North and Centre, no fewer than 12,000 Soviet guerrillas operated under strict military principles, while in the Ushachi area to the south there were some 15,000 partisans. A third centre, the Senno-Chasniki, consisted of 14,000 men, and a fourth, above Minsk, of some 15,000. Never were these to be destroyed. Their menace became acute during the latter part of 1943 and early 1944, when their activities aided the Red Army in its advances. In October 1943, when a powerful Soviet attack was begun against the Vitebsk sector of the German front, the Soviet Kalinin Front asked for close co-operation between combat units and the partisans. A report from 3rd Panzer Army, dated 18 October, notes the effect of this.

> 'The development at the front has demonstrated that the partisans and the Red Army demolition squads have been assigned the task of preparing the way for the Red Army. In the operational plans of the Red Army the two partisan areas, Senno-Lepel and Rossono, seem to serve two different objectives. In the Senno-Lepel region the partisans have recently begun to destroy all road communications. The Vitebsk-Lepel road has always

been the object of strong disruptive activities by the partisans. . . . Destruction of bridges through fire and demolitions has occurred in assembly line fashion. Recently, however, the partisans have no longer restricted themselves to this highway and the roads leading to our own strongpoints, but have extended their activities to all roads leading from the front to the rear which could at any time be used by German troops; these roads have been made impassable through digging ditches, plowing up [the road surface], demolitions, mining, and roadblocks. . . . The intention is clearly to prevent German troops from withdrawing further to the rear; this is confirmed by all reports concerned with this subject. The permanent nature of these destructions and their continuation even while the German forces are disengaging themselves and withdrawing indicate that the Red Army . . . is not planning to continue its advance into this region, but rather intends to use the area as a buffer against which the withdrawing German armies would be pressed.

The transportation network in the Rossono area presents a remarkable contrast to this situation. Here the bridges over the Drissa and in the interior are demolished; there are roadblocks, but evidence of total destruction . . . is completely lacking. No changes in the road situation have been observed for a long time. A reconstruction of roads would not meet with any great difficulty, since the civilian population and the partisans . . . could be utilised for this purpose at short notice. . . . Statements by deserters and intelligence agents indicate that the Red Army is planning to penetrate into the Rossono area, while similar opinions have not been advanced for the Senno-Lepel region.'[8]

Despite this, the Germans were able to hold the front at Vitebsk, and Soviet plans came to naught.

The danger that the guerrillas of the Polotsk Lowland had presented to their line of retreat caused the Germans to mount vigorous counteraction after the Red Army's offensive had spent itself. Two operations were planned for April against the partisans in the Ushachi area, followed by another in the Lepel-Borisov area, by which the Germans hoped to secure their lines of retreat and weaken the partisans to such an extent that attacks on roads and railways would fall off dramatically. To achieve this, they were prepared to expend a considerable amount of scarce supplies and to risk a Red Army attack while even scarcer combat units were undertaking security operations. In mid-April, 20,000 men, soldiers as well as SS men, attacked the Ushachi partisan stronghold in two operations, *Frühlingsfest* (Spring Festival) and *Regenschauer* (Rain Shower). After several weeks, guerrilla losses were estimated to be 7,000 dead and over 7,000 taken prisoner, resulting in the complete dispersal and almost total destruction of all the brigades in the area. The 3rd Panzer Army's escape routes lay open. However, the third operation against the partisan grouping between Borisov and Lepel, code-named *Kormoran* (Cormorant), was not begun until 22 May – too late; the guerrillas had just undertaken a major attack which succeeded in temporarily paralysing the railways. By the time *Kormoran* had finished, on 20 June, it was to be only a few days before the Red Army overran the Polotsk Lowland; the major German efforts required to eliminate the guerrillas had come too late.

The Yelnya-Dorogobuzh area, situated immediately to the south-west of Smolensk, was perhaps the only major success recorded by the Germans in their active anti-partisan operations. It was the first area where guerrilla forces, amounting to 10,000 men, were powerful enough to deny a large slice of territory, up to 3,000 square miles, to the enemy, and it was also the first, and last, instance in which the Germans crushed a movement of such a magnitude. They did so because there they fulfilled the two essentials of anti-partisan warfare: they employed enough troops both to destroy the bands and to occupy the pacified area in sufficient strength to prevent their return; and they adopted political measures to retain the loyalty of the population, or at least to prevent them from supporting the guerrillas.

The Yelnya-Dorogobuzh area, itself, was of minor interest to the invader. Lying well north of the rich black soil region, it had little agricultural value, being covered in large part by thick forest and swamp. However, it was of great strategic importance because the vital Smolensk-Moscow and Smolensk-Roslavl railways lay to the north and south respectively, while the Smolensk-Sukhinichi line dissected the area. Moreover, the very fact that here, directly behind the central front, large partisan forces had established an autonomous region, and had even equipped themselves with tanks, naturally alarmed the Germans. On 20 February 1942, von Schenkendorff noted in his war diary: '10th Panzer Division reports. . . . The division is carrying out reconnaissance in the direction of Dorogobuzh. Results: the area east of the Dnepr is infested with well-armed partisans under unified command. The roads are heavily mined. The whole male population is being recruited and is trained in special training areas. It would appear that the partisans are constantly reinforced by airborne troops.'[9] Minor operations against the guerrillas proved ineffective. On 13 March, von Schenkendorff reported:

> 'The area east of Smolensk and around Dorogobuzh is heavily infested [with partisans]. Dorogobuzh has been in enemy hands

> since 15 February 1942. The enemy is in control of the whole area up to the Dnepr and has already crossed the Dnepr several times with combat patrols. In the north he is moving against the arterial highway.
>
> On orders of the Commander in Chief of Army Group Centre, the Bicycle Squadron 213 was sent to Glinka ... to clear up there. It had to be withdrawn after a few days when the localities in the vicinity were occupied by partisans and encirclement was threatened.'[10]

Such difficulties were simply because sufficient troops had not been made available to counter the guerrilla threat. This was recognised by the commander of Korück 559, the rear of 4th Army, who reported on 25 February 1942:

> 'Formerly, when the army area was almost pacified, I had at my disposal one and two-thirds divisions aside from the two gendarmerie detachments which were available for employment. Now, when the danger is getting greater by the day, I have only three guard battalions, two gendarmerie detachments, and the service troops.... In spite of all preparations we suffer many disappointments because the enemy is stronger and has heavy weapons....
>
> The daily small-scale operations no longer lead to our goal. It is true that they inflict casualties on the enemy, but the enemy can always fill these gaps again. The employment of the rest of my troops – the butcher companies, parts of the prisoner-of-war guard companies, and the agricultural administration – resulted in the killing of more than 300 of the enemy last week and more than 500 the week before. These apparently relatively high casualties are nevertheless only a drop of water on a hot stone and hardly make themselves felt.'[11]

Decisive action was clearly required.

The first major anti-partisan operation in the Yelnya-Dorogobuzh area, code-named *München* (Munich), lasted from 19 March to the end of the month. Three divisions, of which two were panzer divisions and one a security division, were assigned to the attack, although in the event only the last was used. The operation was not a great success. The German garrison at Yelnya was relieved, but the town of Dorogobuzh remained in partisan hands and the guerrilla movement was far from defeated. However, a deep salient had been made into partisan territory, and this was to prove valuable in the next major anti-partisan operation, code-named *Hanover*. This, the largest of the war, was undertaken by two corps together with other units, amounting in all to nine divisions, of which three were panzer, a police regiment and the *Graukopf* Brigade, a total of some 40,000 men – well over twice the number of Soviet partisans in the area, some 15,000 in all. Air support, in the form of both bombing and reconnaissance missions, was generous. The operation ran very much according to plan. Starting on 24 May, a strong cordon was formed around the partisan area, which was then cleared in three advances moving from east to west; fighting ended in the last week of June. Immediately before, and during the period of the operation, some 10,500 guerrillas were killed or captured; the security forces suffered 2,200 casualties, of whom only 550 were killed.

But, however successful 'Hanover' had been, there remained the danger that, once the combat forces had been withdrawn to the front line, the 2,000 guerrillas that remained, hiding, in the area would be reinforced from outside and, aided by the civilians, continue their activity on the same scale as before. This was not to be. The Germans, having anticipated the need for constant watch and careful search, continued to leave forces in the area. Every effort was made to prevent the Soviets from reforming the movement by air: warning stations were established to look for enemy transport aeroplanes, and a special mobile reserve was formed to deal with air drops that local units were too small to handle. The Luftwaffe also took steps to intercept Red Air Force supply missions. Even more important was the attitude towards the Russians adopted by the Germans; it was in marked contrast with that in other regions. In the spring of 1942, the army units began to distinguish between partisan deserters and prisoners, promising humane treatment to the former in contrast with their previous practice of shooting them. Moreover, the first relaxation of the Commissar Order was carried out in the Yelnya-Dorogobuzh area; political officials were henceforth not automatically killed on capture or surrender. The result of these two measures was that desertions from the partisan bands were significantly more numerous than elsehere. During operations, German units were instructed not to indulge in indiscriminate reprisals but to confine themselves solely to destroying partisans. They were helped by the unusually well-defined military nature of the Yelnya-Dorogobuzh guerrillas, who could not be easily confused with the ordinary civilians. Furthermore, after the operations, the Germans realised the need for effective political pacification and continued to make a sharp distinction between partisans and their sympathisers on the one hand, and the rest of the population on the other. Collective punishment was avoided; propaganda was disseminated, intended to alienate the people from the partisans and their cause; and authority was placed in the indigenous auxiliary police. What the commitment of large forces over a long period of time – two corps for two months, followed by a strong military presence in the area – had achieved was confirmed and consolidated by a sensible attitude towards the population. But these dual prerequisites for success were seldom seen in German security policy.

Conclusion

It would be pleasant, for the writing of this book, to conclude by proving that German occupation policy in the East, far from pacifying the population, brought upon its practitioners the full fury of guerrilla warfare – warfare that severely dislocated their supply lines and led to considerable strategic consequences for the course of the war. This, however, would be only partially true. The Germans did, in fact, succeed, through a combination of energy and resourcefulness, in securing their lines of communication for the expenditure of relatively few combat-worthy soldiers; the outcome of the war in Russia was therefore affected very little by the activities of Soviet guerrillas.

Success in the elimination of the partisan menace was, however, to elude the Germans; indeed, by their measures, they actually ensured the continuance and development of the very movement that they were trying to destroy. Certainly the Soviets invested considerable resources in the partisan struggle, resources which might have been put to more use, militarily, at the front, but they were better able to do so than were the Germans, for whom acute scarcity of men and material was a major problem. At a time when the Third Reich, heavily outnumbered in men and material, was fighting for its existence – as it was clearly doing once its soldiers had set foot on Soviet soil – any diversion, however small, of scarce manpower and equipment, or of the attention of already hard-pressed military commands, was bound to be harmful. The irony, from the German point of view, was that the guerrilla war was so unnecessary. Its very existence proved the futility and brutality of German occupation policy, which squandered the valuable potential that lay in the East.

Appendix 1

OKW Directive for Special Areas, Case 'Barbarossa', 13 March 1941

1. **Area of operations and executive power**

1. The authorisation to issue orders and the regulations regarding supply for an area of operations within the Armed Forces shall be set up by the High Command of the Armed Forces in East Prussia and in the General Government at the latest four weeks before operations are started. The proposal by the High Command of the Army is being made in time, after an agreement with the Commander of the Luftwaffe has been reached.

   It is not contemplated to declare East Prussia and the General Government an area of operations. However, in accordance with the unpublished Führer orders from 19 and 21 October 1939, the Commander-in-Chief of the Army shall be authorised to take all measures necessary for the execution of his military aim and for the safeguarding of the troops. He may transfer his authority on to the commanders of the Army Groups and Armies. Orders of that kind have priority over all orders issued by civilian agencies.
2. The Russian territory which is to be occupied shall be divided up into individual states with governments of their own, according to special orders, as soon as military operations are concluded. From this the following is inferred:
   a. The area of operations, created through the advance of the Army beyond the frontiers of the Reich and the neighbouring countries is to be limited in depth as far as possible. The Commander-in-Chief of the Army has the right to exercise the executive power in this area, and may transfer his authority on to the commanders of the Army Groups and Armies.
   b. In the area of operations, the Reichsführer SS is, on behalf of the Führer, entrusted with special tasks for the preparation of the political administration, tasks which result from the struggle which has to be carried out between two opposing political systems. Within the realm of these tasks, the Reichsführer SS shall act independently and under his own responsibility. The executive power invested in the Commander-in-Chief of the Army and in agencies determined by him shall not be affected by this. It is the responsibility of the Reichsführer SS that through the execution of his tasks military operations shall not be disturbed. Details shall be arranged directly through the OKH with the Reichsführer SS.
   c. As soon as the area of operations has reached sufficient depth, it is to be limited in the rear. The newly occupied territory in the rear of the area of operations is to be given its own political administration. For the

present, it is to be divided, according to its genealogic basis and to the positions of the Army Groups, into North (Baltic countries), Centre (White Russia), and South (Ukraine). In these territories the political administration is taken care of by Reich Commissars who receive their orders from the Führer.

3. For the execution of all military tasks within the areas under the political administration in the rear of the area of operations, commanding officers who are responsible to the Commander-in-Chief of the Armed Forces shall be in command.

   The commanding officer is the supreme representative of the Armed Forces in the respective areas and the bearer of the military sovereign rights. He has the tasks of a Territorial Commander and the rights of a supreme Army commander or a commanding general. In this capacity he is responsible primarily for the following tasks:

   a. Close co-operation with the Reich Commissar in order to support him in his political task.
   b. Exploitation of the country and securing its economic values for use by German industry (see para. 4).
   c. Exploitation of the country for the supply of the troops according to the needs of the OKH.
   d. Military security of the whole area, mainly airports, routes of supply, and supply-dumps against revolt, sabotage, and enemy paratroops.
   e. Traffic regulations.
   f. Billeting for armed forces, police and organisations, and for PoWs in as much as they remain in the administrative areas.

   The commanding officer has the right, as opposed to the civilian agencies, to issue orders which are necessary for the execution of the military tasks. His orders supersede all others; also those of the Reich Commissars.

   Service directives, mobilisation orders, and directives on the distribution of the necessary forces shall be issued separately.

   The time for the assumption of command by the commanding officers will be ordered as soon as the military situation shall allow a change in the command without disrupting military operations. Until such time, the agencies set up by the OKH remain in office, operating according to the principles valid for the commanding officers.

4. The Führer has entrusted the uniform direction of the administration of economy in the area of operations and in the territories of political administration to the Reichs Marshal who has delegated the Chief of the 'Wi Rü Amt' with the execution of the task. Special orders on that will come from the OKW/Wi Rü Amt.
5. The majority of the Police Forces shall be under the jurisdiction of the Reich Commissars. Requests for the employment of police forces in the area of operations on the part of the OKH are to be made as early as possible to the OKW/Operational Staff/Section Defence.
6. The behaviour of the troops towards the population and the tasks of the military courts shall be separately regulated, and commanded.

2. **Personnel, Supply, and Communication Traffic:**

7. Special orders shall be issued by the OKW Operational Staff for the measures necessary before the beginning of operations for the restriction of travel, delivery of goods, and communications to Russia.
8. As soon as operations begin, the German-Soviet Russian frontier and at a later stage the border at the rear of the area of operations will be closed by the OKH for any and all non-military traffic with the exception of the police organisations to be deployed by the Reichsführer SS on the Führer's orders. Billeting and feeding of these organisations will be taken care of by the OKH-General Quartermaster who may for this purpose request from the Reichsführer SS the assignment of liaison officers.

   The border shall remain closed also for leading personalities of the highest government agencies and agencies of the Party. The OKW/Operational Staff shall inform the highest government and Party agencies of this fact. The Commander of the Army and the agencies under him shall decide on exceptions.

   Except for the special regulations applying to the police organisations of the Reichsführer SS, applications for entrance-permits must be submitted to the Commander-in-Chief of the Army exclusively.

3. **Regulations regarding Romania, Slovakia, Hungary, and Finland.**

9. The necessary arrangements with these countries shall be made by the OKW, together with the Foreign Office, and according to the wishes of the respective high commands. In case it should become necessary during the course of the operations to grant special rights, applications for this purpose are to be submitted to the OKW.
10. Police measures for the protection of the troops are permitted, independently from the granting of special rights. Further orders in this shall be issued later.
11. Special orders shall be issued at a later date for the territories of these countries, on the following subjects:

    Procurement of food and feed.
    Housing and machinery.
    Purchase and the shipment of merchandise.
    Procurement of funds and wage-control.
    Salaries.
    Request for indemnity-payments.
    Postal and telegraph services.
    Traffic.
    Jurisdiction.

    Requests of units of the Armed Forces and agencies of the OKW from the respective governments regarding these subjects, are to be submitted to the OKW/Operational Staff/Section Defence not later than 27 March 1941.

4. Directives regarding Sweden.

12. As Sweden can become only a transient-area for troops, no special authority is to be granted to the commander of the German troops. However, he is entitled and compelled to secure the immediate protection of RR-transports against sabotage and attacks.

Chief of the High Command of the Armed Forces
Keitel

Appendix 2

OKW Order for the Exercise of Military Jurisdiction and Procedure in area 'Barbarossa', and Special Military Measures, 13 May 1941

The application of martial law aims in the first place at maintaining discipline.

The fact that the operational areas in the East are so far-flung, the battle strategy which this necessitates, and the peculiar qualities of the enemy, confront the courts martial with problems which, being short-staffed, they cannot solve while hostilities are in progress, and until some degree of pacification has been achieved in the conquered areas, unless jurisdiction is confined, in the first instance, to its main task.

This is possible only if the troops take ruthless action themselves against any threat from the enemy population.

For these reasons I herewith issue the following order effective for the area 'Barbarossa' (area of operations, army rear area, and area of political administration):

1. Treatment of offences committed by enemy civilians:

1. Until further notice the military courts and the courts martial will not be competent for crimes committed by enemy civilians.
2. Guerrillas will be relentlessly liquidated by the troops, whilst fighting or escaping.
3. Likewise all other attacks by enemy civilians on the Armed Forces, its members and employees, are to be suppressed at once by the military, using the most extreme methods, until the assailants are destroyed.
4. Where such measures have been neglected or were not at first possible, persons suspected of criminal action will be brought at once before an officer. This officer will decide whether they are to be shot.

   On the orders of an officer with the powers of at least a Battalion Commander, collective despotic measures will be taken without delay against localities from which cunning or malicious attacks are made on the Armed Forces, if circumstances do not permit of a quick identification of individual offenders.
5. It is expressly forbidden to keep suspects in custody in order to hand them over to the courts after the reinstatement of civil courts.
6. The commanders of the Army Groups may by agreement with the competent Naval and Air Force commanders reintroduce military jurisdiction for civilians, in areas which are sufficiently settled.

   For the area of the 'Political Administration' this order will be given by the Chief of the High Command of the Armed Forces.

2. Treatment of offences committed against inhabitants by members of the Armed Forces and its employees.

1. With regard to offences committed against enemy civilians by members of the Wehrmacht and its employees prosecution is not obligatory even where the deed is at the same time a military crime or offence.
2. When judging such offences, it must be borne in mind, whatever the circumstances, that the collapse of Germany in 1918, the subsequent sufferings of the German people, and the fight against National Socialism which cost the blood of innumerable supporters of the Movement, were caused primarily by Bolshevik influence and that no German has forgotten this fact.
3. Therefore the judicial authority will decide in such cases whether a disciplinary penalty is indicated, or whether legal measures are necessary. In the case of offences against inhabitants it will order a court martial only if maintenance of discipline or security of the Forces call for such a measure. This applies for instance to serious offences originating in lack of self-control in sexual matters, or in a criminal disposition, and to those which indicate that the troops are threatening to get out of hand. Offences which have resulted in senseless destruction of billets or stores or other captured material to the disadvantage of our Forces should as a rule be judged no less severely.

   The order to institute proceedings requires in every single case the signature of the Judicial Authority.
4. Extreme caution is indicated in assessing the credibility of statements made by enemy civilians.

3. Within their sphere of competence military commanders are personally responsible for seeing that –

1. Every commissioned officer of the units under their command is instructed promptly and in the most emphatic manner on principles set out under I above.
2. Their legal advisers are notified promptly of these instructions and of verbal information in which the political intentions of the High Command were explained to commanders.
3. Only those court sentences are confirmed which are in accordance with the political intentions of the High Command.

4. Security

Once the camouflage is lifted this decree will be treated as 'Most Secret'.

By order

Chief of the High Command of the Armed Forces
Keitel

Appendix 3

OKW Directive on Communist Insurrection in Occupied Territories, 16 September 1941

1. Since the beginning of the campaign against Soviet Russia, Communist insurrection movements have broken out everywhere in the areas occupied by Germany. The type of action taken is growing from propaganda measures and attacks on individual members of the Armed Forces, into open rebellion and wide-spread guerrilla warfare.

   It can be seen that this is a mass movement centrally directed by Moscow, who is also responsible for the apparently trivial isolated incidents in areas which up to now have been otherwise quiet.

   In view of the many political and economic crises in the occupied areas, it must, moreover, be anticipated, that nationalist and other circles will make full use of this opportunity of making difficulties for the German occupying forces by associating themselves with the Communist insurrection.

   This creates an increasing danger to the German war effort, which shows itself chiefly in general insecurity for the occupying troops, and has already led to the withdrawal of forces to the main centres of disturbance.
2. The measures taken up to now to deal with this general insurrection movement have proved inadequate. The Führer has now given orders that we take action everywhere with the most drastic means in order to crush the movement in the shortest possible time.

   Only this course, which has always been followed successfully throughout the history of the extension of influence of great peoples can restore order.
3. Action taken in this matter should be in accordance with the following general directions:
   a. It should be inferred, in every case of resistance to the German occupying forces, no matter what the individual circumstances, that it is of Communist origin.
   b. In order to nip these machinations in the bud, the most drastic measures should be taken immediately on the first indication, so that the authority of the occupying forces may be maintained, and further spreading prevented. In this connection it should be remembered that a human life in unsettled countries frequently counts for nothing and a deterrent effect can be attained only by unusual severity. The death penalty for 50–100 Communists should generally be regarded in these cases as suitable atonement for one German soldier's life. The way in which sentence is carried out should still further increase the deterrent effect. The reverse course of action, that of imposing relatively lenient penalties, and of being content, for purposes of deterrence, with the threat of more severe measures, does not accord with these principles

and should therefore not be followed.

c. The political relations between Germany and the country in which the disturbance is taking place, are no criterion for the censuring of the military authorities in occupation. Rather, it should be borne in mind and so represented in propaganda, that stern measures also rid the inhabitants of the Communist criminals, and are thus to their own advantage. Clever propaganda of this kind will consequently not result in the severe measures against the Communists having an undesirable reaction on the well-disposed sections of the population.

d. Forces formed from the local inhabitants will generally fail to accomplish such acts of violence. They should on no account receive further support, for this involves increased danger to our own troops. On the other hand, the fullest use can be made of rewards and remuneration for the population, in order to ensure their co-operation in a suitable way.

e. Where, in exceptional cases, court martial proceedings should be instituted in connection with Communist insurrections or other offences against the German occupying forces, the most severe penalties are indicated. In this connection only the death penalty can constitute a real deterrent. In particular, acts of espionage, deeds of sabotage, and attempts to enter the Armed Forces of a foreign power, should, as a matter of principle, be punished by death. Sentence of death should also, as a general rule, be passed in cases of illicit possession of arms.

4. The Commanding Officers in the occupied territories are seeing to it that these principles are made known without delay to all military establishments concerned in dealing with Communist measures of insurrection.

Chief of the High Command of the Armed Forces
Keitel

Appendix 4

The 'Reichenau Order' on the Conduct of Troops in the Eastern Territories, 10 October 1941

High Command of the Army 28.10.41

Subject: Conduct of Troops in the Eastern Territories

By order of the Commander-in-Chief of the Army, an enclosed copy of an order by Commander, 6th Army, on the conduct of the troops in Eastern territories which has been described by the Führer as excellent, is being forwarded with the request to issue corresponding instructions on the same lines if this has not already been done.

By order
Army Quartermaster-General Wagner

Army Command 6. Army H.Q., 10.10.41

Subject: Conduct of Troops in Eastern Territories.

Regarding the conduct of troops towards the Bolshevistic system, vague ideas are still prevalent in many cases. The most essential aim of war against the Jewish-Bolshevistic system is a complete destruction of their means of power and the elimination of Asiatic influence from the European culture. In this connection the troops are facing tasks which exceed the one-sided routine of soldiering. The soldier in the Eastern territories is not merely a fighter according to the rules of the art of war but also a bearer of ruthless national ideology and the avenger of bestialities which have been inflicted upon German and racially related nations.

Therefore the soldier must have full understanding for the necessity of a severe but just revenge on subhuman Jewry. The Army has to aim at another purpose; i.e. the annihilation of revolts in hinterland which, as experience proves, have always been caused by Jews.

The combating of the enemy behind the front line is still not being taken seriously enough. Treacherous, cruel partisans and unnatural women are still being made prisoners-of-war and guerrilla fighters dressed partly in uniforms or plain clothes and vagabonds are still being treated as proper soldiers, and sent to prisoner-of-war camps. In fact, captured Russian officers talk even mockingly about Soviet agents moving openly about the roads and very often eating at German field kitchens. Such an attitude of the troops can only be explained by complete thoughtlessness, so it is now high time for the commanders to clarify the meaning of the present struggle.

The feeding of the natives and of prisoners-of-war who are not working for the Armed Forces from army kitchens is an equally misunderstood humanitarian act as is the giving of cigarettes and bread. Things which the people at home can spare under great sacrifices and things which are being brought by the Command to the front under great difficulties, should not be given to the enemy by the soldier not even if they originate from booty. It is an important part of our supply.

When retreating the Soviets have often set buildings on fire. The troops should be interested in extinguishing of fires only as far as it is necessary to secure sufficient numbers of billets. Otherwise the disappearance of symbols of the former Bolshevistic rule, even in the form of buildings, is part of the struggle of destruction. Neither historic nor artistic considerations are of any importance in the Eastern territories. The command issues the necessary directives for the securing of raw materials and plants, essential for war economy. The complete disarming of the civil population in the rear of the fighting troops is imperative considering the long and vulnerable lines of communications. Where possible, captured weapons and ammunition should be stored and guarded. Should this be impossible because of the situation of the battle, so the weapons and ammunition will be rendered useless. If isolated partisans are found using firearms in the rear of the army drastic measures are to be taken. These measures will be extended to that part of the male population who were in a position to hinder or report the attacks. The indifference of numerous apparently anti-soviet elements which originates from a 'wait and see' attitude, must give way to a clear decision for active collaboration. If not, no one can complain about being judged and treated a member of the Soviet system.

The fear of the German counter-measures must be stronger than the threats of the wandering Bolshevistic remnants. Being far from all political considerations of the future the soldier has to fulfil two tasks:

1. Complete annihilation of the false Bolshevistic doctrine of the Soviet State and its armed forces.
2. The pitiless extermination of foreign treachery and cruelty and thus the protection of the lives of military personnel in Russia.

This is the only way to fulfil our historic task to liberate the German people once for ever from the Asiatic-Jewish danger.

Commander-in-Chief, 6th Army
von Reichenau

Appendix 5

11th Army Order from General von Manstein, 20 November 1941

Since 22 June the German people have been engaged in a life and death struggle against the Bolshevist system.

This struggle is not being carried on against the Soviet Armed Forces alone in the established form laid down by European rules of warfare.

Behind the front, too, the fighting continues. Partisan snipers dressed as civilians attack single soldiers and small units and try to disrupt our supplies by sabotage with mines and infernal machines. Bolshevists left behind keep the population freed from Bolshevism in a state of unrest by means of terror and attempt thereby to sabotage the political and economic pacification of the country. Harvests and factories are destroyed and the city population in particular is thereby ruthlessly delivered to starvation.

Jewry constitutes the middle man between the enemy in the rear and the still fighting remainder of the Red Armed Forces and the Red leadership. More strongly than in Europe, it holds all the key positions in the political leadership and administration, controls trades and guilds, and further forms the nucleus for all unrest and possible uprisings.

The Jewish-Bolshevist system must be exterminated once and for all. Never again must it encroach upon our European living space.

The German soldier has therefore not only the task of crushing the military potential of this system. He comes also as the bearer of a racial concept and as the avenger of all the cruelties which have been perpetrated on him and on the German people.

The fight behind the lines is not yet being taken seriously enough. Active co-operation of all soldiers must be demanded in the disarming of the population, the control and arrest of all roving soldiers and civilians, and the removal of Bolshevist symbols.

Every instance of sabotage must be punished immediately with the severest measures and all signs thereof must be reported.

The food situation at home makes it essential that the troops should as far as possible be fed off the land and that furthermore the largest possible stocks be placed at the disposal of the homeland. Particularly in enemy cities a large part of the population will have to go hungry. Nevertheless, nothing which the homeland has sacrificed itself to contribute may, out of a misguided sense of humanity, be given to prisoners or to the population – so long as they are not in the service of the German Wehrmacht.

The soldier must appreciate the necessity for harsh punishment of Jewry, the spiritual bearer of the Bolshevist terror. This is also necessary in order to nip in the bud all uprisings which are mostly attributable to Jews.

It is the task of leaders at all levels to keep constantly alive the meaning of the present struggle. Support for the Bolshevist fight behind the front by way of thoughtlessness must be prevented.

It is to be expected that non-Bolshevist Ukrainians, Russians, and Tartars will be converted to the New Order. The non-participation of numerous, alleged anti-Soviet elements must give place to a definite decision in favour of active co-operation against Bolshevism. Where it does not exist it must be forced by suitable measures.

Voluntary co-operation in the reconstruction of occupied territory is an absolute necessity for the achievement of our economic and political aims.

It has as its condition a just treatment of all non-Bolshevist sections of the population, some of whom have for years fought heroically against Bolshevism.

The ruling of this country demands from us results, strictness with ourselves, and submergence of the individual. The bearing of every soldier is constantly under observation. It can make enemy propaganda ineffective or give it a spring-board. If the soldier in the country takes from the peasant the last cow, the brood sow, the last chicken, or the seed, then no restoration of the economy can be achieved.

In all measures it is not the momentary success which is decisive. All measures must, therefore, be judged by their effectiveness over a period of time.

Respect for religious customs, particularly those of Mohammedan Tartars, must be demanded.

In pursuance of those concepts there are other measures besides to be carried out by the later administration. The enlightenment of the population by propaganda, encouragement of personal initiative, e.g., by prizes, extensive detailing of the population towards fighting the partisans, and expansion of the local auxiliary police must be given more significance.

For the achievement of this objective the following must be demanded:

Active co-operation of soldiers in the fight against the enemy in the rear.
No soldier to go about alone at night.
All motor vehicles to be equipped with adequate armament.
A self-assured, but not overbearing attitude from all soldiers.
Restraint towards prisoners and the other sex.
No waste of food.

Severest action to be taken:

Against despotism and self-seeking.
Against lawlessness and lack of discipline.
Against every transgression of the honour of a soldier.

Commander-in-Chief, 11th Army
von Manstein

Appendix 6

OKW Directive for the Prosecution of Offences against the Reich or against the Occupation Authorities in the Occupied Territories, 7 December 1941

With the beginning of the Russian campaign, communist elements and other anti-German circles increased their attacks on the Reich and the occupation authorities in the occupied territories. The extent and the danger of these activities compel to most severe measures against the guilty for the purpose of intimidation.

For the time being the following directions shall be observed:

1. In regard to offences committed by non-German civilians in the occupied territories against the Reich or the occupation authorities which endanger their security or efficiency, the death sentence is adequate as a matter of principle.
2. The offences referred to in section I are to be tried in the occupied territories only if it is likely that the guilty persons, at least the main offenders, will be sentenced to death and if the proceedings and the execution of the death sentences can be carried out quickly. Otherwise the offenders, at least the main offenders, are to be brought to Germany.
3. Guilty persons who are brought to Germany are to be subject to court-martial proceedings there only if specific military interests make it necessary. German or foreign authorities making inquiries are to be told that the guilty persons had been arrested and that the state of the proceedings did not permit to give further information.
4. The commanders in the occupied territories and the legal representatives are personally responsible for the execution of this decree within the framework of their competence.
5. The Chief of the High Command of the Armed Forces determines in which occupied territories this decree is to be applied. He is authorised to explain, to make provisions for the execution of the decree, and to supplement it. The Reich Minister of Justice issues the provisions for the execution of the law for his district.

Chief of the High Command of the Armed Forces
Keitel

Appendix 7

Führer War Directive No. 46. Instructions for Intensified Action against the Bands in the East, 18 August 1942

A. General Considerations

1. In recent months banditry in the East has assumed intolerable proportions, and threatens to become a serious danger to supplies for the front and to the economic exploitation of the country.

   By the beginning of winter these bandit gangs must be substantially exterminated, so that order may be restored behind the Eastern front and severe disadvantages to our winter operations avoided.

   The following measures are necessary:

   1. Rapid, drastic, and active operations against the bandits by the co-ordination of all available forces of the Armed Forces, the SS, and Police which are suitable for the purpose.
   2. The concentration of all propaganda, economic, and political measures on the necessity of combating banditry.

2. The following general principles will be borne in mind by all concerned in formulating military, police, and economic measures:
   1. The fight against banditry is an much a matter of strategy as the fight against the enemy at the front. It will therefore be organised and carried out by the same staffs.
   2. The destruction of the bandits calls for active operations and the most rigorous measures against all members of gangs or those guilty of supporting them. Operation orders for action against bandits will follow.
   3. The confidence of the local population in German authority must be gained by handling them strictly but justly.
   4. A necessary condition for the destruction of bandit gangs is the assurance to the local population of the minimum requirements of life. Should this fail, or – what is particularly important – should available supplies not be fairly distributed, the result will be that more recruits will join the bandits.
   5. In this struggle against the bandits the co-operation of the local population is indispensable. Deserving persons should not be parsimoniously treated; rewards should be really attractive. On the other hand, reprisals for action in support of the bandits must be all the more severe.
   6. Misplaced confidence in the native population, particularly in those working for the German authorities, must be strictly guarded against.

Even though the majority of the population is opposed to the bandits, there are always spies to be reckoned with, whose task is to inform the bandits of all action contemplated against them.

B. **Command and responsibility**

1. The Reichsführer SS and the Chief of the German Police.

The Reichsführer SS and Chief of the German Police is the Central authority for the collection and evaluation of all information concerning action against bandits.

In addition, the Reichsführer SS has the sole responsibility for combating banditry in the Reich Commissars' territories. Commanders of the Armed Forces will support him in his tasks arising from this by co-ordinating their measures, and by transferring such staffs, command communications, and supplies as are needed. In so far as is allowed by military security duties, which will be carried out locally as actively as possible, Higher SS and Police Leaders will if necessary assume temporary command of forces of the Armed Forces for use in their operations.

The closest liaison between Higher SS and Police Leaders and commanders of the Armed Forces is an essential condition of success.

2. Army.

The Chief of the Army General Staff is solely responsible for action against bandits in operational areas. In carrying out this task, police units engaged, will come under the Army commanders concerned. The latter will entrust the command of individual operations to Army commanders, or to Higher SS and Police Leaders, according to the situation, the forces engaged, and the seniority of the officers concerned.

C. **Available Forces**

1. Forces of the Reichsführer SS.

The Police and SS formations available and allocated for operations against bandits are intended primarily for active operations. Their employment in other security duties is to be avoided. Efforts will made to reinforce Police and SS formations in the East, and to transfer to the threatened areas a considerable number of establishments of the Reichsführer SS at present employed elsewhere. Formations still at the front, but indispensable for operations against bandits in the rear areas, will be withdrawn from the Army as soon as possible, and placed at the disposal of the Reichsführer SS for duty in their proper areas.

2. Army Forces.

In order to reinforce the garrisons of the vast Eastern territories behind the fighting front, I order as follows:

a. When the General Government becomes a Home Forces area, two reserve divisions will move to the General Government.
b. A total of five reserve divisions will be moved to the spheres of Commander Armed Forces Baltic Territories and Commander Armed Forces Ukraine by 15 October 1942.

c. All formations, units, staffs, establishments, and schools of the Field Army not serving under the Commander of the Replacement Army will be withdrawn by 1 October 1942 from the General Government and transferred to the territories of the Reich Commissioners or to the area of operations. Any necessary exceptions will be approved by the Chief of the High Command of the Armed Forces.

d. The final target is to transfer by the end of October a replacement force of 50,000 men formed from the Reserve Army.

e. The necessary operation orders concerning paragraphs a. to d. will be issued by the Chief of the High Command of the Armed Forces.

3. Air Force.

Commander-in-Chief Air Force will arrange for the transfer of Air Force establishments to the areas threatened by bandits, in order to reinforce the garrison in the Eastern territories.

4. Units formed from the native population.

Native units made up of local people who have particularly distinguished themselves in action against the bandits are to be maintained and extended, provided they are completely reliable and are volunteers. They will not take part in fighting at the front, nor will émigrés or members of the former intelligentsia be enrolled in them.

The Army General Staff will issue general directions covering the internal organisation of these units, where this has not already been done. In matters of rank, uniforms, and training, these directions will follow the general lines laid down for the Turkoman formations. They will then be approved by the Chief of the High Command of the Armed Forces. The wearing of German badges of rank, the Hohetisabzeichen [the Eagle and Swastika], and German military shoulder-straps is forbidden. The dependants of these men are to be provided for. Ration scales for them will be laid down corresponding to the duties they are required to perform. These people will receive preferential treatment in the form of grants of land, which should be as liberal as possible within the limits of local circumstances.

5. Other forces.

The arming of the Reich Labour Service, railwaymen, foresters, agricultural overseers, etc., will, where required, be improved. They should be able to defend themselves with the most effective weapons available.

There must be no German in the area threatened by bandits who is not engaged, actively or passively, in the fight against them.

Adolf Hitler

Appendix 8

11th Army Order for the Organisation and Execution of the Combating of Partisans, 29 November 1941

1. The annihilation of the many located partisan groups, the prevention of the formation of further armed bands, and thus the protection of rear communications are important prerequisites for the final mopping-up and occupation of the Crimea. All formations of the 11th Army, in particular the replacement and supply troops, will take part in the execution of these tasks.
2. In the sectors already defined the execution of this combat task continues to be the responsibility of the Corps HQs and of the Army Rear Command.
3. In order to ensure that throughout the Army Area there will be uniformity in the methods of obtaining information with regard to partisan activities, and to effect the necessary commitments of army units, GHQ has established a Staff for the Combating of Partisans under the command of Major Stephanus of the General Staff, with HQ in Simferopol. It will be directly subordinate to GHQ.
4. Tasks:
   a. Obtaining information on partisan activities throughout the Army Area in close co-operation with Ic/Counter Intelligence Officer (Major Riesen). All HQs will, as quickly as possible, forward reports on partisan activities to the Staff direct. These reports must in every case state the following: Place; time; strength; counter-measures and their effects; which other offices have been informed.
   b. Starting of operations against partisans in the sectors, so far as these operations are not within the scope of the general security tasks of the Corps and the Army High Command; in this connection, if necessary, commitment of detachment Lt-Col. Ewert which is at its disposal. Apart from that the combating of partisans is one of the essential tasks of the Ia (GSO 1).
   c. Setting-up of an appropriate counter-organisation consisting of reliable members of the population and V-men (agents).
   d. Regulating of the direct co-operation of the Corps HQs and divisions, if and when operations have to be carried out near the sector boundaries or beyond them.
   e. Preparing and using propaganda with regard to the combating of partisans in the entire Army area.
5. In an emergency, and unless extensive operations are involved, Major Stephanus of the General Staff is entitled to issue orders on my behalf. In all questions concerning the combating of partisans he will be in direct contact with the Ia's of the Corps HQs and the divisions.
6. All headquarters are to be instructed to give far-reaching assistance to the

'Staff for the Combating of Partisans' and to the *Sonderkommandos* and Army units employed by it, by allotting to them reinforcements and supplies. Section DQMG, GHQ 11th Army has received special orders in this respect.

7. It continues to be the task of all army units to protect themselves against partisan activities and to attack and annihilate minor partisan groups in the vicinity of their quarters. In the mountains, detachments, columns (no single vehicles!) are to be permanently ready for action (machine-guns on lorries ready to fire, etc.). Certain particularly dangerous roads should either be blocked, or the traffic of single vehicles should be stopped at check-points. At the check-points motorised escorts are to be assembled, and the dangerous area is to be crossed in convoy, under their protection. Blocked roads and roads to be used in convoy only will be reported.

   When partisan hiding-places or unoccupied supply and ammunition dumps have been cleared, unnecessary losses have time and again occurred because the covering parties were withdrawn too soon, or because, on leaving the place of operations, the state of alert was lifted too soon.
8. It has already happened that partisans have appeared in German uniforms or women's clothes.
9. Corps HQs will report how many soldiers with a knowledge of the Russian language can be put at the disposal of the 'Staff for the Combating of Partisans'. Employment as interpreters and setting-up of *Sonderkommandos* is intended. Order of commitment will follow. At least two soldiers will report from every division.

The Commander-in-Chief, 6th Army
von Manstein

Appendix 9

Extracts from 11th Army's 'Memorandum on Use of Troops against Partisans', 15 December 1941

1. 1. ....
   2. .... The population must be more frightened of our reprisals than of the partisans.

      The militia which has been formed in some villages has proved its worth. The shooting of militia personnel by the partisans shows how much they dislike this institution. It will therefore be extended.

      There must be ample rewards both in money and kind for deserving militiamen, voluntary guides, and all civilians giving important information about the partisans.

      It must be pointed out to the population again and again that nobody will give them back what the partisans take away, and that the German troops are carrying on the fight against the partisans solely in the interest of the security of the population.
2. 1. ....
   2. Experience has especially been gained in the operation against partisans on the Crimea. That experience has now been recorded in an excellent memorandum issued by an Army Corps. This memorandum and other experience has been collected in the 'Principles of Partisan Warfare' which follow with special reference to the conditions prevailing on the Crimea.
3. 1. Operations against partisans are usually conducted in three stages:
      a. information
      b. attack; destruction of partisan strongholds
      c. protection.

      These three stages will differ in accordance with the number of partisans to be dealt with, the state of the country in and around the scene of action, and the number of our own troops available.

      The weather plays an important part in this.

      When fighting against partisans in a mountainous area nothing except a concentric attack against a partisan stronghold whose location has been established by military intelligence is likely to be successful.

      In open country (woods or fields) it would seem advisable to clear whole areas by forming pockets and sending out patrols.
   2. The following can be used for purposes of information:

      Employment of confidential agents and soldiers in civilian clothes (knowledge of Russian) to interrogate members of the population.

      Statements made by the population.

      Statements made by partisan deserters.

Statements made by relatives of partisans.

Evaluation of documents, maps, etc., found in operations against partisans.

Reports of attacks made by partisans.

The statements of persons who have taken part in the construction of food and ammunition depots are particularly important. If the necessary precautions are taken, it should in most cases be possible to use such persons as guides.

Ground reconnaissance and map study must provide further data. In any case reconnaissance and investigations must be carried out in such an unobtrusive manner, that the partisans are not forewarned and change their positions.

Armed reconnaissance must be strong enough not only to exchange a few shots, but to go over to the attack at any time.

Partisans must never gain the impression that they have defeated the enemy.

Soldiers used for reconnaissance must be specially selected men who are used as far as possible, owing to their profession (gamekeepers, police officers, shepherds, etc.) to recognise all the various trails and peculiarities of the terrain, and who can draw the right conclusion from them. This reconnaissance work can best be compared with a game of 'Red Indians' or 'Robber and Police'. Devotees of hunting in all ranks are particularly suited for this purpose. The results of such reconnaissance must be collected before the operation by the officer in charge so that he is in a position to form a picture of the terrain, of the strength of the enemy, and of the facilities for defence or escape.

. Attack on and destruction of a partisan stronghold:

Very careful preparations must be made for the attack. Mountain equipment (rucksacks, assault kit, compass, binoculars, etc.) must be improvised. Every man must carry non-perishable rations (chocolate, crisp-bread, etc.). Men must be detailed to carry ammunition and food supplies. Every man must carry small arms and hand-grenades.

Medical orderlies must also be detailed.

In every case a base of operations must be set up in the vicinity of the scene of the action which must be known to all men. This base will serve as a command post and supply base for the operation. Arrangements must be made for first aid at this command post.

The better the preparations, the greater the chance of success.

Two kinds of attack must be distinguished:

a. Thorough reconnaissance possible: In this case the attack should be conducted concentrically, either by attacking the strongholds from all sides (avoiding paths in the vicinity of the enemy, advancing under cover of bushes, etc.), or by blocking all exits and then advancing with a strong detachment against the stronghold under cover of small arms and artillery fire. Partisan strongholds are usually constructed in such a way that they have only one approach, which can be easily defended with few weapons. The use of mortars, infantry guns, anti-tank guns, and mountain guns have proved particularly effective in such cases.

b. Thorough reconnaissance impossible (lack of time, inaccessible country, etc.): frontal attack alone promises success. This procedure should be used particularly when a unit reports that partisans have staged an attack in its area and when it is possible to attack the partisans with an adequate force immediately or to pursue them.

c. In both cases the troops should advance making the greatest possible use of cover. It is preferable to move at night or at dawn, rather than advance on the day before, spend the night in prepared positions and attack on the following morning. In the mountains there is always a risk that the partisans may get through the lines.

4. Object: The object is in all cases the annihilation of the partisans and the destruction of their hideouts, their food and ammunition dumps, and their arms.

The operation must in all cases be followed up by reconnaissance of the scene of action on one of the days following, because valuable information can frequently be gained by so doing. Usually partisans return to their demolished hideouts once more, in order to find out whether individual hiding-places have escaped notice.

But they also return to their hideouts after an attack because they think it is now particularly safe. They then attempt to bring their stores into safety.

5. Protection: Operations must be protected by having all arms ready for action from the start to the return to headquarters.

Hedgehog formation must be used when approaching or withdrawing from these strongholds. Partisans have frequently allowed their strongholds and hiding-places to be destroyed, only to attack the returning troops from an ambush. Every man taking part in the operations must be informed beforehand of the following:

Object of the operation,
his personal task in the operation,
action in case of sudden attack,
what action he must take when he is separated from his troop, wounded, or captured.

In this type of warfare, there is no front or rear. (Every man must be equipped for close combat.)

Vehicles which are used as command posts must be protected from all sides by the drivers in such a manner that the vehicles are safe from small arms fire. The parking places for trucks and other vehicles must therefore be chosen with particular care.

Every man must be prepared for 'surprises' in the form of booby traps of all kinds. Billets, food dumps, etc., usually look innocent and are well camouflaged. (No cobwebs on doors and windows.)

Even if no partisans or food dumps are found, individual houses or hiding-places which could be used by the partisans must be thoroughly destroyed.

When approaching or withdrawing from the scene of action, all 'civilians' arousing suspicion in the vicinity of the scene of action will be arrested and searched, and will not be released until the operation has been completed, and they have established their innocence. Where there is the least suspicion, they will be taken along and handed over to the nearest Secret Field Police post. (Exact information must be given as to place, date, time, and special circumstances connected with the apprehension of the person in question.)

6. Every man must be made conscious of the fact that he is fighting a particularly dangerous and highly trained enemy. All the arms available must be used ruthlessly. Utmost severity is necessary.

Misplaced compassion endangers the lives of our troops.

It is wrong to use a standard method in operations against partisans. All the experience gained is bound to be of a general nature; every individual operation will be different from all others.

Attack is trumps.

7. Communications. The use of all possible means of communication will make the task easier and will contribute considerably to the success of the operation. In the event of an attack being launched against a stronghold from all sides, the principal means of communication will usually be a pack wireless set. The firing of Very light signals, when prearranged places have been reached, has proved successful. The disadvantage of this method is that the partisans are thereby warned. The method should therefore only be used when the partisan stronghold has been completely surrounded.

In large-scale operations it is possible to use aircraft to inform headquarters of the position of the various detachments by wireless or message dropping. Air reconnaissance, especially in wooded or mountainous areas, promises success only when the weather is good (low-altitude flying) in the course of an operation. Reconnaissance planes can supply important information on the whereabouts of partisan strongholds by discovering tracks and smoke in uninhabited areas.

8. Treatment of partisans:
   a. Partisans captured in action will be interrogated and then shot (former members of the Red Army) or hanged (civilians). . . .
   b. Partisans who are caught will be hanged without exception. A label will be attached to them with the following legend: 'This is a partisan who did not give himself up!' . . .

Appendix 10

Order of the Central Committee of the Communist Party concerning combat organisation in the Rear of the German Army, 18 July 1941

In the war with Fascist Germany, which has occupied a part of the Soviet territory, combat in the rear area of the German Army acquires particular importance. Its task is to create unbearable conditions for the German invaders, to disorganise their lines of communications, supply, and military units, to paralyse all their measures, to destroy the hoarders and their collaborators, to support everywhere the organisation of partisan cavalry and infantry units and destruction groups; to spread the wide network of our Bolshevik organisation in order to carry out all measures against the Fascist occupiers. In this battle against the Fascist invaders we still have quite a number of methods and opportunities, which have not as yet been utilised, for inflicting severe blows on the enemy. In all these activities we will receive in every town and also in every village willing support from hundreds, even thousands of our brothers and friends who find themselves under the boots of the German Fascists and who are expecting our help in the organisation of the struggle against the occupiers.

To give this combat activity in the rear area of the German Army greater *élan* and fighting force it is necessary that the leaders of the republics and of the oblast and rayon organisations of the Soviet Party [sic] take over the organisation on the spot themselves; they personally must organise the work in the rayons occupied by the Germans, create groups and units of selfless fighters who are already engaged in a battle of annihilation against the enemy's troops and in their destruction. There are still a few cases in which the leaders of the Party and Soviet organisations of the rayons threatened by the Fascists shamelessly leave their combat posts and retreat deep into the rear area to safe positions, thus becoming deserters and pitiful cowards. In the face of these shameful facts the heads of the republic and oblast organisations of the Party are not taking energetic measures. The Central Committee of the VKP(b) demands from all Party and Soviet organisations, especially from all their leaders, that they put an end to such unbearable conditions, and reminds them that the Party and the Government will not hesitate to take the most severe measures in regard to those slackers and deserters; it hopes that the Party organisations will take every step to purge these traitors from the Party organisations, and will concentrate all their efforts on destroying the enemy at the front and in the rear area, and will make every preparation for a victory against the Fascist bands.

In this connection, the Central Committee of the VKP(b) demands that the Central Committees of the Parties of the republics and the oblast and rayon committees of the occupied oblasts and rayons, and those threatened with occupation, carry out the following measures:

1. Particularly reliable, leading Party, Soviet, and Komsomol activists, and also non-Party members devoted to the Soviet régime, who are acquainted with the circumstances in the rayon to which they are to be assigned, must be selected for the organisation of Communist [underground] cells and for assuming leadership in partisan activities and in the destruction campaign. The assignment of workers to certain regions must be carefully prepared and camouflaged; for this purpose each group (two to three men) must get in touch with only one person; groups to be assigned are not to come in contact with one another.
2. In those rayons which are threatened by enemy occupation the leaders of the Party organisation must organise secret underground cells without delay, to which they immediately assign a number of Communists and Komsomol members.

   In order to insure that partisan activities will spread widely in the rear areas of the enemy, the Party organisations must create immediately combat and paratroop units from among those who participated in the Civil War, and from among those comrades who have already distinguished themselves in destruction battalions and in units of the home guard, and also from among workers of the NKVD and NKGB. Communist and Komsomol members who are not used for work in the secret cells must also be enlisted in these groups [combat and paratroop units].

   The partisan units and secret groups must be supplied with arms, ammunition, money, and valuables for this purpose; the necessary supplies have to be buried and hidden ahead of time.

   Signal communications between the partisan units, the secret cells, and the Soviet-side rayons must be established; for this purpose the organisation must be supplied with radio equipment; couriers, codes, etc., must be used; the distribution and preparation of leaflets, slogans, and newspapers must be accomplished on the spot.
3. The Party organisations under the personal guidance of their first secretaries must select experienced fighters; these must be comrades who are devoted to the end to the Party, and who are personally well known to the leaders of the Party organisation, and are experienced in the work of organising and providing leadership for partisan activity.
4. The Central Committees of the republic Communist parties, the oblast committees and district committees must report, through a specially designated [covert] address, to the Central Committee of the VKP(b), the names of those comrades who are selected as leaders of the partisan groups.

   The Central Committee of the VKP(b) demands that the leaders of the Party organisations personally direct the struggle in the German Army's rear, that they arouse the enthusiasm of those persons who are devoted to the Soviet régime by personal examples of bravery and selflessness, so that the whole struggle will be of direct, generous, and heroic assistance to the Red Army which is fighting the Fascists at the front.

Appendix 11

Instruction concerning the Organisation and Activity of Partisan Detachments and Diversionist Groups, issued by the Soviet North-West Front, 20 July 1941

General Directives

1. The partisan movement has arisen as a popular movement in the enemy's rear areas. It is called upon to play a mighty role in our patriotic war. The basic objectives of partisan warfare in the rear of the enemy have been clearly stated by the Chairman of the State Committee for Defence, Comrade Stalin: 'Partisan units, mounted and on foot, must be formed; diversionist groups must be organised to combat the enemy troops, to foment partisan warfare everywhere, to blow up bridges and roads, damage telephone and telegraph lines, set fire to forests, stores, transports. In the occupied regions conditions must be made unbearable for the enemy and all his accomplices. They must be hounded and annihilated at every step and all their measures frustrated.'
2. First and foremost, partisan detachments and diversionist groups must be established in the main operating areas, that is, the areas of greatest concentration of the enemy. The partisan detachments are to be organised as combat units or diversionist groups according to their function.
3. Partisan detachments must be well armed and sufficiently strong for active operations in the enemy rear. The total strength of such a unit may amount to 75–150 men, organised into two or three companies, with the companies divided into two or three platoons.
4. The basic operating sections of the combat units will be the company and the platoon. Their basic duties – carried out as a rule at night or from ambush – are attacks on columns and concentrations of motorised infantry, on dumps and ammunition transports, on airfields, and on railroad transports.

   The operations must be carried out in areas in which forests furnish cover for the units. Such an area can consist of up to two or three administrative rayons; operations are to be carried out only against the main lines of communication of the enemy. Each administrative rayon should contain at least one partisan combat unit.
5. Aside from combat units, diversionist groups of 30–50 men are to be created in each rayon. These will be organised into five to eight groups of three, five, or ten men each. The diversionist groups must be so organised that the partisans of one group do not know those of any of the other groups. The organisation of these groups, above the level of the individual unit, exists only for the purpose of controlling their operations and organising new groups.

6. The basic objectives of the diversionist groups are as follows: the destruction of telephone and telegraph lines, the burning of gasoline dumps and transports, the destruction of railroad lines, the destruction of individual trucks and small groups of vehicles and the capture of documents found on them, the burning of armoured vehicles by means of incendiary bombs, the killing of enemy officers, the spreading of rumours designed to produce panic among the enemy troops (rumours concerning the appearance of Soviet tanks or airborne troops in their rear).
7. In all the areas still occupied by the Red Army, the NKVD [People's Commissariat of the Interior] and NKGB [People's Commissariat of State Security] offices are to organise destruction battalions to combat enemy airborne troops in our rear. In the event that these areas should be evacuated by the Red Army and occupied by the enemy, the destruction battalions must remain in the area and change over to partisan warfare.
8. The local rayon Party and Soviet offices and the representatives of the NKVD and NKGB are fully responsible for the organisation of the destruction battalions and for their conversion into partisan units.

   It is categorically forbidden to dissolve the destruction battalions; if they split up or retreat to our rear area, the head of the above-named offices will be brought to account before the War Tribunal.
9. The primary basis of the organisation of the partisan movement must be the mass formation of combat units and diversionist groups.

Tactical Employment of Partisan Combat and Diversionist Detachments

Only bold and resolute actions of the partisan detachments will guarantee success and bring the Red Army substantial help. The strength of the partisans consists in their having the initiative and in their unexpected actions.

Bases for the actions of the partisan detachments are the ambush and sudden, short raids on the objective after which the detachment scatters into small groups and reunites at the rendezvous. Actions are undertaken only at night or before dawn when the vigilance of the enemy guards slackens. Advance on the objective takes place only at night after the objective and the approach route have been reconnoitred by daylight.

If the objective of the raid is guarded, one must remove the guard quickly and noiselessly (with ranger tactics) or go around him. The partisans ought not to return fire.

After the raid, or if it failed, the partisans escape pursuit and reunite at a previously indicated rendezvous three to five kilometres distant from the operation point.

As a rule, in escape from pursuit one must first take a false direction of march. If the enemy pursues the detachment, a small group of the boldest partisans must be assigned the task of covering the withdrawal of the main group. The covering group must pull back in a false direction. If the pursuing units are foot soldiers, one must surprise them either by using the main group for a flank attack or by proceeding to capture and destroy the objective denuded by the withdrawal of the enemy guards; thus the real mission will be fulfilled.

For their destructive actions in the rear of the enemy, the partisan detachments and diversionist groups must utilise local resources on a broad scale; for example, for the demolition of railway tracks, the rails must be loosened with the help of a wrench, which is available in every signalman's hut. For destruction of communication lines, the poles should be sawed off.

Plain bottles filled with gasoline are to be used to set fire to gasoline tanks or armoured cars (a bundle of rags or twigs, soaked in an inflammable fluid, is to be bound at the bottom of the bottle); the bottles are to be thrown at the fuel tanks and motor vehicles in raids on parking places of the enemy's motorised troops.

Trains can be halted by laying a pyre on the rails. When the train has stopped, it is to be fired on from ambush, and soldiers climbing out must be destroyed by machine-gun and rifle fire as well as by hand-grenades. For the fight against motorised units raids on resting places are to be carried out at night and the personnel as well as the gasoline supply destroyed.

For the fight against the enemy's air force, raids on airfields are to be undertaken and planes destroyed on the ground. Groups of three to five men are to be formed from among the good shots; they will approach the airport under cover and destroy from ambush low-flying planes landing and taking off. In addition to its tasks, the areas of activity are to be laid down for the partisan detachment. These areas must include large woods to screen secret manoeuvres and hiding-places.

Destruction of Traffic Routes and Means of Communication

The most substantial interference in railroad and truck transport is attained through the destruction of bridges (blowing up, undermining, burning).

For the destruction of rails, small groups (three or four men) must be assigned. Derailments must be effected simultaneously on a series of railway sections, thus rendering the repair more difficult. As derailment locations, steep downgrades are to be chosen, where the train moves at high speed and is harder to stop. The loosened rails must be removed from immediately in front of the train so that the engineer will not notice the damaged stretch. Three or four men (who sit in ambush) can do this by tying to the rails strong rope or telegraph wire which can be obtained by destroying communication lines. If the road is double track, it is sufficient to derail one track since thereby both will be blocked. Simultaneously with the destruction of the rails, communication lines running along the railroad must be destroyed by cutting the wires after sawing off the poles. The more poles downed, the harder is the repair.

A good means of interference is linking wires together. This is achieved by joining all wires on the pole by a thin, unobtrusive wire, the end of which leads down the pole and is buried.

Occupation and Destruction of Encampments

The destruction of gasoline and munitions dumps has priority at all times. Usually these dumps are located far from inhabited areas; they are carefully guarded and have good communications connections. For that reason communications with the outside must first be broken in order to occupy and destroy [the dumps].

For the occupation of encampments the following groups ... must be assigned: (a) A group for destruction of communications with the outside. (b) One or a few groups with automatic weapons and grenades to cover the section where the enemy guards are and pin them down. (c) A few groups armed with hand-grenades, gasoline bottles, and rifles for the actual occupation after the destruction of the guards.

The raids are to be carried out only at night or at dawn. In ample time prior to the raid on the camp, daytime reconnaissance must secure information on the position of the posts and guard-room, the telephones and signal arrangements, and the concealed approaches to the camp and the posts. It is essential for the group leaders to acquaint themselves personally with the objective of the action in daylight.

After occupation of the camp, immediate steps are to be taken for its destruction by setting fires at various places (by using gasoline bottles, effectively shooting up gasoline tanks and cisterns with inflammable missiles, and other means).

After completing the task, the detachment concentrates at the rendezvous previously set by the commander.

Ambushes and Raids in the Fight Against Living Enemy Targets

The partisan detachments have unlimited possibilities to carry out sudden short raids from ambush on living targets of the enemy. Such raids engender panic in his ranks, induce him to flight, and create confusion among his units and subdivisions whereby his further movement is held up and serious losses are inflicted on personnel and matériel.

Partisan warfare can be especially effective against troop units marching at night. In most instances, large units of the enemy carry out their marches at night, when they are less threatened by planes. Night raids from ambush are suitably carried out simultaneously by some groups (platoons) with reinforced firing capacity. Such groups can impede the advance of whole divisions and bring about disorder.

Ambushes for raids are best set along roads. The best ambush is the edge of a wood, 150–250 metres from the road, on which movement of enemy columns is expected. Ambushes against living targets should not be arranged near a road, for after the first shots the groups can be attacked by enemy columns.

The region between ambush and road should be open, so that the use of the total fire-power of machine-guns and rifles is assured. The fire should be directed obliquely at the road and preferably by crossfire along the road. This firing system must be sustained within each group. It is a good idea to station on the flanks of the groups, 30–40 metres from the road, two or three skilled grenade-throwers who, after rifle fire against the column has started, throw hand-grenades at it.

The ambush must not be detected by the enemy's security patrols. This is achieved by the arrangement of ambushes 100–150 metres from the road and by absolute quiet within the group (at night the flank guards of the foe are sent out 50–100 metres from the road). Smoking, movements in the group, talking, etc., are categorically forbidden in ambush. The mouth must be covered with the sleeve, cap, or something of the like in case of involuntary coughing.

Firearms attacks are to be carried out only against the main forces and not against forward security units and detachments. The latter must be allowed to pass by. Ambushes in platoons must be organised in intervals of 500–700 metres and the firing attack is to begin simultaneously upon signal of the leader. The position of the leader is with the middle group or with the group which, in the direction of the enemy's advance, is closest to the enemy.

The opening of fire from the first machine-gun of the leader's group can serve as the signal. In the ambush no entrenchments are to be made as these can lead to discovery.

When time permits, matériel abandoned by the enemy must be destroyed. First, the motors of the vehicles are to be ruined by rifle shots. Horses used for the horse-drawn guns must be shot. All light weapons (rifles, machine-guns, munitions as well as hand-grenades) must be taken along for utilisation in future battles. Surplus items are to be wrecked, so that they cannot be used later.

At night it is relatively easy for partisan detachments to bring about a fight of two enemy columns against each other. To achieve this, small partisan groups between the two columns open fire simultaneously on both columns.

Operations against motorcycle riders, infantry transported on motor vehicles, or marching infantry can be especially effective. Small groups of three to five partisans, in ambush along the road at intervals of 100–150 metres, can inflict a serious defeat on the enemy, scatter his columns, and send them fleeing in panic.

For ambushes and raids against columns of motor vehicles a section of the road on a high embankment or with ditches along the road is to be selected. In all cases, the partisans must strive to erect roadblocks with felled trees, destroyed bridges, abandoned vehicles set crosswise, etc. These roadblocks will be useful only if in their vicinity (150–200 metres) in the direction of the foe) ambushes are set up with one or two groups to shoot at the enemy troops as they crowd together.

The partisan detachments and their groups must be mobile and not detectable by the enemy. To increase mobility, detachments and groups must count only on captured vehicles and on those furnished by the population. Vehicles tie the detachment to roads and are more of a hindrance than a help. Riding horses, even when unsaddled, are a good means of locomotion; but as a rule mobility is to be assured by training in rapid marching, tactical march, and especially in night marching.

For marching movements, paths in fields and woods are to be preferred. Inhabited areas must be avoided. It is better to march extra kilometres than to be discovered by the foe.

March discipline must be high. Smoking and conversation are forbidden at night.

On unexpected contact with the foe at night, one should not open fire but rather quickly escape from the foe and change direction several times.

On the detachment's route of march two to three men are to be left behind for 20–30 minutes, in order to learn whether or not the foe or his agents are following its trail. The latter are to be taken prisoner and executed.

For its own security the detachment or group dispatches two to three scouts during the day, 300–500 metres ahead; at night, 100–150 metres ahead. It is desirable to send the scouts on horseback; in this case they are to be 1–1½ kilometres ahead. To the rear the detachments are guarded by two scouts. In the column itself observers are assigned ahead and to the sides for reconnaissance. It is the detachment's duty to avoid unexpected contact with the enemy. If small groups of the enemy are identified, they should be allowed to pass by and the main force should be attacked from ambush. The foe is to be hit wherever he appears.

The well-prepared organisation of rest periods is one of the most important considerations of the detachment in the rear of the enemy. The foe will strive to take the detachment by surprise during its rest. Therefore, the detachments must always be in permanent battle readiness. The particular diversity and tension of the work of the partisan detachments require great attention [to the problem of rest in order to preserve the strength of the partisans.

The authority of the commander of the detachment will be firm if the partisans see in him not only a valiant, bold fighter and a good organiser of sudden raids on the enemy but also a careful, solicitous leader.

The resting-place is as a rule in woods (and thickets), remote from roads and inhabited points and in the winter or at especially rainy times, in isolated buildings (woodsmen's huts, single farms). One should not stay in the same place for more than two successive days. The resting-places (hideouts) must be changed daily if possible.

Immediately before arriving at the chosen resting-place, the detachment (group) must take a marked change of direction in its approach route and leave behind a listening post of two or three men in an ambush to seize people who try to ferret out the detachment.

In case an alarm [is sounded] while [the unit is] at rest, a rendezvous is to be made known beforehand. The partisans rest with their weapons, the commanders among their troops. The resting-place is to be guarded closely on all sides by double posts. If an inhabited region is chosen as a resting-place, it must be enclosed on all sides by guards who do not let inhabitants and members of the detachment pass without special order. The troops of the detachment are to be sheltered in houses and barns in compact groups with their commanders. The commanders are not permitted to have separate quarters.

Consequently, the resting-places must conform to the following requirements: (a) Create the best rest conditions; remain unnoticed by the enemy from the ground and from the air. (b) Good places for detection of unexpected raids by foot troops must exist. (c) Rapid assembling on alarm and the existence of assembly places must be assured. (d) The distance from large roads and inhabited regions must be sufficiently great.

The partisan movement is a mass movement of the whole people. The partisan movement splinters, tires out, and weakens the forces of the enemy and brings about advantageous conditions for the Red Army's counter-attack. The strength of the partisans rests in their activeness, initiative, and boldness. Basic methods of work are sudden night raids from ambushes on enemy units in the rear.

The primary sources of supply for weapons, munitions, and provisions are loot taken from the enemy. Stores which only a limited number of persons know are to be created from surpluses in various hiding-places.

The partisan detachments do not wait for assignment of tasks from above; they operate independently according to the instructions of the great leader of the peoples, Comrade Stalin: 'Create intolerable conditions for the enemy.... Destroy him at every step, undermine all his measures', in order to liberate our fatherland from foreign invasion.

A Note on Sources

Since the conclusion of the Second World War, only a very few works have appeared on the partisan struggle behind German lines in the East. Foremost among them is the excellent *The Soviet Partisan Movement in World War II*, edited by John A. Armstrong, published in 1964, and forming the essence of the research undertaken by the United States Air Force; I have placed much reliance on it, and here acknowledge it as a major source. Other works of much use have been *Communist Guerrilla Warfare* by Aubrey Dixon and Otto Heilbrunn, published in 1954, and *Der Sowjetrussische Partisanenkrieg 1941–44* by Erich Hesse, published in 1969. This present book brings together the various aspects of these, and many other works, which deal with German security policy; it is the first to deal with the Soviet partisan war from the German point of view, and analyses its successes and failure accordingly. For the wider aspects of German policy in the Eastern occupied areas, Alexander Dallin's book, *German Rule in Russia, 1941–1945*, remains the standard work; it is, in my opinion, an excellent book, which, although dealing only cursorily with security measures, presents a first-class picture of National Socialist policies in other fields.

Notes

Chapter 1 – The Rule of Terror

1. J.V. Stalin, *The Great Patriotic War of the Soviet Union*, New York, 1945, p. 15.
2. Martin Bormann's memorandum of a meeting held on 16 July 1941, quoted in *Trial of the Major War Criminals before the International Military Tribunal*, Nuremberg, 1949, vol. 38, p. 88, Document 221-L.
3. Franz Halder, *War Diary*, 19 September 1939.
4. Bormann's memorandum of a meeting held on 2 October 1940; quoted in *Trial of the Major War Criminals*, vol. 7, pp. 224–26, Document USSR 172.
5. Meeting with Military leaders, 3 October 1939; quoted in *Nazi Conspiracy and Aggression*, Washington, 1946, vol. 7, pp. 420–1, Documents EC 344–16 and –17.
6. Hans-Adolf Jacobsen, *Der Zweite Weltkriege im Chronik und Dokumentum*, Darmstadt, 1962, pp. 606–9.
7. For an excellent account of German aims in, and rule over, Russia, see Alexander Dallin, *German Rule in Russia, 1941–45*, London, 1957.
8. J.F.C. Fuller, *The Decisive Battles of the Western World*, London, 1956, vol. 3, p. 435.
9. For a good, short history of Russia, see Lionel Kochan, *The Making of Modern Russia*, London, 1962 (Pelican, 1963).
10. J.F.C. Fuller, *Conduct of War*, London, 1961, p. 262.
11. Ibid., p. 75.
12. Erich Kern, *Dance of Death*, London, 1948, p. 69.
13. *Hitler's Table Talk*, London, 1953, p. 424.
14. Dallin, p. 56; quoted from Nuremberg Document 1037–PS, unpublished.
15. *Hitler's Table Talk*, p.33.
16. Dallin, p. 9; Hitler to Otto Strasser, 21 May 1930.
17. Joseph Goebbels, *Diaries*, Garden City, New York, 1948, p. 206.
18. Noted by Bormann, 16 July 1941; quoted in *Trials of the Major War Criminals*, vol. 38, p. 88, Doc. 221–L.
19. Dallin, p. 67.
20. Halder, 30 March 1941.
21. Ibid.
22. OKW/WFSL/Abt.L (IV/QU) No. 44718/41; Nuremberg Document 050–C; see Appendix 2 for full text.
23. Ibid.
24. OKW/WFSL/Abt.L (IV/QU) No. 44822/41.
25. OKW/Abt Kr.–Verw *Kriegsgefangenwesen*.
26. Dallin, p. 32.
27. OKW/WFSt/Abt.L (IV/Qu) Nr. 44125/41, 13 March 1941; partial text quoted in Appendix I.
28. Dallin, p. 70.

29. Helmut Krausnick et al., *Anatomy of the SS State*, London, 1968, pp. 62–3.
30. Halder, 3 July 1941.
31. Stalin, p. 15.
32. John S. Pustay, *Counterinsurgency Warfare*, New York, London, 1956, p. 26.
33. For a discussion of this aspect of Soviet guerrilla warfare, see T.A. Taracouzio, *The Soviet Union and International Law*, New York, 1935, and John Armstrong (ed.), *The Soviet Partisan Movement in World War II*, Madison, 1964, pp. 4–5, 29–70, 298–320.
34. Henri Michel, *The Shadow War*, London, 1972, p. 268.
35. Armstrong, p. 5.
36. Ibid., p. 662.

Chapter 2 – The Failure of the Partisan Movement – 1941

1. Warlimont, Walter, *Inside Hitler's Headquarters*, London, 1964, p. 206.
2. See Walter Laqueur, *Guerrilla: a historical and critical study*, London, 1977, pp. 44–9.
3. Leo Tolstoy, *War and Peace*, New York, p. 962.
4. Carl von Clausewitz, *Vom Kriege*, Leipzig, 1935, p. 474.
5. See Pustay.
6. V.I. Lenin, *Selections from Lenin*, Vol. II, London, 1929, p. 224.
7. Robert Asprey, *War in the Shadows*, London, 1977, p. 486.
8. Quoted in Armstrong, p. 674.
9. See p. 49.
10. See pp. 50–51.
11. Quoted in Armstrong, p. 407.
12. This work deals only with the Soviet guerrilla movement in the Ukraine, and leaves aside all consideration of the Ukrainian Guerrilla Army, a nationalist movement as much anti-Soviet as Anti-German. It had some success against the invader, in one incident killing the SA Chief, Victor Lutze. Its strength was such that it could engage in open combat with German divisions with some prospect of success.

Chapter 3 – The Revival of the Partisan Movement – 1942

1. Commander of rear area of Army Group Centre, situation report dated 12 February 1944; Imperial War Museum, Document ZG184.
2. OKH, memorandum to OKW, 1 October 1942; Imperial War Museum, Document ZG893.
3. Letter, dated 15 August 1941, in author's possession.
4. Heinz Guderian, *Panzer Leader*, New York, 1957, p. 156.
5. Fuller, *Conduct of War*, p. 263.
6. J.F.C. Fuller, *The Decisive Battles of the Western World*, vol. 3, p. 434.
7. Order No. 0019, 16 July, 1941, quoted in Dallin, p. 64.

8. See Appendix 4 for full text of this order, dated 10 October 1941 and entitled 'The Conduct of Troops in the Eastern Territories'.
9. Dallin, p. 410; see Dallin for the treatment of Russian prisoners-of-war.
10. Ibid, p. 103.
11. Ibid., p. 102.
12. Ibid., p. 304.
13. See German Report Series, *Rear Area Security in Russia*, 1951.
14. Dallin, p. 215.
15. Armstrong, p. 408.
16. Dallin, p. 139.
17. Ibid., p. 159.
18. Aubrey Dixon and Otto Heilbrunn, *Communist Guerrilla Warfare*, London, 1954, p. 22.
19. *Trial of the Major War Criminals*, vol. 2, p. 304.
20. *Nazi Conspiracy and Aggression*, vol. 3, pp. 242–251, Document 294–PS.
21. John Erickson, *Road to Stalingrad*, London, 1976, p. 248.
22. Dixon and Heilbrunn, p. 165.
23. Armstrong, p. 435.
24. Dallin, p. 219.
25. Guderian, p. 156.
26. See ibid., p. 45.
27. Armstrong, p. 144.

Chapter 4 – German Security Policy – 1941

1. OKW/WFSt/Abt.L (IV/Qu) 44125/41 *Richtlinien auf Sondergebieten zur Weisung* Nr. 21 (*Fall Barbarossa*), 13 March 1941. For text, see Appendix 1.
2. See *Nazi Conspiracy and Aggression*, vol. 4, p. 634, Document PS 1997.
3. The *Wehrmachtbefehlshaber* for Ostland was General Friedrich Braemer, and for the Ukraine, Luftwaffe General Karl Kitzinger.
4. By virtue of an agreement between Wagner and Heydrich, dated 26 March 1941; see Dixon and Heilbrunn, pp. 100–101.
5. By virtue of the OKW decree of 13 March 1941; see Appendix 1.
6. The Higher SS and Police Leaders were:
   North – Hans Prützmann
   Centre – Erich von dem Bach-Zelewski, succeeded in October 1942 by Curt von Gottberg.
   South – Friedrich Jeckeln
   Caucasus – Gerret Korsemann
7. *Trial of the Major War Criminals*, vol. 4, p. 17.
8. Halder, 18 September 1941.
9. Dallin, p. 210.
10. See *Nazi Conspiracy and Aggression*, vol. 7, p. 49, Document D–411.
11. Armstrong, p. 357.

12. Ibid., pp. 358–9.
13. Ibid., p. 359.
14. Ibid., pp. 359–60.
15. Ibid., p. 359.
16. Dixon and Heilbrunn, p. 87.
17. Ibid., p. 85.
18. Ibid., pp. 87–8.
19. Erich Hesse, *Der Sowjetrussische Partisanenkrieg*, 1941–1944, Göttingen, 1969, pp. 79–80.
20. See Appendix 2 for full order.
21. Dallin, p. 75.
22. OKW/WFSt/Abt L (IV/Qu) Nr 002060/41; see Appendix 3.
23. OBfhdH/Gen StdH/Ausb-Abt. 1(a) Nr. 1900/41 *Richtlinien für die Partisanen Bekampfung*.
24. Krausnick et al., p. 519.
25. Hesse, p. 76.
26. Dallin, p. 498.
27. Dixon and Heilbrunn, pp. 113–4.
28. Ibid., p. 114; see also Hesse, pp. 25–30.
29. Dixon and Heilbrunn, p. 125.
30. See Appendix 4.
31. Hesse, p. 94. Date of order was 8 November 1941.
32. Dixon and Heilbrunn, p. 141.
33. Ibid., p. 142.
34. Ibid., pp. 142–3.
35. Order of the Day, *Einsatzgruppe* B, 20 November 1941, in author's possession.
36. SS Hauptamt, 2 December 1941, in author's possession.
37. *Trial of the Major War Criminals*, vol. 7, p. 58.
38. Ibid., vol. 3, p. 171–2.
39. Ibid., vol. 7, p. 218.
40. Ibid., vol. 4, pp. 27–8.
41. See Appendix 2.
42. Dixon and Heilbrunn, p. 172.
43. *Nazi Conspiracy and Aggression*, vol. 2, p. 391, Document 3713 PS.
44. Ibid., p. 396.
45. *Trial of the Major War Criminals*, vol. 4, pp. 29–31.
46. *Nazi Conspiracy and Aggression*, vol. 6, p. 1427, Document 3712 PS.
47. *Trial of the Major War Criminals*, vol. 4, p. 36.
48. *Nazi Conspiracy and Aggression*, vol. 2, pp. 396–7, Document 3717 PS.

Chapter 5 – The Partisan Movement 1942–44

1. Goebbels, 6 March 1942.
2. Dixon and Heilbrunn, pp. 53–4.
3. See Appendix 7.

4. Armstrong, p. 185.
5. See pp. 147–150
6. Armstrong, p. 113.
7. Ibid., p. 152.
8. Ibid., p. 154.
9. A. Fydorov, *The Underground Committee Carries On*, Moscow, 1952, p. 424.
10. Dixon and Heilbrunn, pp. 47–8.
11. Armstrong, p. 176.
12. Ibid., p. 173.
13. Ibid., p. 154.
14. Ibid., p. 749.
15. Ibid., p. 187.

Chapter 6 – The Development of German Security Policy 1942–44

1. Dixon and Heilbrunn, p. 139.
2. Armstrong, p. 281.
3. Goebbels entries for 6, 16, 29 March.
4. Dixon and Heilbrunn, p. 48.
5. Ibid., p. 46.
6. Ibid.
7. Ibid., p. 47.
8. Adolf Hitler, *Hitler's Secret Conversations 1941–1944*, New York, 1953, p. 579.
9. Dallin, p. 210.
10. See Appendix 7.
11. Dixon and Heilbrunn, p. 148.
12. Hesse, p. 206.
13. *Trial of the Major War Criminals*, vol. 7, p. 59.
14. Ibid., vol. 4, p. 30.
15. Hesse, p. 206.
16. Report, dated 18 May 1943, written in poor German; author's collection.
17. Krausnick et al. pp. 346–7.
18. *Trial of the Major War Criminals*, vol. 7, pp. 309–11.
19. RFSS, Chef der SS Hauptamt, VS Nr 2140/42, 17 June 1942.
20. *Nazi Conspiracy and Aggression*, vol. 6, p. 131, Document 3428 PS.
21. Krausnick, p. 66.
22. *Nazi Conspiracy and Aggression*, Supplement A, p. 668, Document 3943 PS.
23. Imperial War Museum, Document INT, 758.
24. Dixon and Heilbrunn, p. 85.
25. Ibid.
26. German Report Series, *Combat in Russia Forests and Swamps*, Washington, 1951, pp. V–VI.

27. Letter, dated 18 July 1943, in author's possession.
28. Armstrong, p. 160.
29. Dixon and Heilbrunn, p. 74.
30. Goebbels, pp. 374–5.
31. Armstrong, p. 226.
32. Ibid., p. 219.
33. Ibid.
34. See Appendix 7.
35. See pp. 80–81.
36. Heinz Höhne, *The Order of the Death's Head*, London 1969, p. 363.
37. *Trial of the Major War Criminals*, vol. 9, p. 281.
38. Ibid., vol. 4, p. 22.
39. Ibid., vol. 2, p. 18.
40. Dallin, p. 87.
41. Ibid., p. 550.
42. *Nazi Conspiracy and Aggression*, vol. 8, p. 207, Document 12–135.
43. Ibid., p. 205.
44. See pp. 7, 48, 80–81.
45. *Nazi Conspiracy and Aggression*, vol. 2, p. 392, Document 3714–PS.
46. Krausnick et al., p. 523.
47. *Trial of the Major War Criminals*, vol. 9, p. 307.
48. Hesse, pp. 205–6.
49. *Nazi Conspiracy and Aggression*, vol. 2, p. 392, Document 3713 PS.
50. Armstrong, pp. 631–2; Bräutigam's memorandum was dated 27 July 1944.
51. Ibid., p. 573.
52. Ibid., p. 575; instructions from Rosenberg dated 27 October 1942.
53. Ibid., p. 576.
54. Ibid.
55. Dallin, p. 241; von Kleist's instructions were dated 15 December 1942.
56. Armstrong, p. 576.
57. Ibid.; date of order was 5 December 1942.
58. Ibid., p. 581; date of order 8 September 1942.
59. Ibid., p. 583.
60. Ibid., p. 584.
61. Ibid., p. 617.
62. Krausnick et al. p. 522.
63. Merkblatt Nr. 69/2 *Bandenbekampfung*, OKW Nr. 03268/44 WFSt/Op., 6 May 1944. See Appendix to Dixon and Heilbrunn.
64. Ibid.
65. Ibid.

Chapter 7 – 'Untermensch' with Iron Crosses

1. Dallin, pp. 518–9; Nuremberg Document 1685 PS, unpublished.
2. Ibid., p. 518.
3. Ibid., p. 548.

4. Ibid., p. 550; date of order was 17 February 1943.
5. Ibid., p. 550.
6. George Fischer, *Soviet Opposition to Stalin*, Cambridge, Mass., 1953, p. 46.
7. Dixon and Heilbrunn, p. 130.
8. *Hitler's Table Talk*, p. 354.
9. *Trial of the Major War Criminals*, vol. 38, p. 88, Document 221–L.
10. Fischer, p. 179.
11. Ibid., p. 45.
12. *Trial of the Major War Criminals*, vol. 37, p. 663, Document 17–L.
13. Dallin, p. 582.
14. Fischer, p. 50.

Chapter 8 – 'Passive' Security – the Success

1. See Appendix 10 for full order. See also Appendix 11 for Partisan methods.
2. Armstrong, p. 494.
3. Hermann Teske, *Die silbernen Spiegel*, Heidelberg, 1952, p. 112.
4. Goebbels, 29 April 1942.
5. Dixon and Heilbrunn, p. 73.
6. Armstrong, p. 497.
7. German Report Series, *Rear Area Security in Russia*, pp. 34–5.
8. Kovpak, p. 23.

Chapter 9 – 'Active' Security – the Failure

1. *Trial of the Major War Criminals*, vol. 15, p. 402, Document GB485.
2. Armstrong, pp. 374–5.
3. Ibid., p. 428.
4. Ibid., p. 382.
5. Ibid., p. 379.
6. Ibid., p. 505.
7. Ibid., p. 512.
8. Ibid., p. 541–2.
9. Ibid., p. 541–2.
10. Ibid., p. 424.
11. Ibid., p. 424.

Bibliography

Books

ARMSTRONG, JOHN (ed.): *The Soviet Partisan Movement in World War II.* Madison: University of Wisconsin Press, 1964; Ontario: Burns and MacEachern, 1964.

ARMSTRONG, JOHN: *Ukrainian Nationalism: 1939–1945.* New York: Columbia University Press, 1955; London: Oxford University Press, 1955; New York and London: Columbia University Press, 1963.

DALLIN, ALEXANDER: *German Rule in Russia, 1939–1945: A Study of Occupation Policies.* London: Macmillan, 1957; New York: St. Martin's Press, 1957.

The Kaminsky Brigade: 1941–1944. Cambridge, Mass.: Russian Research Center, Harvard University, 1956.

DIXON, AUBREY, C. and HEILBRUNN, OTTO: *Communist Guerrilla Warfare.* London: George Allen & Unwin, 1954.

EARLE, EDWARD MEAD (ed.): *Makers of Modern Strategy.* Princeton: Princeton University Press, 1943; London: Oxford University Press, 1943; Toronto: Ryerson Press, 1943.

ERICKSON, JOHN: *The Soviet High Command: A Military-Political History.* New York: St. Martin's Press, 1962; London: Macmillan, 1962; Toronto: Macmillan, 1962.

The Road to Stalingrad. London: Weidenfeld and Nicolson, 1975; New York: Harper & Row, 1975.

FISCHER, GEORGE: *Soviet Opposition to Stalin.* Cambridge Mass.: Harvard University Press, 1952; Toronto: S.J.R. Saunders, 1952; London: Oxford University Press, 1953.

FOOT, M. R. D.: *Resistance: An Analysis of European Resistance to the Nazis, 1940–45.* London: Eyre Methuen, 1976; New York: McGraw Hill, 1977.

FULLER, J. F. C. (Major-General): *The Decisive Battles of the Western World.* Volume III. London: Eyre and Spottiswoode, 1954–1956; New York: Funk & Wagnalls, 1954–56, as *Military History of the Western World.*; Toronto: McClelland, 1954–1956.

Conduct of War. London: Eyre and Spottiswoode, 1961; New Brunswick: Rutgers University Press, 1961; New York: Duell, 1963.

FYODOROV, A.: *The Underground Committee Carries On.* L. Stoklitsky (trans.). Moscow: Foreign Languages Publishing House, 1952.

GARTHOFF, RAYMOND L.: *Soviet Military Doctrine.* Glencoe, Illinois: The Free Press, 1953; London: George Allen & Unwin, 1954 as *How Russia Makes War.*

GILBERT, FELIX (ed.): *Hitler Directs His War.* New York: Oxford University Press, 1950; London and Toronto: Oxford University Press, 1951.

GOEBBELS, PAUL JOSEPH: *The Goebbels Diaries, 1942–1943*. Louis P. Lochner (trans.), New York: Doubleday, 1948; London: Hamish Hamilton, 1948.
GREENE, T. N. (Lieutenant-Colonel) (ed.): *The Guerrilla – And How to Fight Him*. New York: Frederick A. Praeger, 1962.
GREINER, HELMUTH: *Die Oberste Werhmachtsführung 1939–43*. Wiesbaden: Limes, 1951.
GUDERIAN, HEINZ: *Panzer Leader*. Constantine Fitzgibbon (trans.). New York: Dutton, 1952; London: Michael Joseph, 1952; Toronto: Collins, 1952.
HALDER, FRANZ: *Kriegstagebuch*. Stuttgart: W. Hohlhammer, 1964; Trans. for International Military Tribunal, 1946.
HAWEMANN, WALTER (ed.): *Hitler's Lagebesprechungen*. Stuttgart: Deutsche Verlags-Anstalt, 1962.
HESSE, ERICH: *Der Sowjetrussische Partisanenkrieg 1941–44*. Göttingen: Musterschmidt Verlag, 1969.
HIGGINS, TRUMBULL: *Hitler and Russia: The Third Reich in a Two-Front War, 1937–1943*. New York: The Macmillan Company, 1966; London: Collier-Macmillan, 1966.
HITLER, ADOLF: *Mein Kampf*. John Chamberlain, Sidney B. Fay and others (Editorial Sponsors). New York: Reynal and Hitchcock, 1939; Toronto: McClelland, 1939.
Hitler's Secret Conversations, 1941–1944. Norman Cameron and R. H. Stevens (trans.). New York: Farrar, Straus & Cudahy, 1953; London: Weidenfeld and Nicolson, 1953.
HOWELL, EDGAR M.: *The Soviet Partisan Movement: 1941–1944*. Washington DC: Dept of the Army, 1956.
IGNATOV, P. Z.: *Partisans of the Kuban*. J. Fineberg (trans.). London: Hutchinson, 1945.
INTERNATIONAL MILITARY TRIBUNAL: *Trial of the Major War Criminals before the International Military Tribunal*. (42 vols.). Nuremberg: Secretariat of the Tribunal, 1947/49.
KAMENTSKY, JOHR: *Hitler's Occupation of the Ukraine, 1941–1944*. Milwaukee, Wisconsin: Marquette University Press, 1956.
KOLKOWICZ, ROMAN: *The Soviet Military and the Communist Party*. Princeton: Princeton University Press, 1967.
KOVPAK, S. A. (Major-General): *Our Partisan Course*. Ernst and Mira Lesser (trans.). London: Hutchinson, 1947.
KUHNRICH, HEINZ. *Der Partisanen Krieg in Europa, 1939–1945*. Berlin: Dietz Verlag, 1965.
LAQUEUR, WALTER: *Russia and Germany: A Century of Conflict*. Boston: Little, Brown and Company, 1965; London: Weidenfeld and Nicolson, 1965.
Guerrilla: A Historical and Critical Study. Boston: Little, Brown and Company, 1976; London: Weidenfeld and Nicolson, 1977.
LITTLEJOHN, DAVID: *The Patriotic Traitors*. London: Heinemann, 1972; New York: Doubleday, 1972.
VON LUTTICHAU, CHARLES V. P. (ed.): *Guerrilla and Counter-guerrilla Warfare in Russia During World War II*. Washington DC: Office of the Chief

of Military History, Dept of the Army, 1963.

VON MANSTEIN, ERICH: *Lost Victories.* Anthony G. Powell (trans.). Chicago: Henry Regnery Company, 1958; London: Methuen, 1958.

MAVROGODATO, RALPH and ZIEMKE, EARL: *The Partisan Movement in the Polotsk Lowland.* Maxwell Air Force Base, Alabama: Human Resources Research Institute, December 1954.

MICHEL, HENRI: *The Shadow War.* London: Deutsch, 1972; New York: Harper & Row, 1972.

NEUMANN, PETER: *Other Men's Graves.* Constantine Fitzgibbon (trans.). London: Weidenfeld and Nicolson, 1958; Toronto: Ambassador Books, 1958; New York: William Sloane, 1959, as *The Black March.*

OSANKA, FRANKLIN MARK (ed.): *Modern Guerrilla Warfare.* New York: The Free Press of Glencoe, 1962.

PARET, PETER and SHY, JOHN W.: *Guerrillas in the 1960s.* New York: Frederick A. Praeger, 1962; London: Pall Mall, 1962; Ontario: Burns and MacEachern, 1962.

PONOMARENKO, Lieut-Gen.: *Simonov, Konstantin, and Others Behind the Front Lines.* No translator given. London: Hutchinson, 1945.

PUSTAY, JOHN S.: *Counterinsurgency Warfare.* New York: The Free Press, 1965; London: Macmillan, 1965.

REDELIS, VALDIS: *Partisanenkrieg: Mittelabschnitt der Ostfront 1941/43.* Heidelberg: Scharnhorst Buchkameradschaft, 1958.

REITLINGER, GERALD: *The House Built on Sand. The Conflicts of German Policy in Russia, 1939–1945.* London: Weidenfeld and Nicolson, 1960; New York: Viking Press, 1960; Toronto: McClelland, 1960.

SCHRAMM, PERCY ERNST (ed.): *Kriegestagebuch des Oberkommandos der Wehrmacht.* (8 vols.). Frankfurt am Main: Bernard und Graefe Verlag fuer Wehrwesen, 1963.

STALIN, J. V.: *The Great Patriotic War of the Soviet Union.* New York: International Publishers, 1945; Toronto: Progress Books, 1945; London: Hutchinson, 1946 as *War Speeches; Orders of the Day and Answers to Foreign Press Correspondents During the Great Patriotic War, July 3 1941 – June 22 1945.*

STALLING, GERHARD (ed.): *Bilanz des Zweiten Weltkrieges.* Hamburg: Gerhard Stalling Verlag, 1953.

TARACOUZIO, TIMOTHY ANDREW: *The Soviet Union and International Law.* New York: The Macmillan Company, 1935; London: Macmillan, 1935; Toronto: Macmillan, 1935.

TELPUCHOWSKI, BORIS SEMJONOIVITSCH: *Die Sowjetische Geschichte des Grossen Vaterlandischen Krieges, 1941–1945.* Frankfurt am Main: Bernard und Graefe Verlag fuer Wehrwesen, 1961.

TESKE, HERMANN: *Die silbernen Spiegel.* Heidelberg: Kurt Vowinckel, 1952.

TREVOR-ROPER, H. R. (ed.): *Hitler's War Directives 1939–45.* London: Sidgwick & Jackson, 1964; New York: Holt, Rinehart, and Winston, 1965, as *Blitzkrieg to Defeat: Hitler's War Directives, 1939–1945.*

US DEPARTMENT OF THE ARMY: *Combat in Russian Forests and Swamps*. Washington DC, July 1951.

Effects of Climate on Combat in European Russia. Washington DC, February 1952.

Military Improvisations During the Russian Campaign. Washington DC, August 1951.

Rear Area Security in Russia: The Second Soviet Front Behind the German Lines. Washington DC, July 1951.

Russian Combat Methods in World War II. Washington DC, November 1950.

Small Unit Actions During the German Campaign in Russia. Washington DC, July 1953.

Terrain Factors in the Russian Campaign. Washington DC, July 1951.

US GOVERNMENT PRINTING OFFICE: *Nazi Conspiracy and Aggression*. (8 vols.). Washington DC: 1946.

WERTH, ALEXANDER: *Russia at War, 1941–1945*. Toronto: Smithers & Bonellie, 1960; New York: E. P. Dutton and Co. Inc., 1964; London: Barrie & Rockliff, 1964.

WHITE, FEDOTOFF D.: *The Growth of the Red Army*. Princeton: Princeton University Press, 1944.

ZIEMKE, EARL F.: *Stalingrad to Berlin: The German Defeat in the East*. Office of the Chief of Military History, United States Army, Washington DC, 1968.

Articles and Periodicals

AUGUR (pseud.): 'Die rote Partisanerbewegung'. *Allgemeine Schweizerische Militärzeitung*, CXV, June–July 1949.

CODO, ENRIQUE MARTINEZ: 'Guerrilla Warfare in the Ukraine'. *Military Review*, XL, November 1960.

DALLIN, ALEXANDER and MAVROGODATO, RALPH S.: 'Rodionov: A Case Study in Wartime Redefection'. *American Slavic and East European Review*, XVIII, 1959.

GARTHOFF, RAYMOND L.: 'Unconventional Warfare in Communist Strategy'. *Foreign Affairs*, Vol. 40, No. 4, July 1962.

GOLZ, HERBERT: 'Erfahrungen aus dem Kampf gegen Banden'. *Wehrkunde*, IV, April 1955.

GUETTE, ADOLF: 'Kampf hinter der Front'. *Truppenpraxis*, II, October 1960.

HEYSING, GUENTER: 'Partisanen-Hochburg Minsk'. *Deutsche Soldatenzeitung*, Jg. 4, Nr. 17, 1954.

KREIDEL, HELLMUTH: 'Partisanenkampf in Mittelrussland'. *Wehrkunde*, IV, September 1955.

KUEHNRICH, HEINZ: 'Die Darstellung der Partisanenbewegung in der Westdeutschen Historiographie'. *Zeitschrift fuer Geschichtswissenschaft*, VIII, January 1962.

SIMPSON, KEITH: 'German Experiences of Rear Area Security on the Eastern Front'. *Royal United Services Institution Journal*, December 1976.

TESKE, HERMANN: 'Die Eisenbahn als operatives Fuehrungsmittel in Krieg gegen Russland', *Wehrwissenschaftliche Rundschau*, II, Sept.–Oct. 1951.

'Der Wert von Eisenbahnbruecken im zweiten Weltkrieg'. *Wehrwissenschaftliche Rundschau*, IV, April 1954.

'Partisanen gegen die Eisenbahn'. *Wehrwissenschaftliche Rundschau*, III, October 1953.

Index